COACHWORK ON
ROLLS-ROYCE
& BENTLEY
1945-1965

COACHWORK ON
ROLLS-ROYCE
& BENTLEY
1945-1965

By James Taylor

Herridge & Sons

FOREWORD AND ACKNOWLEDGMENTS

This is a book about the coachwork on Rolls-Royce and Bentley models with separate chassis built after 1945. These cars have been written about countless times in many good books, but the focus here is rather different. It is on the coachbuilders and the contribution they made to helping these two British marques remain at the peak of the motor industry for so long.

I have therefore chosen to arrange the information in alphabetical order of coachbuilder, although I have deliberately separated British coachbuilders from the smaller number of those outside Britain who bodied these chassis. Each coachbuilder had its own way of describing designs and of numbering them, and there is therefore some variety in the way I have tackled their output; in each case, I have chosen an approach that seemed appropriate to that subject, rather than adopting a rigidly consistent approach throughout the book.

I suspect that many readers of this book will be only too familiar with the different chassis produced by Rolls-Royce and Bentley in this period, but I thought it wise to include a chapter that provides an outline history anyway, if only for the benefit of those who are less familiar with the subject. In that chapter, I have included specification tables and, of course, chassis number sequences because chassis numbers are central to the business of identifying individual bodies.

Wherever possible, I have tried to give an indication of how many bodies were built of any particular type. It is not always possible to be precise. In a few cases, there is dispute over the identification of a particular body; and anyone who is already familiar with the subject will know how often authorities disagree on precise numbers. So where totals for a particular body type are shown, they should be treated with caution; generally, the method adopted in this book is to quote a total where most authorities agree on one, and to give an approximate figure where they do not.

Finding photographs to illustrate this book has been a challenge, not least because there simply are none known of some bodies. Much of the colour photography was provided by my highly talented colleague Simon Clay, and I am very grateful to him. Some excellent pictures also came from well-known Rolls-Royce and Bentley enthusiast Klaus-Josef Rossfeldt. Others came from WikiMedia Commons, and special thanks must go to those photographers who have made their work available for public use through this medium.

In many cases, the original coachbuilder's black-and-white record photographs remain the most satisfactory option, one key advantage being that they do illustrate exactly how the cars looked when they were new. However, as is increasingly the case nowadays, many old photographs have passed through so many hands and are now so widely available on the internet that it is often impossible to attribute sources. All reasonable efforts have been made to determine copyright ownership, but I apologise if anyone's copyright has been inadvertently infringed.

James Taylor
Oxfordshire,
July 2019

Published in 2019
by Herridge & Sons Ltd
Lower Forda, Shebbear
Beaworthy, Devon EX21 5SY

© Copyright James Taylor 2019

Design by Ray Leaning, MUSE Fine Art & Design

ISBN 978-1-906133-89-4
Printed in China

Contents

Chapter One

Chassis and Standard Coachwork

This is a book about bespoke coachwork on Rolls-Royce and Bentley chassis built in the two decades after the Second World War, but it is impossible to look at that subject without some understanding of the chassis themselves and of the "standard" coachwork that was available for many of them.

By the late 1930s, the car division of Rolls-Royce was suffering from low profitability. Analysis within the company drew the fairly obvious conclusion that the three models then current – Rolls-Royce 25/30, Rolls-Royce Phantom III, and Bentley 4¼-litre – had too little in common with one another. For the future, then, rationalising components would reduce manufacturing costs, and various options were considered. Over the next few years, and then immediately after the war, there were several schemes for a rationalised range of chassis, but the one that actually entered production in 1946 was very much stripped down and simplified.

The war itself had a major effect on the choice of models introduced in 1946. Britain was about to embark on a period of austerity as it recovered from the war, and this was no time for large and extravagant new models. What was needed was one large chassis suitable for owners who wanted grand and formal coachwork, and one smaller chassis for those who wanted a car more suitable for everyday use. These two chassis could share essentially the same design, the major difference between them being in the length of the wheelbase, and in fact the design was developed from the one drawn up at the end of the 1930s for the Bentley MkV saloon, of which only a handful were made before hostilities put an end to production.

A basic six-cylinder engine design was created, incorporating an efficient combustion chamber design involving a combination of overhead inlet and side exhaust valves. This design was deliberately intended to be expandable, to give a greater capacity if that was needed later in the engine's life, and it was also designed to be made available as an eight-cylinder if there was a call for such an engine. There was scope to create a four-cylinder engine from the same basic design and, although no such engine ever appeared in a car made at the Rolls-Royce factory in Crewe, a four-cylinder version of the engine would be made standard for the British Army's purpose-built Austin Champ.

Traditionally, Rolls-Royce and Bentley had made only chassis, leaving the coachwork to be constructed by a specialist in the craft to meet the requirements of the individual customer. But during the 1930s it had become increasingly apparent that not every customer wanted to go through the somewhat elaborate (and costly) exercise of having coachwork individually designed; many were content with designs that the coachbuilders built in small volumes or batches, with perhaps minor variations to preserve the illusion of individuality. It was also during the 1930s that the volume car makers had gone over to stamping out car bodies from steel instead of building them laboriously by hand in the traditional way. It was cheaper by far, and it often produced a stronger body that was also less prone to the rattles and creaks that inevitably set in as a coachbuilt body got older.

Rolls-Royce had not ignored all this. In conjunction with Park Ward, a coachbuilder in which it had owned a major share since 1933, it investigated more modern designs that used a greater quantity of steel in their construction. Although the word "standardised" was not one the company would have wanted to be used within earshot of its customers, there was no doubt that it was moving towards the concept as the 1930s

The "standard steel' Body on the Bentley MkVI chassis was discreet and conservative. It reflected the styling trends of the mid-1940s but quickly began to look dated as more modern designs appeared.

wore on. So by the time serious planning began for the post-war models, this thinking also had to be taken into account.

Silver Wraith and MkVI

All these ideas came together to create the plan for post-war chassis production. The smaller model would have a 120-inch (10ft) wheelbase and the six-cylinder engine with twin carburettors to provide spritely performance. The initial plan was that this chassis could be used for both a Rolls-Royce model (planned as the Silver Dawn) and a Bentley (planned as the MkVI). The larger model would have the same engine, but with a single carburettor and a 127-inch wheelbase. This was only barely enough for more formal coachwork (the wheelbase of the pre-war Rolls-Royce Wraith was 136 inches, and that was the smaller model of the time) but it would make the chassis more adaptable. The new post-war Rolls-Royce would be called the Silver Wraith.

The Silver Wraith would be made available for bespoke coachwork in the usual way, but the smaller chassis would break new ground and would have a standardised saloon body that would be built by Pressed Steel, who built volume-production bodies for many of the lesser British chassis makers. There would of course also be bare chassis available in the traditional way for customers who wanted bespoke coachwork. As planning proceeded, however, so concerns arose about the planned standardised coachwork; the company was concerned that traditional Rolls-Royce buyers would be deterred by the idea of buying such a thing. So the decision was taken to make the smaller chassis available only as a Bentley, to avoid tarnishing the Rolls-Royce name by this use of standardised bodywork. As a result, the Silver Dawn was removed from the production

plans and would not appear until later.

So the new post-war range was announced in April 1946 as the Rolls-Royce Silver Wraith and the Bentley MkVI. The intention was always that they should remain in production with only running modifications for some years, as Rolls-Royce was a low-volume manufacturer and only in this way could the company amortise the costs of development and tooling and still turn in a profit. So the major changes to those first production models were introduced gradually, and over a period of time.

Buyers of the MkVI expected a high standard of comfort and interior appointments, and there was no doubt that the "standard steel" body hit the mark in that respect. Plain leather upholstery was the fashion of the time.

The owner-driver Rolls-Royce followed some years after the Bentley MkVI, but the Silver Dawn was in fact the same car, with a less powerful engine and of course the Rolls-Royce radiator grille and other badges.

THE BENTLEY CRESTA PROJECT

In the late 1940s, Walter Sleator of Franco-Britannic Autos in Paris identified a ready market on the European continent for a sleek coupé design on Bentley chassis. After discussions with the factory, a specification was drawn up that included a lowered bonnet line and a steeply raked steering column. Again at Sleator's request, left-hand drive was made optional, although not before 1949 when it became available on the standard MkVI chassis as well.

The first Cresta coupé was designed and built by Pinin Farina in Italy, who built three examples in 1948. The contract for the production bodies was nevertheless awarded to Facel Metallon that year, and a plausible explanation is that the French authorities would not permit exhibits at the Paris Salon which had originated in countries that had been enemies of the French in 1939-1945; a French-built body, even if designed by an Italian, was by contrast acceptable. For good measure, however, the Facel body was displayed on neutral territory, at the 1949 Geneva show.

Facel Metallon built ten more bodies between 1948 and early 1951. However, Crewe had been working in the mean time on its own interpretation of a high-performance coupé, and production of the Cresta models ceased to make way for the Bentley Continental.

Silver Dawn, R Type, Continental and long-wheelbase Silver Wraith

The first changes came in April 1949, when the two-model range was made up to three models by the introduction of the Rolls-Royce Silver Dawn. The main impetus for this came from America, where Rolls-Royce felt that the Bentley name was not sufficiently well known to justify the high price they would have to charge there for the MkVI model. As a Rolls-Royce, though, the car had prestige – and so the Silver Dawn became the first post-war chassis to be available with left-hand drive (although the Bentley and Silver Wraith would soon follow). It also had the single-carburettor engine from the Silver Wraith, to help distinguish it from the Bentley in markets where the two cars would be sold side by side. The Bentley, of course, had to have better performance because of the marque's distinguished sporting history.

The next set of changes came in October 1951, when a big-bore, 4.5-litre development of the original six-cylinder engine became standard in all three chassis. This was a prelude to further developments during 1952, which saw changes to all three existing chassis and the introduction of a fourth model as well. Primarily to suit changing tastes in coachwork, where customers were now expecting more boot space, the tail of the Bentley MkVI and Rolls-Royce Silver Dawn chassis was extended and the standard steel saloon body was modified with an appropriately larger boot. The Silver Dawn remained a Silver Dawn, but the Bentley was briefly known by its factory development name of MkVII before the name R Type became popular – a name derived from the fact that the new chassis was introduced with those numbered in the R series.

The Silver Wraith grew, too. With the Silver Dawn ready to attract customers who wanted the Rolls-Royce name on an everyday car, it was safe to increase the wheelbase of the larger chassis to something much more appropriate for formal or limousine coachwork. So the "long-wheelbase" Silver Wraith, with an extra six inches between axle centres, became available. However, in this case the changeover was not a clean one, and the older short-wheelbase chassis continued to be built until well into 1953 alongside the newer type.

The new model during 1952 was in some ways symbolic of the easing of post-war austerity – even though rationing in Britain would not end until 1953. It was called the Bentley Continental, and was intended as a high-speed, long-distance touring car that would be particularly suitable for the unrestricted roads on the European continent. Britain, sadly, was still several years from developing anything remotely

Two-tone paintwork was becoming fashionable, and it suited the Silver Dawn very well indeed. This is a late example, registered in May 1954. (Simon Clay)

A criticism of the Bentley MkVI and early Silver Dawn was a lack of boot space. Coachbuilders had shown the way forward by extending the rear of the chassis, and Crewe did the same in 1952, modifying the rear of the "standard steel" body to suit. This is a Bentley R Type saloon from that first year.

similar in the form of its motorways. The chassis was a development of the existing 120-inch wheelbase type with the 4.5-litre twin-carburettor engine, but with higher gearing and other modifications. It would become known as the R Type Continental because most examples were contemporary with the Bentley R Type, although in fact all those built up to June 1953 actually had a chassis that was more akin to the MkVI type.

Most important in the whole concept of the car was weight saving, and in the beginning it was available only with a lightweight two-door fastback saloon body that had been designed at Rolls-Royce and was built for them by HJ Mulliner. The Continental was the very epitome of what would today be called a supercar. It was exclusive, expensive, had very high performance (120mph was in the realms of fantasy in 1952) and was

a stunningly attractive design with enormous presence. When, later, Rolls-Royce released Continental chassis for bodying by other coachbuilders, they insisted that only two-door coachwork should be constructed.

The seat belts would not have been fitted when this car was new, but the rest of the interior is characteristic of a late Silver Dawn. (Simon Clay)

Over time, however, the original lightweight, high-performance nature of the car became a little blurred as customers ordered weighty items such as stronger bumpers, more comfortable seats, and other equipment that had not been part of the original concept.

Phantom IV

The Rolls-Royce Phantom IV chassis was built in very limited numbers. This was the very first example – which was originally intended to be the only one.

Meanwhile, Rolls-Royce had begun production of yet another new model, although this one was simply out of reach of the vast majority of the company's customers. One of the cars originally planned as part of the post-war rationalised range was a full-size Limousine chassis powered by the eight-cylinder (5.6-litre) derivative of the post-war engine, but, for a variety of reasons, this had been sidelined. However, when Rolls-Royce received an order during 1949 from HRH Princess Elizabeth and her husband the Duke of Edinburgh for a large limousine, the idea was resurrected and was given the name of Phantom IV.

The first example of the new chassis, on a massive 145-inch wheelbase, was delivered to the Royal couple in July 1950. As *The Autocar* reported in its issue of

The Bentley R Type Continental was a supercar of its day. This is actually the first example, affectionately known as Olga because of its registration number, OLG 490. This lightweight fastback body by HJ Mulliner was the only option for the first cars, but bodies by other coachbuilders became available later.

7 July, "it is possible that Rolls-Royce may now be encouraged to embark on the production of further examples of this superb chassis. It must be said, however, that at present no other orders are being accepted." That did not stop the enquiries coming in, and eventually Rolls-Royce relented. In the end a further 17 Phantom IV chassis were built between 1951 and 1956, of which one was only ever used as a delivery truck around the Rolls-Royce works. All the others were for heads of state or royalty only, notably in the Middle East but also in Spain.

Later Continentals, Silver Cloud and S Type

The next major development was in 1954, when the six-cylinder engine was bored out once again to 4.9 litres and was put into the last two series of the Bentley Continental chassis. The idea was partly to compensate for the increasing weight of coachwork (as mentioned earlier), but this engine had also been developed with

The 4.9-litre six-cylinder engine of the Silver Cloud was the final derivative of the design that had been new immediately after the 1939-1945 war. (Simon Clay)

The new owner-driver models appeared in 1955. This overhead view shows the sturdy chassis of a Rolls-Royce Silver Cloud.

More than 60 years after its introduction, the "standard steel" saloon body on the Silver Cloud is still one of the most attractive designs ever made. This left-hand-drive example is on chassis LSHF241, and again benefits from two-tone paintwork. (Simon Clay)

the next new chassis in mind. This would replace the Rolls-Royce Silver Dawn, the Bentley R Type and the Bentley Continental, and it would follow the trend towards greater commonality. In fact, when the Rolls-Royce Silver Cloud and Bentley S Type were introduced in 1955, they were identical in all but radiator grille and marque identification.

Dimensionally, the new models had an extra three inches in the wheelbase to provide more room within the body, but overall they were much the same size as the models they replaced. Most importantly, they came with a quite extraordinarily well-proportioned standard saloon body, designed once again by Rolls-Royce (in

the person of chief designer John Blatchley) and built by Pressed Steel. Bare chassis were made available for coachbuilders in the usual way, and there was also a special Continental version of it, with a slightly more powerful engine and taller gearing to make it better suited to the high-speed, long-distance touring with which the Continental name was associated.

Improvements and changes came, as always, slowly. Power was increased slightly in 1957, and in that year a long-wheelbase chassis was also introduced, offering an extra four inches to make the same 127 inches as the original short-wheelbase Silver Wraith. The Silver Wraith itself, by then of course in long-

For the first time, Bentley and Rolls-Royce had no differences other than visual identification. This picture shows the Bentley S Type on the left, next to a Rolls-Royce Silver Cloud, when both were new.

From 1957, a long-wheelbase chassis became available for chauffeur-driven work. The extra four inches of length gave more legroom in the rear. They had been inserted so carefully into the original body design that it is not always easy to recognise a long-wheelbase Silver Cloud at first glance.

wheelbase form with a 133-inch wheelbase, would remain in production for another two years or so, but its replacement was already in the design stages.

Silver Cloud II, S2 and Phantom V

Meanwhile, Rolls-Royce had been working on an entirely new engine for the next generation of new models. With the 4.9-litre size introduced in 1954, the existing six-cylinder reached the limit of its development, and the decision had been made that its replacement should have eight cylinders but in a vee formation. The American market had become an important one for Rolls-Royce sales, and all the prestige marques originating in that country (and many of the bread-and-butter marques as well) depended on V8 engines. Rolls-Royce could therefore not realistically offer anything with fewer cylinders.

The new engine was ready by 1959, and was a straightforward design with a single central camshaft, a 90-degree angle between the cylinder banks, and a twin-carburettor fuel system. With a swept volume of 6.23 litres, it had also been designed for later increases in size – although in 1959 no-one could have imagined that it would still be in production for some Bentley models in the early 21st century. The new V8 was announced in August 1959 for the Rolls-Royce Silver Cloud II, Bentley S2, and Bentley Continental S2 chassis, the latter now differing from the standard

Rolls-Royce considered that there was now a worthwhile demand for a seven-seater Limousine, and developed the Phantom V chassis to meet it. This style of coachwork was the default option, but it was built by hand in the traditional way. The chassis was of course made available to other coachbuilders as well.

type mainly in its taller gearing and more steeply raked steering column. The new engine also went into another new model, which directly replaced the Silver Wraith. This was called the Rolls-Royce Phantom V.

The Phantom V chassis was yet another development

With the arrival of the new V8 engine in 1959, the Silver Cloud became a Silver Cloud II and the Bentley became an S2. As this 1961 Silver Cloud II shows, there were no external features to distinguish these new models from their six-cylinder predecessors. (Simon Clay)

of the standard chassis, this time extended to the same 145 inches of wheelbase that had served for the very limited-production Phantom IV. Ideally suited to Limousine coachwork, therefore, it was predominantly bodied with such styles, and the default option after 1961 was a supremely elegant seven-passenger design originally drawn up by Park Ward but latterly produced by the Rolls-Royce-owned Mulliner, Park Ward division. Although the Phantom V chassis was also made available for bespoke coachwork, the only

independent British coachbuilder still functioning in the first half of the 1960s was James Young, which did not leave customers with very much choice.

Silver Cloud III, S3, and Phantom VI

One final set of changes would occur before the end of the period that this book encompasses, and they were made in 1963. At that stage, the V8 engine was slightly uprated for all models, and the mainstream chassis were renamed the Rolls-Royce Silver Cloud III and

This Silver Cloud III chassis was specially prepared for the Earls Court Motor Show in 1964, where the picture was taken.

The Silver Cloud III (and Bentley S3) models were recognisable by new front-end details, with paired headlamps, a shorter radiator grille, and a tapered bonnet. (Simon Clay)

The Phantom V chassis was replaced by the Phantom VI in 1968. The "standard" body, now built by the HJ Mulliner, Park Ward division of Rolls-Royce, retained the design of the one drawn up for the Phantom V. Paired headlamps had been added to the Phantom V in 1963, to ensure the big limousine retained a family resemblance to the then-new Silver Cloud III. This is a 1971 example, PRH4662. (Simon Clay)

Bentley S3. Long-wheelbase variants of both remained available, and there was a Bentley Continental S3 too, although this no longer had a more powerful engine or higher gearing than the standard chassis. Instead, it was supplied with a steeper steering column rake (to allow lower coachwork) and a more comprehensive set of dashboard instruments.

The mainstream chassis continued with the same design of standard saloon bodies as before, although they were distinguished by a slightly shorter radiator grille, a sloping bonnet line and – most obviously – by paired headlamps that were doubtless inspired by the fashion for these in the USA. The paired headlamps were also grafted onto the front end of all Phantom V chassis at the start of the VA series in 1963 to enable the big Limousine to retain its family resemblance. A subsequent development was that a version of the

Silver Cloud III chassis with the raked steering column of the S3 Continental was made available in 1964, so more or less eliminating the uniqueness of the Bentley.

The mainstream chassis – Silver Cloud and Bentley S3 in both standard and Continental guises – were all replaced in autumn 1965 by the new Rolls-Royce Silver Shadow and Bentley T Type models, although production of the older chassis continued into 1966 to meet orders for coachbuilt bodies. The Phantom V meanwhile remained in production until 1968, when it underwent a number of revisions and became a Phantom VI. With the latest Silver Shadow version of the V8 engine, the Phantom VI always came with coachwork by the in-house coachbuilders Mulliner, Park Ward, and remained in production as a splendid anachronism until 1990 – the last Rolls-Royce model to have a separate chassis and drum brakes.

The completed chassis of the Silver Wraith prototype 1-SW-1 awaits its coachwork.

SPECIFICATIONS

ROLLS-ROYCE SILVER WRAITH

ENGINE

(A to E series)
4257cc six-cylinder, with overhead inlet and side exhaust valves
88.9mm bore x 114.3mm stroke
Cast iron block and aluminium alloy cylinder head
Seven main bearings
6.4:1 compression ratio
Stromberg dual downdraught carburettor

(F series and later short wheelbase, and long-wheelbase to DLW162)
4566cc six-cylinder, with overhead inlet and side exhaust valves
92mm bore x 114mm stroke
Cast iron block and aluminium alloy cylinder head
Seven main bearings
6.4:1 compression ratio; 6.75:1 optional on short-wheelbase H series and long-wheelbase B series
Stromberg dual downdraught carburettor (to WSG6); single Zenith downdraught carburettor from WSG7

(Long-wheelbase from LDLW163)
4887cc six-cylinder, with overhead inlet and side exhaust valves
95.25mm bore x 114mm stroke
Cast iron block and aluminium alloy cylinder head
Seven main bearings
6.4:1 compression ratio; 6.75:1 optional on B series and standard from C series; 8:1 from FLW60
Stromberg dual downdraught carburettor (to WSG6); single Zenith downdraught carburettor from WSG7

TRANSMISSION
Four-speed manual gearbox, no synchromesh on first gear
Ratios: 2.985:1, 2.02:1, 1.343:1, 1.00:1, reverse 3.15:1
11-inch single-dry-plate clutch
Four-speed automatic gearbox with fluid coupling optional from short-wheelbase H series and standard from late long-wheelbase D series
Ratios: 3.82:1, 2.63:1, 1.45:1, 1.00:1, reverse 4.30:1
Axle ratio
Short wheelbase   3.727:1
                  3.416:1 optional on some export chassis
                  from F series
Long wheelbase   3.727:1
                  3.416:1 optional
                  4.25:1, E series
                  4.375:1, F series onwards

STEERING, SUSPENSION AND BRAKES
Cam-and-roller steering; power assistance optional on long-wheelbase F series and later
Independent front suspension, with coil springs, wishbones, anti-roll bar and lever-arm hydraulic dampers
Live rear axle with semi-elliptic leaf springs and driver-controlled lever-arm hydraulic dampers
Drum brakes front and rear, 12.25in x 2.6in, with hydraulic operation at the front and mechanical operation at the rear; mechanical servo assistance

WHEELS AND TYRES
Short wheelbase
17-inch steel disc wheels with 5in rims and 6.50 x 17in cross-ply tyres. Some export chassis from F series onwards had 16-inch steel disc wheels with 5in rims and 7.50 x 16 cross-ply tyres
Long wheelbase
16-inch steel disc wheels with 5in rims and 7.50 x 16 cross-ply tyres

DIMENSIONS
Overall length	17ft 2in short wheelbase
	17ft 9.5in long wheelbase
Wheelbase	10ft 7in short wheelbase
	11ft 1in long wheelbase
Track, front	4ft 10in
Track, rear	4ft 11.5in short wheelbase
	5ft 4in long wheelbase
Height and width	Dependent on body fitted

CHASSIS NUMBER SEQUENCES
Chassis were numbered sequentially within each series, always omitting the number 13. On left-hand-drive chassis, an L was inserted before the letter prefix, eg LWHD50, LDLW105.

Short wheelbase models

Series	Chassis numbers	Series	Chassis numbers
A	WTA1 to WTA85	C	WGC1 to WGC101
	WVA1 to WVA81	D	WHD1 to WHD101
	WYA1 to WYA87	E	WLE1 to WLE35
B	WZB1 to WZB65		WME1 to WME96
	WAB1 to WAB65	F	WOF1 to WOF76
	WCB1 to WCB73	G	WSG1 to WSG76
C	WDC1 to WDC101	H	WVH1 to WVH 116
	WFC1 to WFC 101		

Long wheelbase models

Series	Chassis numbers	Series	Chassis numbers
A	ALW1 to ALW51	E	WLW1 to ELW101
B	BLW1 to BLW101	F	FLW1 to FLW101
C	CLW1 to CLW43	G	GLW1 to GLW26
D	DLW1 to DLW172	H	HLW1 to HLW52

There were 1883 Rolls-Royce Silver Wraith chassis, of which 1244 were short-wheelbase types and 639 were long-wheelbase types.

SPECIFICATIONS

BENTLEY MKVI

ENGINE

(A to L series)
4257cc six-cylinder, with overhead inlet and side exhaust valves
88.9mm bore x 114.3mm stroke
Cast iron block and aluminium alloy cylinder head
Seven main bearings
6.4:1 compression ratio
RHD models: two SU H4 carburettors (to B81HP), or two SU H6 carburettors (from B83HP)
LHD models: one Stromberg dual downdraught carburettor

(M series onwards)
4566cc six-cylinder, with overhead inlet and side exhaust valves
92mm bore x 114mm stroke
Cast iron block and aluminium alloy cylinder head
Seven main bearings
6.4:1 compression ratio; 6.75:1 from SMF62
RHD models: two SU H6 carburetors
LHD models: one Stromberg dual downdraught carburettor

TRANSMISSION

Four-speed manual gearbox, no synchromesh on first gear
Ratios: 2.98:1, 2.02:1, 1.34:1, 1.00:1, reverse 3.15:1
10-inch single-dry-plate clutch
Axle ratio 3.727:1

STEERING, SUSPENSION AND BRAKES
Cam-and-roller steering
Independent front suspension, with coil springs, wishbones, anti-roll bar and lever-arm hydraulic dampers
Live rear axle with semi-elliptic leaf springs and driver-controlled lever-arm hydraulic dampers
Drum brakes front and rear, 12.25in x 2.6in, with hydraulic operation at the front and mechanical operation at the rear; mechanical servo assistance

WHEELS AND TYRES
16-inch steel disc wheels with 5in rims and 6.50 x 16in cross-ply tyres

DIMENSIONS
Overall length	15ft 11.5in or 16ft 4.5in, depending on bumper type
Wheelbase	10ft 0in
Track, front	4ft 8.5in
Track, rear	4ft 10.5in
Height and width	Dependent on body fitted

CHASSIS NUMBER SEQUENCES
Chassis series beginning with 1 used odd numbers only, always omitting 13. Series beginning with 2 used even numbers only. There were normally (but not invariably) two sets of suffix codes in each chassis series, and these typically (but not invariably) were not issued in alphabetical order, so that (for example) the AK series came before the AJ series. On left-hand-drive chassis, an L was inserted before the letter suffix, eg B176LLJ.

Series	Chassis numbers	Series	Chassis numbers
A	B2AK to B254AK	H	B1HP to B251HP
	B1AJ to B247AJ	J	B2JO to B250JO
B	B2BH to B400BH		B1JN to B251JN
	B1BG to B401BG	K	B2KM to B200KM
C	B2CF to B500CF		B1KL to B201KL
	B1CD to B501CD	L	B2JL to B400LJ
D	B2DA to B500DA		B1LH to B401LH
	B1DZ to B501DZ	M	B2MD to B400MD
E	B2EY to B500EY		B1MB to B401MB
	B1EW to B501EW	N	B2NZ to B500NZ
F	B2FV to B500FV		B1NY to B501NY
	B1FU to B601FU	P	B2PV to B300PV
G	B1GT to B401GT		B1PU to B301PU
H	B2HR to B250HR		

Note: There were two additional cars in the above series. These were B256AK (formerly experimental chassis 1-B-VI) and B403MB (formerly experimental chassis 4-B-VI). There were 5202 Bentley MkVI chassis.

SPECIFICATIONS

ROLLS-ROYCE SILVER DAWN

ENGINE

(A to B series)
4257cc six-cylinder, with overhead inlet and side exhaust valves
88.9mm bore x 114.3mm stroke
Cast iron block and aluminium alloy cylinder head
Seven main bearings
6.4:1 compression ratio
Stromberg dual downdraught carburettor

(C series onwards)
4566cc six-cylinder, with overhead inlet and side exhaust valves
92mm bore x 114mm stroke
Cast iron block and aluminium alloy cylinder head
Seven main bearings
6.4:1 compression ratio; 6.75:1 from SMF62
Stromberg dual downdraught carburettor to SFC100; Zenith
downdraught carburettor from SFC102

TRANSMISSION

Four-speed manual gearbox, no synchromesh on first gear
Ratios: 2.98:1, 2.02:1, 1.34:1, 1.00:1, reverse 3.15:1
10-inch single-dry-plate clutch (A and B series);
11-inch clutch (C series onwards)
Four-speed automatic gearbox with fluid coupling optional from SMF2
Ratios: 3.82:1, 2.63:1, 1.45:1, 1.00:1, reverse 4.30:1
Axle ratio 3.727:1; 3.416:1 from SRH2

STEERING, SUSPENSION AND BRAKES

Cam-and-roller steering
Independent front suspension, with coil springs, wishbones, anti-roll
bar and lever-arm hydraulic dampers
Live rear axle with semi-elliptic leaf springs and driver-controlled lever-
arm hydraulic dampers
Drum brakes front and rear, 12.25in x 2.6in, with hydraulic operation
at the front and mechanical operation at the rear; mechanical servo
assistance

WHEELS AND TYRES

16-inch steel disc wheels with 5in rims and 6.50 x 16in cross-ply tyres

DIMENSIONS

Overall length	16ft 4.5in (A to D series) or 16ft 11.5in (E series onwards), or 17ft 6in (E series onwards, with heavy export bumpers)
Wheelbase	10ft 0in
Track, front	4ft 8.5in
Track, rear	4ft 10.5in
Height and width	Dependent on body fitted

CHASSIS NUMBER SEQUENCES

Chassis series beginning with 1 used odd numbers only, always omitting
13. Series beginning with 2 used even numbers only. On left-hand-drive
chassis, an L was inserted before the letter prefix, eg LSTH79.

Series	Chassis numbers	Series	Chassis numbers
A	SBA2 to SBA138	F	SNF1 to SNF125
	SCA1 to SCA163	G	SOG2 to SOG100
B	SDB2 to SDB140		SPG1 to SPG101
C	SFC2 to SFC160	H	SRH2 to SRH100
D	SHD2 to SHD60		STH1 to STH101
E	SKE2 to SKE50	J	SUJ2 to SUJ130
	SLE1 to SLE51		SVJ1 to SVJ 133
F	SMF2 to SMF76		

There were 761 Rolls-Royce Silver Dawn chassis.

SPECIFICATIONS

BENTLEY R TYPE

ENGINE
4566cc six-cylinder, with overhead inlet and side exhaust valves
92mm bore x 114mm stroke
Cast iron block and aluminium alloy cylinder head
Seven main bearings
6.4:1 compression ratio; 6.75:1 from B93TO
Two SU H6 carburettors

TRANSMISSION
Four-speed manual gearbox, no synchromesh on first gear
Ratios: 2.98:1, 2.02:1, 1.34:1, 1.00:1, reverse 3.15:1
11-inch single-dry-plate clutch
Four-speed automatic gearbox with fluid coupling optional from B2RT
(LHD), B2SR (RHD export) and B134TN (Home market)
Ratios: 3.82:1, 2.63:1, 1.45:1, 1.00:1, reverse 4.30:1
Axle ratio 3.727:1; 3.416:1 optional from B445SP

STEERING, SUSPENSION AND BRAKES
Cam-and-roller steering
Independent front suspension, with coil springs, wishbones, anti-roll
bar and lever-arm hydraulic dampers
Live rear axle with semi-elliptic leaf springs and driver-controlled
lever-arm hydraulic dampers
Drum brakes front and rear, 12.25in x 2.6in, with hydraulic operation
at the front and mechanical operation at the rear; mechanical servo
assistance

WHEELS AND TYRES
16-inch steel disc wheels with 5in rims and 6.50 x 16in cross-ply tyres

DIMENSIONS
Overall length	16ft 7.5in, 16ft 11.5in or 17ft 6in, depending on bumper type
Wheelbase	10ft 0in
Track, front	4ft 8.5in
Track, rear	4ft 10.5in
Height and width	Dependent on body fitted

CHASSIS NUMBER SEQUENCES
The sequences for the R Type standard chassis followed on from those
for the Bentley MkVI chassis.

Chassis series beginning with 1 used odd numbers only, always
omitting 13. Series beginning with 2 used even numbers only. There
were normally (but not invariably) two sets of suffix codes in each
chassis series, and these typically (but not invariably) were not issued in
alphabetical order, so that (for example) the SR series came before the
SP series. On left-hand-drive chassis, an L was inserted before the letter
suffix, eg B386LSR.

Series	Chassis numbers	Series	Chassis numbers
R	B2RT to B120RT	W	B2WH to B300WH
	B1RS to B121RS		B1WG to B301WG
S	B2SR to B500SR	X	B2XF to B140XF
	B1SP to B501SP	Y	B1YA to B331YA
T	B1TO to B401TO		B2YD to B330YD
	B2TN to B600TN	Z	B1ZX to B251ZX
U	B1UL to B251UL		B2ZY to B250ZY
	B2UM to B250UM		

Note: There were two additional cars in the above series. These were
B122XRT (formerly experimental chassis 14-B-VII) and B124XRT
(formerly experimental chassis 12-B-VII).
There were 2322 Bentley R Type chassis.

SPECIFICATIONS

BENTLEY R TYPE CONTINENTAL

ENGINE

(A to C Series)
4566cc six-cylinder, with overhead inlet and side exhaust valves
92mm bore x 114mm stroke
Cast iron block and aluminium alloy cylinder head
Seven main bearings
7.27:1 compression ratio (to BC18A); 7.1:1 (BC19A to BC3C); 7.2:1 (from BC4C)
Two SU H6 carburettors

(D and E Series)
4887cc six-cylinder, with overhead inlet and side exhaust valves
95.25mm bore x 114mm stroke
Cast iron block and aluminium alloy cylinder head
Seven main bearings
7.2:1 compression ratio
Two SU HD8 carburettors

TRANSMISSION
Four-speed manual gearbox, no synchromesh on first gear
Ratios: 2.98:1, 2.02:1, 1.34:1, 1.00:1, reverse 3.15:1
10-inch single-dry-plate clutch
Four-speed automatic gearbox with fluid coupling optional from BC1D
Ratios: 3.82:1, 2.63:1, 1.45:1, 1.00:1, reverse 4.30:1
Axle ratio 3.077:1

STEERING, SUSPENSION AND BRAKES
Cam-and-roller steering
Independent front suspension, with coil springs, wishbones, anti-roll bar and lever-arm hydraulic dampers
Live rear axle with semi-elliptic leaf springs and driver-controlled lever-arm hydraulic dampers
Drum brakes front and rear, 12.25in x 2.6in, with hydraulic operation at the front and mechanical operation at the rear; mechanical servo assistance

WHEELS AND TYRES
16-inch steel disc wheels with 5in rims and 6.50 x 16in cross-ply tyres

DIMENSIONS
Overall length	17ft 2.5in (early bumpers) or 17ft 7.5in (heavy export type bumpers)
Wheelbase	10ft 0in
Track, front	4ft 8.5in
Track, rear	4ft 10.5in
Height and width	Dependent on body fitted

CHASSIS NUMBER SEQUENCES
Chassis were numbered sequentially within each series, always omitting the number 13. On left-hand-drive chassis, an L was inserted before the letter suffix, eg BC46LC.

Series	Chassis numbers	Series	Chassis numbers
A	BC1A to BC25A	D	BC1D to BC74D
B	BC1B to BC25B	E	BC1E to BC9E
C	BC1C to BC78C		

Note: There was one additional car in the above series. This was BC26A (formerly experimental chassis 9-B-VI).
There were 208 Bentley R Type Continental chassis.

SPECIFICATIONS

ROLLS-ROYCE PHANTOM IV

ENGINE

(A and B series)
5675cc eight-cylinder, with overhead inlet and side exhaust valves
89mm bore x 114mm stroke
Cast iron block and aluminium alloy cylinder head
Nine main bearings
6.4:1 compression ratio
Stromberg dual downdraught carburettor

(C series)
6515cc eight-cylinder, with overhead inlet and side exhaust valves
95.25mm bore x 114mm stroke
Cast iron block and aluminium alloy cylinder head
Nine main bearings
6.4:1 compression ratio
Stromberg dual downdraught carburettor

TRANSMISSION
Four-speed manual gearbox, no synchromesh on first gear
Ratios: 2.985:1, 2.02:1, 1.343:1, 1.00:1, reverse 3.15:1
11-inch single-dry-plate clutch
Four-speed automatic gearbox with fluid coupling from 4BP5
Ratios: 3.82:1, 2.63:1, 1.45:1, 1.00:1, reverse 4.30:1
Axle ratio 4.25:1

STEERING, SUSPENSION AND BRAKES
Cam-and-roller steering
Independent front suspension, with coil springs, wishbones, anti-roll bar and double-acting hydraulic dampers
Live rear axle with semi-elliptic leaf springs and driver-controlled lever-arm hydraulic dampers
Drum brakes front and rear, 12.25in x 2.6in, with hydraulic operation at the front and mechanical operation at the rear; mechanical servo assistance

WHEELS AND TYRES
17-inch steel disc wheels with 5in rims and 7.00 x 17in cross-ply tyres

DIMENSIONS
Overall length	19ft 1.5in
Wheelbase	12ft 1in
Track, front	4ft 10.5in
Track, rear	5ft 3in
Height and width	Dependent on body fitted

CHASSIS NUMBER SEQUENCES
Chassis series beginning with 1 used odd numbers only. Series beginning with 2 used even numbers only. All chassis had right-hand drive.

Series	Chassis numbers	Series	Chassis numbers
A	4AF2 to 4AF22	C	4CS2 to 4CS6
B	4BP1 to 4BP7		

There were 18 Rolls-Royce Phantom IV chassis.

SPECIFICATIONS

ROLLS-ROYCE SILVER CLOUD AND BENTLEY S

ENGINE
4887cc six-cylinder, with overhead inlet and side exhaust valves
95.25mm bore x 114mm stroke
Cast iron block and aluminium alloy cylinder head
Seven main bearings
6.6:1 compression ratio
8:1 for North America only from SDD136 (Silver Cloud)
    and B120EG (Bentley)
8:1 standard from SFE9 (Silver Cloud) and B257EK (Bentley)
8:1 on all long-wheelbase models
Two SU HD6 carburettors with 6.6:1 compression ratio
Two SU HD8 carburettors with 8:1 compression ratio

TRANSMISSION
Four-speed automatic gearbox with fluid coupling
Ratios: 3.82:1, 2.63:1, 1.45:1, 1.00:1, reverse 4.30:1
Axle ratio 3.42:1

STEERING, SUSPENSION AND BRAKES
Cam-and-roller steering
Power assistance optional, initially for export only, from mid-C series (Silver Cloud) and late B series (Bentley); standard on long-wheelbase models
Independent front suspension, with coil springs, wishbones, anti-roll bar and opposed-piston hydraulic dampers
Live rear axle with semi-elliptic leaf springs and driver-controlled hydraulic dampers
Drum brakes front and rear, 11.25in x 3.0in, with hydraulic operation at the front and hydro-mechanical operation at the rear; mechanical servo assistance; twin master cylinders and duplicated front hydraulic circuits from SYB50 (Silver Cloud), B245BC (Bentley) and on all long-wheelbase chassis

WHEELS AND TYRES
15-inch steel disc wheels with 6in rims and 8.20 x 15 cross-ply tyres

DIMENSIONS
Overall length	17ft 8in
	17ft 11.75in long wheelbase
Wheelbase	10ft 3in
	10ft 7in long wheelbase
Track, front	4ft 10in
Track, rear	5ft 0in
Height and width	Dependent on body fitted

CHASSIS NUMBER SEQUENCES
On the standard cars, chassis series beginning with 1 used odd numbers only, always omitting 13. Series beginning with 2 used even numbers only. There were two sets of suffix codes in each chassis series, and these were sometimes issued in alphabetical order and sometimes not. On left-hand-drive chassis, an L was inserted before the letter prefix, eg LSXA25.

Standard models: Rolls-Royce

Series	Chassis numbers	Series	Chassis numbers
A	SWA2 to SWA250	E	SGE2 to SGE500
	SXA1 to SXA251		SFE1 to SFE501
B	SYB2 to SYB250	F	SHF1 to SHF249
	SZV1 to SZB251		SJF2 to SJF250
C	SBC2 to SBC150	G	SKG1 to SKG125
	SCC1 to SCC151		SLG2 to SLG126
D	SDD2 to SDD450	H	SMH1 to SMH265
	SED1 to SED451		SNH2 to SNH262

Standard models: Bentley

Series	Chassis numbers	Series	Chassis numbers
A	B2AN to B500AN	E	B2EG to B650EG
	B1AP to B501AP		B1EK to B651EK
B	B2BA to B250BA	F	B2FA to B650FA
	B1BC to B251BC		B1FD to B651FD
C	B2CK to B500CK	G	B1GD to B125GD
	B1CM to B500CM		B2GC to B126GC
D	B2DB to B350DB	H	B1HB to B45 HB
	B1DE to B351DE		B2HA to B50HA

On the long-wheelbase models, chassis were numbered consecutively, always omitting the number 13. On left-hand-drive chassis, an L was inserted before the letter prefix, eg LBLC22 (Rolls-Royce), LALB28 (Bentley).

Long-wheelbase models: Rolls-Royce

Series	Chassis numbers	Series	Chassis numbers
A	ALC1 to ALC26	C	CLC1 to CLC47
B	BLC1 to BLC51		

Note: There was one additional car in the above series. This was ALC1X (formerly experimental chassis 28-B).

Long-wheelbase models: Bentley

Series	Chassis numbers
A	ALB1 to ALB36

SPECIFICATIONS

BENTLEY S CONTINENTAL

All details as for standard Bentley S, except:

ENGINE

Compression ratio 7.25:1; 8:1 from BC21BG

TRANSMISSION

Four-speed manual gearbox optional on early chassis, no synchromesh on first gear
Ratios: 2.669:1, 1.539:1, 1.216:1, 1.00:1, reverse 2.861:1
11-inch single-dry-plate clutch
Axle ratio 2.92:1 (all chassis)

STEERING AND BRAKES

Power assistance optional from early B series
Twin master cylinders and duplicated front hydraulic circuits from BC16BG

CHASSIS NUMBER SEQUENCES

Chassis omitting the number 13. On left-hand-drive chassis, an L was inserted before the letter suffix, eg BC4LCH.

Series	Chassis numbers	Series	Chassis numbers
A	BC1AF to BC101AF	E	BC1EL to BC51EL
B	BC1BG to BC101BG	F	BC1FM to BC51FM
C	BC1CH to BC51CH	G	BC1GN to BC31GN
D	BC1DJ to BC51DJ		

Note: There was one additional car in the above series. This was BC102AF (formerly experimental chassis 27-B).
There were 431 Bentley S Continental chassis.

SPECIFICATIONS

ROLLS-ROYCE SILVER CLOUD II & III, AND BENTLEY S2 & S3

ENGINE

6230cc V8 with overhead valves
104.14mm bore x 91.44mm stroke
Aluminium alloy block and cylinder heads
Five main bearings
8:1 compression ratio (Silver Cloud II and Bentley S2)
9:1 for Silver Cloud III and Bentley S3, but 8:1 retained for countries where 100 octane petrol was unavailable
Two SU HD6 carburettors (Silver Cloud II and Bentley S2)
Two HD8 carburettors (Silver Cloud III and Bentley S3)

TRANSMISSION

Four-speed automatic gearbox with fluid coupling
Ratios: 3.82:1, 2.63:1, 1.45:1, 1.00:1, reverse 4.30:1
Axle ratio 3.89:1

STEERING, SUSPENSION AND BRAKES

Power-assisted cam-and-roller steering
Independent front suspension, with coil springs, wishbones, anti-roll bar and double-acting hydraulic dampers
Live rear axle with semi-elliptic leaf springs, Z-type control rod, and driver-controlled hydraulic dampers
Drum brakes front and rear, 12.25in x 2.6in, with hydraulic operation at the front and hydro-mechanical operation at the rear; mechanical servo assistance

WHEELS AND TYRES

15-inch steel disc wheels with 6in rims and 8.20 x 15 cross-ply tyres

DIMENSIONS

Overall length	17ft 8in
	18ft 0in long-wheelbase models
	Silver Cloud III and Bentley S3 models were typically an inch shorter overall because of smaller over-riders; North American cars and some coachbuilt cars retained the additional inch
Wheelbase	10ft 3in
	10ft 7in long-wheelbase models
Track, front	4ft 10.5in
Track, rear	5ft 0in
Height and width	Dependent on body fitted

CHASSIS NUMBER SEQUENCES : ROLLS-ROYCE SILVER CLOUD II AND BENTLEY S2

On the standard cars, chassis series beginning with 1 used odd numbers only, always omitting 13. Series beginning with 2 used even numbers only. There were two sets of suffix codes in most chassis series, and these were issued in alphabetical order. On left-hand-drive Rolls-Royce chassis, an L was inserted before the letter prefix, eg LSAE583; on left-hand-drive Bentley chassis, the L was inserted before the letter suffix, eg B445LBR.

Standard models: Rolls-Royce Silver Cloud II

Series	Chassis numbers	Series	Chassis numbers
A	SPA2 to SPA326	C	SXC1 to SXC671
	SRA1 to SRA325	D	SYD2 to SYD550
B	STB2 to STB500		SZD1 to SZD551
	SVB1 to SVB501	E	SAE1 to SAE685
C	SWC2 to SWC730		

Note: There was one additional car in the above series. This was SAE687 (formerly experimental chassis 30-B).
There were 2418 standard Rolls-Royce Silver Cloud II chassis.

Standard models: Bentley S2

Series	Chassis numbers	Series	Chassis numbers
A	B1AA to B325AA	C	B1CT to B445CT
	B2AM to B326AM		B2CU to B756CU
B	B1BR to B501BR	D	B1DV to B501DV
	B2BS to B500BS		B2DW to B376DW

There were 1863 standard Bentley S2 chassis.

CHASSIS NUMBER SEQUENCES : ROLLS-ROYCE SILVER CLOUD II AND BENTLEY S2 LONG-WHEELBASE MODELS

On the long-wheelbase models, chassis were numbered consecutively, always omitting the number 13. On both Rolls-Royce and Bentley chassis, left-hand drive was indicated by an L ahead of the letter prefix, eg LLCC2, LLBA9.

Long-wheelbase models: Rolls-Royce Silver Cloud II

Series	Chassis numbers	Series	Chassis numbers
A	LCA1 to LCA176	C	LCC1 to LCC 101
B	LCB1 to LCB101	D	LCD1 to LCD125

There were 299 long-wheelbase Rolls-Royce Silver Cloud II chassis.

Long-wheelbase models: Bentley S2

Series	Chassis numbers	Series	Chassis numbers
A	LBA1 to LBA26	B	LBB1 to LBB33

There were 57 long-wheelbase Bentley S2 chassis.

CHASSIS NUMBER SEQUENCES : ROLLS-ROYCE SILVER CLOUD III AND BENTLEY S3

All Rolls-Royce chassis series begin with 1 and use odd numbers only, always omitting the number 13. All Bentley chassis series begin with 2 and use even numbers only. On left-hand-drive Rolls-Royce chassis, an L was inserted before the letter prefix, eg LCSC85B; on left-hand-drive Bentley chassis, the L was inserted before the letter suffix, eg B40LJP. There was no B series for the standard chassis of either model.

Standard models: Rolls-Royce Silver Cloud III

Series	Chassis numbers	Series	Chassis numbers
A	SAZ1 to SAZ61	H	SHS1 to SHS357
C	SCX1 to SCX877	J	SJR1 to SJR623
D	SDW1 to SDW601	K	SKP1 to SKP423
E	SEV1 to SEV495	Coachbuilt	CSC1B to CSC141B
F	SFU1 to SFU803		CSC1C to CSC83C
G	SGT1 to SGT659		

Notes: There was no chassis numbered CSC83B. There was an additional chassis numbered LCSC83C (with left-hand drive): built for the Shah of Iran as a Bentley Continental S3 numbered BC56LXE, it was delivered as a Rolls-Royce.
There were 2555 standard Rolls-Royce Silver Cloud III chassis.

Standard models: Bentley S3

Series	Chassis numbers	Series	Chassis numbers
A	B2AV to B26AV	F	B2FG to B350FG
C	B2CN to B828CN	G	B2GJ to B200GJ
D	B2DF to B198DF	H	B2HN to B400HN
E	B2EC to B530EC	J	B2JP to B40JP

There were 1286 standard Bentley S3 chassis.

CHASSIS NUMBER SEQUENCES: ROLLS-ROYCE SILVER CLOUD III AND BENTLEY S3 LONG-WHEELBASE MODELS

All Rolls-Royce chassis series begin with 1 and use odd numbers only, always omitting the number 13. All Bentley chassis series begin with 2 and use even numbers only. On left-hand-drive chassis, an L was inserted before the letter prefix on both Rolls-Royce and Bentley models, eg LCAL1 (Rolls-Royce).

Long-wheelbase models: Rolls-Royce Silver Cloud III

Series	Chassis numbers	Series	Chassis numbers
A	CAL1 to CAL83	E	CEL1 to CEL105
B	CBL1 to CBL61	F	CFL1 to CFL41
C	CCL1 to CCL101	G	CGL1 to CGL29
D	CDL1 to CDL95		

There were 254 long-wheelbase Rolls-Royce Silver Cloud III chassis.

Long-wheelbase models: Bentley S3

Series	Chassis numbers	Series	Chassis numbers
A	BAL2 to BAL30	C	CCL2 to CCL22
B	BBL2 to BBL12		

There were 323 long-wheelbase Bentley S3 chassis.

SPECIFICATIONS

BENTLEY CONTINENTAL S2 & S3

There were no significant technical or dimensional differences between the Continental chassis and the standard equivalent, except that early S2 Continentals (to BC99BY) had taller 2.92:1 axle gearing. Thereafter the gearing was the same 3.89:1 as the standard chassis. However, all S2 and S3 Continentals had a more steeply raked steering column and more comprehensive instrumentation than their standard equivalents.

CHASSIS NUMBER SEQUENCES
BENTLEY S2 CONTINENTAL

Chassis were numbered sequentially within each series, always omitting the number 13. On left-hand-drive chassis, an L was inserted before the letter suffix, eg BC59LCZ.

Series	Chassis numbers	Series	Chassis numbers
A	BC1AR to BC151AR	C	BC1CZ to BC139CZ
B	BC1BY to BC101BY		

There were 388 Bentley Continental S2 chassis.

CHASSIS NUMBER SEQUENCES
BENTLEY S3 CONTINENTAL

All chassis series begin with 2 and use even numbers only. On left-hand-drive chassis, an L was inserted before the letter suffix, eg BC44LXA.

Series	Chassis numbers	Series	Chassis numbers
A	BC2XA to BC174XA	D	BC2XD to BC28XD
B	BC2XB to BC100XB	E	BC2XE to BC120XE
C	BC2XC to BC202XC		

Notes: There was no chassis numbered BC56XE. This was built as BC56LXE but was delivered as a Rolls-Royce, with chassis number LCSC83C.

There were 311 Bentley Continental S3 chassis.

SPECIFICATIONS

ROLLS-ROYCE PHANTOM V

ENGINE

6230cc V8 with overhead valves
104.14mm bore x 91.44mm stroke
Aluminium alloy block and cylinder heads
Five main bearings
8:1 compression ratio
9:1 from VA series; 8:1 retained for countries where 100 octane petrol unavailable
Two SU HD6 carburettors

TRANSMISSION

Four-speed automatic gearbox with fluid coupling
Ratios: 3.82:1, 2.63:1, 1.45:1, 1.00:1, reverse 4.30:1
Axle ratio 3.89:1

STEERING, SUSPENSION AND BRAKES

Power-assisted cam-and-roller steering
Independent front suspension, with coil springs, wishbones, anti-roll bar and double-acting hydraulic dampers
Live rear axle with semi-elliptic leaf springs and driver-controlled hydraulic dampers
Drum brakes front and rear, 11.25in x 3.0in, with hydraulic operation at the front and hydro-mechanical operation at the rear; mechanical servo assistance

WHEELS AND TYRES

15-inch steel disc wheels with 6in rims and 8.90 x 15 cross-ply tyres

DIMENSIONS

Overall length	19ft 10in (19ft 9in for some VA series and later cars)
Wheelbase	12ft 1in
Track, front	5ft 0.875in
Track, rear	5ft 4in
Height and width	Dependent on body fitted

CHASSIS NUMBER SEQUENCES

The chassis numbers were issued in two distinct main sequences. In the earlier sequence, chassis series beginning with 1 used odd numbers only, and series beginning with 2 used even numbers only. There were two sets of suffix codes in some chassis series, and only one in others. In the later sequence, the numbers were sequential. The number 13 was always omitted. On left-hand-drive chassis, an L was inserted before the letter suffix, eg 5LAS3.

1st Series	Chassis numbers	2nd Series	Chassis numbers
A	5AS1 to 5AS101	A	5VA1 to 5VA123
	5AT2 to 5AT100	B	5VB1 to 5VB51
B	5BV1 to 5BV101	C	5VC1 to 5VC51
	5BX2 to 5BX100	D	5VD1 to 5VD101
C	5CG1 to 5CG79	E	5VE1 to 5VE51
		F	5VF1 to 5VF183

There were 516 Rolls-Royce Phantom V chassis.

SPECIFICATIONS

ROLLS-ROYCE PHANTOM VI

The Phantom VI chassis shared the specification of the earlier Phantom V until spring 1978, when the following mechanical changes were made.

ENGINE

6750cc V8 with overhead valves
104.14mm bore x 99.1mm stroke
Aluminium alloy block and cylinder heads
Five main bearings
8:1 compression ratio (Silver Cloud II and Bentley S2)
9:1 for Silver Cloud III and Bentley S3, but 8:1 retained for countries
  where 100 octane petrol was unavailable
Two SU HD6 carburettors (Silver Cloud II and Bentley S2)
Two HD8 carburettors (Silver Cloud III and Bentley S3)

TRANSMISSION

Three speed GM400 automatic gearbox with torque converter
Ratios: 2.5:1, 1.5:1, 1.0:1, reverse 2:1

BRAKES

Operation by high-pressure hydraulic system

CHASSIS NUMBER SEQUENCES

Phantom VI chassis numbers used a new standardised system that had been established for the Silver Shadow in 1965. This has a three-letter prefix, either PRH or PRX and a four-digit serial number. The prefix codes break down as follows:

P Phantom
R Rolls-Royce
H Home specification (ie RHD)
X Export specification (ie LHD)

The first three Phantom VIs were PRH4108, PRH4503 and PRH4504, all numbered within the series also used for the Rolls-Royce Silver Shadow and Bentley T series. A special sequence was then allocated to the Phantom VI, running from 4549 to 4874. Two numbers in this sequence were not used: 4670 and 4699.

With the introduction of the 6.75-litre engine in 1978, a new sequence of numbers was reserved for the Phantom VI. This ran from PGH101 to PGH134

From October 1980, all Phantom VI models had standardised VINs. The first one was SCAPM0000AWX01332, and the last (in 1990) was SCAPM01A2LWH10426. These numbers were in the same sequence as other models from Crewe until 1987, when they were allocated a separate sequence that started at 10415.

SCA	Rolls-Royce
P	Phantom VI
M	Limousine (later included Landaulette as well)
T	Landaulette
0	Engine type (always a 0 outside North America before 1987)
0	6230cc or 6750cc V8
1	6750cc V8 from 1987
0	Restraint system (always a 0 outside North America before 1987)
0	Check digit (0-9 or X) (always a 0 outside North America before 1987)
A	1980 MY (none built 1981)
C	1982 MY (etc)
W	Willesden factory
H	RHD
X	LHD

There were 374 Rolls-Royce Phantom VI chassis.

Chapter Two

Coachbuilt Bodies

Glamour has always been an important element in bespoke coachwork, and this Park Ward Drophead Coupé on a Rolls-Royce Silver Wraith chassis encapsulates the concept. (Simon Clay)

Many coachbuilders who worked on the Rolls-Royce and Bentley chassis in this period could trace their origins back to the days of carriage building, when their craft was to build a carriage that would be pulled by a horse or horses. As the 20th century got under way and demand for horse-drawn vehicles dried up, so they turned to building bodies – coachwork – for motor car chassis.

As the volume car makers gradually began to make standardised bodies in-house, or to agree contracts with coachbuilders for standardised designs to be built in quantity, so the coachbuilding business began to reduce. But the makers of grander chassis, in all the countries where cars were manufactured, generally preferred to focus on the job they were good at and to

entrust coachwork to those surviving firms who still did the job by hand and to much higher standards of finish, style and equipment than was practicable by the latest mass-production methods. Rolls-Royce and Bentley were among them.

The advent of monocoque structures in the later 1930s ate further into the coachbuilding business, and some of the older firms closed for good. Then, as the 1939-45 war ended, there were more changes in the trade. Skilled men were not as easy to find as they had been earlier; nor was business. Even Rolls-Royce turned to volume-produced standardised bodies for the post-war Bentley, the MkVI that became available in 1946. And although Rolls-Royce and Bentley were certainly not alone in calling on traditional coachbuilding skills,

More drophead glamour from Park Ward, this time on a 1952 Rolls-Royce Silver Dawn chassis. (Rolls-Royce Motor Cars Ltd)

they quite soon became the major customers for the work of those coachbuilders who remained in business.

There were at least 56 coachbuilders who worked on Rolls-Royce and Bentley chassis in the period from 1945-1965, most of them in Britain but (as Chapter 4 shows) several overseas as well. The table later in this chapter lists them. Their numbers gradually declined as mergers and unfavourable market conditions took their toll, but there were five major British companies who continued to work on Rolls-Royce and Bentley chassis for most of the two decades that this book covers. They were Freestone & Webb, Hooper, HJ Mulliner, Park Ward, and James Young, who, in due

course, became known as the "Big Five".

Yet even their numbers gradually shrank. Freestone & Webb, the smallest of the five, closed down in 1958. Hooper followed in 1959. HJ Mulliner lost its independence in 1961, being bought out by Rolls-Royce and merged with Park Ward (already owned by Rolls-Royce Ltd and acting as the in-house bespoke coachbuilding division), and the two companies emerged as a wholly-owned subsidiary called Mulliner, Park Ward. Last of the five to remain independent and active was James Young, but even that company closed its doors when Rolls-Royce went over to monocoque construction for the new Silver Shadow models in 1965.

THE DICTATES OF FASHION

Coachbuilding, rather like clothes, was always subject to the dictates of fashion. If a particular coachbuilder's new design caught the public imagination, it would not be long before others borrowed elements of it, adapted it, or (in a few cases) came up with an outright copy.

In order to keep ahead of their rivals, and of course in order to present fresh and interesting new designs to their potential customers, coachbuilders in Britain showed their latest offerings at the annual Earls Court motor show in London. This was always held in the autumn, usually during October, and a new body ordered on the spot could often be ready for delivery by Christmas or early in the new year unless there were complications. Most coachbuilders revised or replaced their "standard" designs – the ones built in low volumes – every year or two in order to retain that freshness which is so important to fashion.

Always striving to be different and ahead of the game, several coachbuilders aimed to produce new designs for the first post-war British motor show, in 1948. James Young showed a radical new design (right), but it did not catch on. (Anton van Luijk/Wikipedia Commons)

Bespoke in a different way: this drophead coachwork was actually converted from the standard four-door Saloon under Rolls-Royce auspices.

The coachbuilding process

The process of creating a coachbuilt body for a Rolls-Royce or Bentley chassis remained much the same throughout the 20 years covered in this book, and was in fact much the same as it had been since the dawn of the 20th century. A customer would probably make contact initially with a Rolls-Royce and Bentley dealer, who would be able to advise on which of the coachbuilders might be able to provide a body of the kind required.

Not every coachbuilt body was an entirely bespoke creation, of course. In order to keep quantities up and costs down, most of the coachbuilders had developed designs that could be built in small batches, with minor variations to suit a customer's wishes. Some of the bigger dealers – Jack Barclay in London was one – tended to keep examples of these in stock so that a customer could, in effect, buy a coachbuilt model straight from the showroom floor. The quantities in which such bodies were built varied enormously: a popular one might attract 50 or more orders over a period of years, but there might be no more than two or three examples of the less popular designs.

Truly individual bodies became rarer during the 1950s, but for those who wanted something more individual (and that might include a particular minor variation on a low-quantity "stock" design), the whole purchasing process would take much longer. From the time a customer placed an order for a chassis to the time that chassis had been fitted with coachwork, tested and approved by Rolls-Royce, and finally delivered, might take several months. In the late 1940s, when materials shortages were common and could have a major impact on manufacturing industries of all kinds, there might be further delays.

For a truly bespoke body, the first stage was for the customer to talk to the coachbuilder's chief designer, who would sketch out roughly what was required in pencil. Interview concluded, the designer or one of his staff would then make an ink drawing that contained the important internal dimensions. This, typically, might be given a unique design number. A copy of this drawing would then be sent to the customer for approval, and further copies with amendments would follow if the customer requested changes. Eventually, the customer would approve a coloured rendering of the completed vehicle, typically a water colour wash, and then copies of all the relevant drawings and illustrations would be sent on to Rolls-Royce for approval. This approval was critical: Rolls-Royce understandably wanted to protect the integrity of their chassis and were also concerned about warranties. So without that prior approval the coachbuilder could not proceed, and to enforce that the company could decline to supply the chassis for bodying.

No doubt a price was discussed and agreed at this point, and now the coachbuilder would move on to the next stage, which was to create a full-size drawing of the planned coachwork. At Freestone & Webb, this full-size drawing occupied a whole wall of the Drawing Office, and would include several elevations on the same sheet of paper. This was not just an artist's impression of the way the finished car would look. It was a precision drawing from which the body would

be built, and any dimensional errors here would lead to similar errors in the finished coachwork.

Once approved in-house, the full-size drawing was passed to the Setting-Out Department, which would use it to make the templates from which the frame members for the new body would be made. Traditional frames were made from seasoned ash, although this was in short supply in the late 1940s and compromises had to be made. The wood available in those difficult times was not always ideal for the job, and often rotted prematurely, leading to failure of the frame and eventually its collapse.

Some companies of course used metal framing, or a mixture of wood and metal, and this "composite" construction gradually became the norm in the 1950s. Park Ward was a pioneer of all-metal framing, Hooper's Teviot design used all-metal framing from 1950, and HJ Mulliner became a pioneer of frames that depended on aluminium extrusions. Composite frames might use T-section steel for the centre pillars to add rigidity to an otherwise timber structure. Freestone & Webb were still using composite frames when they closed in 1958, with box-section pillars made of aluminium alloy to reduce weight; James Young depended on composite frames until 1966. The wooden sections of these frames were generally mated through lap joints, although there would also be some mortise and tenon joints, such as where the cant rail met the pillar. All timber joints were screwed and glued, and were also reinforced by steel brackets.

Dimensional accuracy was crucial, because bodies were generally constructed away from the chassis up

to the point where the framing was complete. After the chassis had been delivered from Crewe, the body would then be mounted to it, typically using special rubber mountings that helped absorb any flexing and also reduced the transmission of road noise into the passenger compartment.

Chassis arrived from Crewe in driveable form, with engine and transmission already installed, with the radiator shell, bonnet, engine side panels and bulkhead in place, and with the steel floor, rear seat pan, boot platform and spare wheel housing spot-welded together. The factory provided bumpers, wheel trims, instruments, lights and tools as part of the package. Sometimes, Crewe would also supply the front wings and other pressings of a "standard steel" body (where one existed) to be integrated into the coachbuilder's work. Otherwise, the complex wing structures were usually made on wooden jigs – a practice that had grown up after war work in 1939-1945 had made the benefits of jig-building more apparent and more widespread.

The body would then be carefully mounted in place. With the doors still off, skilled trimmers got to work on the interior. Coach fitters had already produced the metal parts needed for such things as occasional seat mechanisms and picnic table components, while cabinet makers in the Wood Shop had created the dashboard and other interior wood trim panels – including, of course, those for the division if one was to be fitted. Most coachbuilders had their own distinctive style for interior woodwork, creating exquisite results by using carefully matched veneers on a solid wood

Some highly individual designs brought their own surprises. This Saloon was built by the Italian coachbuilder Bertone on a Bentley chassis in 1953. (Simon Clay)

Even though many coachbuilders relied on core designs that could be built in small batches, there was always room for individualisation. This Park Ward Drophead Coupé on a Bentley MkVI chassis was specially built for King Fredrik IX of Denmark in 1950. (Anton van Luijk/ Wikimedia Commons)

or plywood base. Seats were again the work of skilled craftsmen (and sometimes women), created specifically for each body, and other interior trim would be added to the body as it came together.

Doors would then be hung and carefully "fitted" to the body to achieve even gaps and smooth lines. Window frames, which in this period were typically separate structures that were bolted into the lower door sections, would also have to be adjusted to achieve the perfect fit that a customer expected. They would have been made in-house from brass strip brazed together and, like the door hinges, would be heavily chrome-plated over deposits of copper and nickel.

The metal used for the outer panels was usually half-hard aluminium, which was easy for the skilled panel-beaters to work by hand, was light in weight, and was also durable. Body panels would be beaten and manipulated into shape in position on the frame before being joined by welding. Outer door handles might be made in-house to a unique design (James Young's handles with their distinctive square push-buttons were an example), or might be standard production items provided by Crewe (as was usually the case at Park Ward).

Once fully panelled, the body would then be taken to the Paint Shop. At least 20 coats of paint would be sprayed on by hand, including six coats of cellulose lacquer – or more if the paint was a metallic type. Rubbing down between coats and after the final coat would again be done by hand, and the whole process might take a week or longer because each coat of paint had to be left to dry naturally.

The paint process was meticulous, and produced a finish that was visibly superior to the processes used in mass production. Little had changed since the 1930s.

On the first day, primer would be applied. On the second day, the finish would be inspected and stopper applied as necessary. The third day would be devoted to rubbing down – by hand, of course – to achieve a perfectly smooth finish. The fourth day would typically see the undercoat or surface sealer applied. The top coats, of which there could be several, would not be put on until the fifth day. Fine lining might follow, and of course would be hand-applied by another skilled craftsman. Any rectification at this stage could delay the process further, but in an ideal world the body would be polished on the sixth day.

Once the coachbuilder had completed assembly work, a Rolls-Royce representative would always inspect the car before it could be signed off. The inspection would include a road test, designed to detect squeaks and rattles, and might be followed by some rectification work. A final polish followed this inspection process, and then delivery to the supplying dealer (or direct to the customer, as appropriate) would follow only once everything had been completed to the satisfaction of both chassis maker and coachbuilder.

That, then, would end the coachbuilder's direct involvement, although most coachbuilders were only too pleased to welcome customers who came back for minor alterations or additions to their coachwork. Modifications could and did range from the very minor to major changes such as to the wing lines, and even to quite radical transformations, such as from drophead coupé to fixed-head coupé. It is also important to remember that these cars were not thought of as indivisible and immutable wholes in the way that has since become the norm. Body and chassis had come from separate makers and could be separated again. So it sometimes happened that a well-liked body was transferred to an owner's new chassis, the old one perhaps then being sold to a specialist dealer. Sometimes, an accident-damaged body had to be replaced. Equally, it was not unknown for owners to tire of the body they had originally bought and to change it for a new one.

The evolution of coachwork between 1945 and 1965

As the first chassis became available from Crewe during 1946, British coachbuilders had very little to offer that was new. The first bodies that appeared on Rolls-Royce Silver Wraith and Bentley MkVI chassis were mostly continuations and adaptations of pre-war styles, and many of them had the razor-edge lines that had been so popular in the late 1930s. These essentially conservative design elements would remain in Limousine coachwork for longer than elsewhere, no doubt because of a conservative outlook among the buyers of such vehicles. Chrome embellishment was rare because of supply difficulties associated with chromium plating, and these early bodies generally appeared rather plain by later standards. Front and rear wings were typically separate pressings and their lines were not continued into the doors. They were often joined by running-boards below the doors, and sometimes these running-boards were concealed by an outsweep at the bottom of the door panels.

Not a lot of progress was evident in design before 1948, and the main impetus for progress that year was that the first post-war motor shows were scheduled. The Geneva Show in March was important for attracting European customers – and of course government policy of the time put a heavy emphasis on export success – while the Earls Court Show in London in October was important for attracting business from the home market. So coachbuilders made a particular effort to come up with something new or, at the very least, something that was eye-catching even if it was a little extravagant. In those times of austerity, extravagance seemed like a world away and was automatically of interest even if it also attracted disapproval.

An influential design around this time was the first Hooper Teviot, with very neat lines that hinted at a smoothing out of the harsher elements of razor-edge styles. The first ones had actually been built early in 1948, and the design would continue to evolve and to remain a shape that others emulated for several more years. By contrast, Park Ward and James Young both used the 1948 Earls Court show to display modern full-width styles that were American in inspiration and doubtless avant-garde, but which simply lacked the grace and elegance of more traditional designs. They had little influence on their peers and sold poorly.

By 1949, new designs were increasingly enclosing the rear wheels, with either full or cutaway spats. Wing lines were raised at the front and flowed back across the doors, typically suppressing external running-boards, and they sometimes met rear wings which were increasingly becoming little more than pressings on the body sides. Major influences in this period were the Park Ward style (which appeared on an experimental body in 1949 and became a "production" style later), and the Hooper "Empress", which was actually called the New Look on its 1949 introduction. With this design and others that emulated it, the rear wings disappeared as separate volumes because the body sides were pushed outwards to give more rear seat width.

The search for new coachwork solutions was very much on by the end of the 1940s, and it was HJ Mulliner who made the next major step forward.

As demand for bespoke coachwork slowed right down in the 1950s, the remaining coachbuilders struggled to find new features that would appeal. These cowled and recessed lights were from Hooper, on a rare body for the Bentley Continental chassis. (Simon Clay)

Their development of Lightweight construction in 1950, using Reynolds Metal instead of timber to create the body frame, was a breakthrough that did not go un-noticed at Rolls-Royce. When the chassis maker wanted lightweight coachwork to improve the performance of the model that became the first Bentley Continental, it was HJ Mulliner who were awarded the contract to build it – though with styling from Rolls-Royce itself. The new Lightweight bodies were formidably expensive, and HJ Mulliner continued to

in the products from British coachbuilders, but one of the first designs to have it was the famous Mulliner Lightweight saloon, originally designed for Rolls-Royce Silver Wraith chassis. By 1954, it had become commonplace.

The visual counterbalance of that longer boot became attractive in other areas, too. The "standard-steel" Bentley MkVI saloon body built by Pressed Steel had followed those pre-war visual principles, and by the early 1950s was beginning to look rather dated. Several coachbuilders felt the need to create longer rear ends than the chassis was designed to take, and supported these by extending the chassis rails themselves. Rolls-Royce took the hint, so their Silver Dawn and R Type Bentley incorporated a longer tail as standard, plus the so-called "big boot" body.

The new proportions with larger boots would eventually become standard fare, and the standard saloon coachwork for the 1955 Rolls-Royce Silver Cloud was a supremely elegant reflection of this. But in the meantime there were some interesting anomalies.

The anomalies

During the late 1940s, a loophole in government regulations led to the popularity of shooting brake type bodies, typically made of wood to minimise costs; if certain rules were met, these qualified as commercial vehicles and were therefore exempt from Purchase Tax. Many were built on pre-war chassis whose bodies had deteriorated beyond repair, and many were somewhat crudely built by what were essentially carpentry firms rather than by coachbuilders. Nevertheless, they set a trend. In the late 1940s and early 1950s, bodies of this style began to appear on brand-new Rolls-Royce and Bentley chassis, their owners perhaps always intending to replace them with something more

The coachbuilders gradually fell by the wayside during the period covered by this book. This beautiful drophead design for the Bentley S2 Continental was originally the work of Park Ward, but that coachbuilder (already under Rolls-Royce ownership) was merged with HJ Mulliner in the early 1960s, and the design became a Mulliner, Park Ward product. (John Sweney/WikiMedia Commons)

build more conventional composite bodies for many more years, but the new method of construction was associated with a new style as well.

Most closed bodies of the late 1940s followed the pre-war practice of having a sloping rear panel with the luggage boot let into this and extending from it. Meanwhile, American influence was beginning to affect the European industry in the shape of "three-box" styling (where a projecting boot visually counterbalanced the projecting bonnet), as pioneered on the 1947-model Studebakers whose basic design came from the Raymond Loewy industrial design studio. It took a long time for this to become common

Some designs were built in tiny numbers. There was just one of these two-door bodies by HJ Mulliner, using their "lightweight" construction. Built on Bentley MkVI chassis B75KL, it was delivered to a Swiss customer in 1951.

luxurious and more conventional when post-war austerity eased. Inevitably, the major coachbuilders were asked to provide their own interpretations of the style. Harold Radford also depended on it for his first Countryman models of 1948-1949 – although these had wooden cladding on otherwise standard composite coachbuilt bodies.

The idea that coachwork could be changed or replaced at will is alien to today's world of monocoque bodies, but in a world where body and chassis were separate entities it led to some interesting developments. In the later 1940s and early 1950s, there are several documented instances of a body being replaced or swapped from one chassis to another. There are several undocumented but suspected instances, too, many of them attributed to firms such as Coopers of Putney. Coopers would buy unwanted bodies that had been removed when a chassis was rebodied. They would also buy "end of run" bodies from some of the major coachbuilders; these would typically be batch-built designs where a number had been built for stock but a few had remained unsold by the time they had been replaced in the coachbuilder's catalogue. Coopers' speciality was fitting these bodies to whatever chassis their customers brought along, and adapting them (usually quite skilfully) to fit chassis for which they

This Limousine on a Rolls-Royce Phantom V chassis was new to the Duke of Kent in 1963, but during later ownership by the Al-Fayed family was painted in the colours of Harrods, the London store that they owned. (Simon Clay)

More modifications: in this case, a Phantom V Limousine was converted into a large Cabriolet by specialist Claus Inhoven, who did similar work on several Silver Clouds as well. (Klaus-Josef Rossfeldt)

Sometimes, coachwork was expected to be discreet rather than glamorous. This James Young Limousine on a Rolls-Royce Silver Wraith chassis demonstrates how that could be achieved with such a large car. (Simon Clay)

in the body sides. Front end design took some time to catch up, hindered to a degree by the tall radiator grilles associated with the Rolls-Royce and Bentley marques, and there were some rather strange attempts to make the front of the car look different. By about 1953, some of the latest curvaceous designs were let down by unimaginative frontal styling, with headlamps simply let into curved wing fronts. So new features began to appear, Hooper and Freestone & Webb being pioneers of cowled wing fronts with the headlamps let into specially formed sections. At the rear, by 1954 the influence of the American taste for tail fins was apparent, and a few coachbuilders began to incorporate discreet fin-like projections on the rear wings of otherwise conventionally styled bodies. The most extreme example of this trend was probably Freestone & Webb's use of a gap between the boot and rear wings, allowing the latter to take on shapes that would otherwise have been difficult to blend into the lines of the boot.

had not been designed. This produced some strange combinations and has made tracing the provenance of some vehicles very difficult. It was a step up from another practice prevalent among small coachbuilders of the time, which was to create "replica" bodies – new bodies in rough imitation of old styles to replace worn-out bodies on older but still serviceable chassis.

Inevitably, with the progression to full-width bodies and three-box designs, separate wings disappeared and "wings" were delineated by curvaceous pressings

By the early 1960s, nearly all the independent coachbuilders had gone, and the styling trends were very much set by the in-house Mulliner, Park Ward body division. Mostly, designs remained quite conservative, and the elegant Flying Spur (originally an HJ Mulliner design) and grand Limousine bodies on the Phantom V chassis (originally by Park Ward) more or less defined the era. But there was one notable new design, which was the Koren style for the Bentley Continental (and later also Rolls-Royce) chassis. Sweeping away the curves of the 1950s, these very modern-looking bodies with their straight-through

Some designs became timeless classics. This is James Young's SCT100 Limousine, the so-called "baby Phantom", on a long-wheelbase Rolls-Royce Silver Cloud chassis from 1965. (Simon Clay)

Another timeless classic from this era was the original fastback body built by HJ Mulliner for the first Bentley Continental chassis. This is it, on chassis BC5C from 1953. (Simon Clay)

wing lines were actually beautifully proportioned – and yet they were always a controversial alternative to the more traditional designs.

Then, as separate chassis disappeared from Crewe (the exception being the low-volume Phantom V and later Phantom VI types), standard bodywork became the norm. The development of styles after 1965 is beyond the scope of this book, but it is interesting that the "standard" Rolls-Royce Silver Shadow and its Bentley equivalent had quite plain lines, while their equally standard but hand-built equivalents depended on the subtle use of curves.

THE COST OF COACHBUILDING

Individual coachbuilders did not disclose the prices of their creations in the catalogue of the Earls Court Motor Show in the 1950s, but the price of the complete vehicle was published when their coachwork was shown on the Rolls-Royce or Bentley stands. The prices listed here are total costs including Purchase Tax, and those for standard Rolls-Royce and Bentley saloons of the time are shown for comparison. Generally speaking, for coachbuilt cars the coachwork cost rather more than the chassis. Note that the actual cost of a coachbuilt car could vary quite considerably if individual features were included in the specification.

1955

Rolls-Royce Silver Cloud (standard saloon)	£4796 10s 1d
Silver Wraith Park Ward Touring Saloon	£7325 5s 10d
Silver Wraith HJ Mulliner Touring Limousine	£7359 17s 6d
Silver Wraith Hooper seven-passenger Limousine	£7502 7s 6d
Bentley S Type (standard saloon)	£4669 0s 10d
Bentley Continental Park Ward Drophead Coupé	£6765 14s 2d
Bentley Continental HJ Mulliner Saloon	£7027 15s 10d

1956

Rolls-Royce Silver Cloud (standard saloon)	£5386 7s 0d
Silver Wraith Park Ward Touring Saloon	£7906 7s 0d
Silver Wraith HJ Mulliner Touring Limousine	£8071 7s 0d
Silver Wraith Hooper Enclosed Limousine	£8093 17s 0d
Bentley S Type (standard saloon)	£5243 17s 0d
Bentley Continental Park Ward Saloon	£7163 17s 0d
Bentley Continental HJ Mulliner Saloon	£7606 17s 0d

1957

Rolls-Royce Silver Cloud (standard saloon)	£5693 17s 0d
Silver Cloud LWB with division (standard)	£6893 17s 0d
Silver Wraith HJ Mulliner Touring Limousine	£8438 17s 0d
Silver Wraith Hooper seven-passenger Limousine	£8708 17s 0d
Bentley S Type (standard saloon)	£5543 17s 0d
Bentley Continental Park Ward Drophead Coupé	£7493 17s 0d
Bentley Continental HJ Mulliner Saloon	£7913 17s 0d

1958

Rolls-Royce Silver Cloud (standard saloon)	£5693 17s 0d
Silver Cloud LWB with division (standard)	£6893 17s 0d
Silver Cloud HJ Mulliner Drophead Coupé	£8326 7s 0d
Silver Wraith Park Ward seven-passenger Limousine	£8708 17s 0d
Bentley S Type (standard saloon)	£5543 17s 0d
Bentley Continental Park Ward Drophead Coupé	£7493 17s 0d
Bentley Continental Park Ward Saloon	£7913 17s 0d
Bentley S Type HJ Mulliner Six-light Saloon	£8033 17s 0d

COACHWORK STYLES AND TERMS

This table is intended as a layman's guide to the meaning of the most common terms used to describe styles of coachwork on post-war Rolls-Royce and Bentley chassis. Others were often created by combining terms listed below.

However, a few words of warning are necessary. Most important is to understand that these terms were not immutably fixed, and that the coachbuilders themselves used different terms to describe the same thing. One reason for these differing uses of terminology was undoubtedly to make a design sound exotic, special, and above all, different from that offered by a rival company.

The second thing to understand is that the descriptions used for some bodies have been applied only by commentators, and not by the coachbuilders themselves. They are therefore to some extent subjective. That subjectivity is not and cannot be absent from some of the descriptions used in this book.

Note, too, that some designs were drawn up to be adaptable, so that a Saloon might also be made available as a Saloon with Division, or a Touring Limousine might be created by modifying a seven-passenger Limousine design.

All-weather

The name is at least partially self-explanatory. An All-weather body was essentially an open four-door type, with effective weather protection in the shape of a folding roof or "head" and, typically, winding windows in the doors. These bodies were rare in the post-war period.

Cabriolet

Cabriolet was the French term for what most British coachbuilders called a Drophead Coupé. French coachwork was highly regarded in the 1930s and to call a design a Cabriolet gave it a certain additional glamour even by the 1950s.

Close-coupled

If a design was described as close-coupled, it meant that the front and rear seats were closely coupled – a rather euphemistic way of saying that there was not much legroom for rear-seat passengers.

Coupé

Literally, the word means "cut", and it comes from French and from the days of horse-drawn vehicles. Between 1945 and 1965, a Coupé body typically had two doors and a fixed roof, although it was likely to have an overall outline that generally resembled that of a saloon. The distinction between Two-door Saloon and Coupé is sometimes a fine one, but a Coupé would typically have a more deliberately sporting appearance. James Young specialised in what they called Saloon Coupés, a term explained below.

De Ville

De Ville styles were formal bodies intended for chauffeur-drive use. The words are French and translate as "for town" but really indicated that the owner would sit in the back (typically in a closed compartment) while the chauffeur would be exposed in a front section with no roof and, sometimes, no side windows either. A De Ville roof is a fabric or metal panel that fits over the otherwise exposed driving compartment.

Drophead Coupé

First, the idea of Coupé implied a two-door design. The "head" or roof was designed to "drop", or fold away behind the rear seats. The roof would be made of fabric and its folding mechanism might be supported by external bars, often called hood irons or pram irons.

Fixed-head Coupé

The Fixed-head Coupé was a particular type of Coupé which was designed to look as if it was or could be a Drophead Coupé. Some bodies did little more than add a fixed roof section to what was otherwise a Drophead Coupé design. Several carried dummy hood irons, and some had the roof covered in fabric to look more convincingly like the folding type used on a Drophead Coupé.

Landaulette

Some coachbuilders preferred to spell the word as "landaulet", which perhaps sounded less French. Essentially, a Landaulette body was a (usually) large Saloon with division or a Limousine where the roof section above the rear seat could be folded down. The Laundaulette was particularly used for parade duties, where the rear seat occupants wanted to be seen by those outside the car. The concept is almost unthinkable in the modern era, when any celebrity so clearly on view would be at risk of injury from thrown objects or, worse, of assassination.

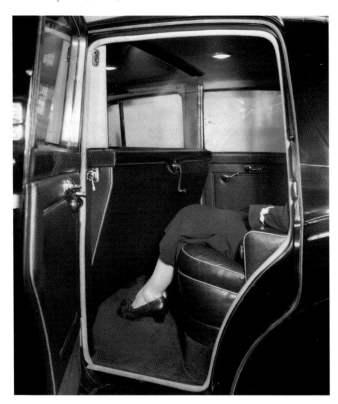

A Division was sometimes used to separate the chauffeur from the rear-seat passengers, although it was more commonly found in Limousines with their greater rear legroom than in Saloons like this Bentley MkVI.

Limousine

A Limousine is a formal closed body, typically with six windows and often with a division as well. Limousines typically (but not invariably) incorporated a pair of folding occasional seats in the rear compartment that could increase the seating capacity to seven – although these additional seats were not usually anywhere near as comfortable as the main seats.

Pillarless

In a pillarless saloon body, the central pillars are eliminated and the front and rear doors shut against each other. When open, they offer unimpeded access to the interior, which was a key attraction of the design. Vanvooren were the acknowledged leaders of this type, although they did not invent pillarless construction, which was already available in the UK by 1933. Another attraction of pillarless construction was weight saving, although that was sometimes countered by the additional body reinforcement needed to maintain rigidity.

Saloon

Strictly speaking, a Saloon is a fully-enclosed four-door body with a six-light design, although the term was often used as shorthand for the four-light Sports Saloons that several coachbuilders constructed for Bentley chassis.

Saloon Coupé

A Saloon Coupé body has two doors and a fixed roof, but the name suggests that it was too upright-looking to be considered a simple Coupé. Even so, the difference between Saloon Coupé, Two-door Saloon, and Coupé sometimes needs persuasive explanation. James Young was a regular user of the Saloon Coupé description.

Saloon with Division

The division would be a feature of a formal body, and was usually a partition between the passenger compartment in the rear and the driving compartment in the front, present to give the rear-seat occupants greater privacy. (It would not do to have the chauffeur, a mere servant, listening to the conversations of the no doubt titled owners.) A Limousine body had the same layout but was generally larger.

Sedanca

A Sedanca design was the same thing as a De Ville type; in other words, the driver's compartment was exposed while the passengers in the rear had some form of weather protection. None of that prevented some bodies being called by the Sedanca de Ville name, and these were closed four-door types with a De Ville front section and the ample proportions of a Limousine.

Sedanca Coupé

The term Coupé de Ville would do just as well to describe a car with an open driving position and a fixed roof over the rear seats, but some coachbuilders preferred this form of words.

Sports Saloon

A Sports Saloon might or might not be very sporting. The key factor was that it had only four side windows, which distinguished it from the more formal six-window Saloon and Limousine.

Touring Limousine

Theoretically, a Touring Limousine offered much the same space as a Limousine but had a larger luggage boot. In order to accommodate this, the rear seat might be moved further forwards, so reducing rear legroom slightly.

Touring Saloon

A Touring Saloon was not quite the same thing as a simple Saloon, typically being expected to have a larger boot (for all the luggage needed on tour). This term was also sometimes used to describe what might otherwise have been a Touring Limousine (with division) where rear legroom was less than the term Limousine suggested

Limousine bodies typically had occasional seats that could be folded out when needed. Here is one in an HJ Mulliner Limousine on a Rolls-Royce Silver Wraith chassis.

Instruments were supplied by Rolls-Royce with the chassis, but coachbuilders could style the dashboard as they wished (within reason). This set of instruments is on the beautifully veneered dashboard of the James Young Limousine in the lower picture on page 38. Even the modern ICE head unit does not look out of place. (Simon Clay)

THE COACHBUILDERS

These were the coachbuilders who constructed coachwork on Rolls-Royce and Bentley chassis when those chassis were new and still in production between 1946 and 1965. There were no fewer than 56 of them.

Several chassis were subsequently rebodied when those original bodies wore out or ceased to meet their owners' requirements. Some "spare" bodies – built for stock but left unsold as new designs replaced them – ended up with another type of coachwork specialist, of whom the best known was Coopers in Putney. These companies fitted the new-old-stock bodies onto whatever chassis their customers brought through the door, and this has complicated the historical record in more than one case.

Motor Shows were always vital to coachbuilders, because they afforded the opportunity to display their latest designs. This is the Mulliner, Park Ward "Koren" coupé, newly updated with paired headlamps at the 1963 Earls Court show.

Abbott	J Cairns
Aburnsons	James Young
Alpe & Saunders	Jones Bros
Baker & Son	Kong
Bertone	Mulliner, Park Ward
Beutler	Mulliners
Brewster	Park Ward
Chapron	Pinin Farina
Cooper	Poberejsky
David Joel	Radford
Denby	Reall
Dottridge	Rippon
Duncan	Ronald Kent
Eadon	Roos
Epps Bros	Saoutchik
Facel Metallon	Scottish CWS
Figoni & Falaschi	Seary & McReady
Franay	Simpson & Slater
Freestone & Webb	Van den Plas (Brussels)
Ghia	Vanden Plas
Graber	Vanvooren
Gurney Nutting	Vignale
Gustaf Nordberg	Vincents
Harwood	Wendler
HJ Mulliner	Westminster
Holland	Windover
Hooper	Woodall Nicholson
Inskip	Worblaufen

… and even today, the identity of the coachbuilders for a few chassis remains unknown.

Chapter Three

Coachwork by British Coachbuilders A-Z

By far the greater proportion of coachwork on post-war Rolls-Royce and Bentley chassis came from British coachbuilders. This chapter lists them in alphabetical order, and for the larger companies breaks down each coachbuilder's output into appropriate categories to aid understanding.

ABBOTT

Edward D Abbott was a sales executive at Page & Hunt, a coachbuilder at Wrecclesham near Farnham, and had responsibility for liaison with London dealers. When Page & Hunt went into receivership in 1929, he was able to take over the company and to re-establish it under his own name.

Although early Abbott activities focussed on bus bodies and on the retail dealership side of the business, car coachwork continued. It was probably Abbott's earlier knowledge of London car dealers that enabled him to get coachwork contracts for some of the more prestigious chassis of the 1930s. These included Rolls-Royce, for which the company produced 16 bodies in the 1930s, and Bentley, for which there were at least two bodies, both for the racing motorist Eddie Hall.

Abbott created this sleek and highly distinctive style for the R Type chassis, and although it was not a Continental, it certainly had the looks to suggest that it was. This example is on chassis B2RT, the very first production R Type, and was displayed at the 1952 Earls Court Motor Show. (Simon Clay)

The long, tapering tail of the Abbott saloon body helped to give the impression of a streamlined shape. Later examples of this design were even better looking after losing an inch of height from the roof. (Simon Clay)

A major customer was the Rootes Group, for whom Abbott built drophead coupé coachwork in batches.

Low-volume batch building remained a goal after the war, and Abbott continued to work for Rootes, also securing a contract to build drophead bodies for the Healey 2.4-litre chassis in 1951 – although there were only 77 of these in three years. Like other small coachbuilders of the time, Abbott picked up other work where it could. There were at least three re-bodies on Rolls-Royce chassis, one a sports saloon on a 20/25, one supposedly the hearse body on a Wraith, and the third a van body on a Silver Ghost! By 1950 it was still open to one-off commissions, and among

the bodies it built on the Bentley MkVI chassis was a wooden estate type.

Abbott worked on chassis from Crewe between 1948 and 1954. Most of its bodies were for the Bentley MkVI chassis, and most of those 21 bodies were drophead coupés. Next most numerous were 16 bodies (a disputed total) on the Bentley R Type, of which just one was a drophead coupé and the others were sleek two-door saloons with a deliberately Continental look about them. The company built just two bodies for the Rolls-Royce Silver Wraith, both of them two-door styles on the short-wheelbase chassis. By late 1954, Abbott had achieved its aim of a low-

The interior of the Abbott saloon body had the appropriate combination of leather and figured wood, but the design was functional rather than overtly luxurious. (Simon Clay)

volume contract for a major chassis maker, in this case Ford, for whom it now converted Consul, Zephyr and Zodiac saloons into Farnham estates. So the company decided not to offer coachwork for the later Silver Cloud and Bentley S generation of chassis.

The company's first commission to build on a post-war chassis from Crewe did not come until 1948, when it built a drophead coupé on a Bentley MkVI chassis for an Egyptian customer. This was delivered in May 1948, but there are unfortunately no known pictures of it. Nevertheless, it is likely to have shared the design of the company's later drophead coupé bodies for the MkVI, of which there were 16 in all. This design was in place by autumn 1948, when it was displayed at the Earls Court Show on chassis B443CD. The design was elegant and very much of its time, with voluminous front wings sweeping back across the doors to meet rear wings that in most cases probably carried wheel spats.

There were of course detail variations among these 16 drophead coupés: B146DA, for example, had differently positioned headlights and no wheel spats. Two of them (B265DZ and B177KL) are known to share design number 3768, and it may well be that this was the basic design number of all of them. Abbott showed them no fewer than four times at Earls Court. After B443CD in 1948 came B265DZ in 1949, B353GT (probably) in 1950, and B10MD in 1951. That last named was equipped with a hydraulically operated hood mechanism, and was also the last

Abbott body on a MkVI. Nevertheless, the same basic drophead coupé style would appear again in 1952 on a Rolls-Royce Silver Wraith (WOF50), suitably adjusted for the longer wheelbase.

There were commissions for three fixed-head coupés on the MkVI chassis in the late 1940s, too. These were on B387BG (delivered in December 1948), B389DZ (January 1950) and B454EY (November 1949). Unfortunately, no pictures of B387BG or B454EY are known to exist, and no details of their body style or styles are available. Perhaps they shared the styling of B389DZ, the last one delivered. There was a single fixed-head coupé on a Silver Wraith chassis

Abbott built several of these drophead coupé bodies on the Bentley MkVI chassis, some with minor variations. This one is on chassis B265DZ, and was pictured at the Earls Court Motor Show in 1949.

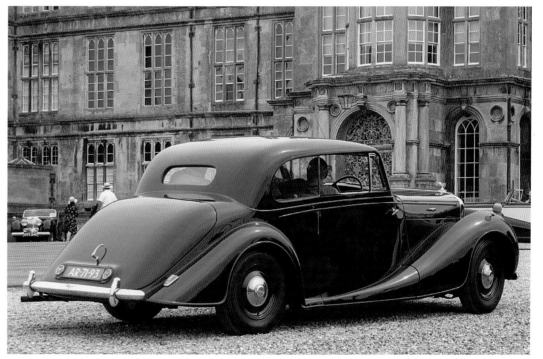

Fixed-head Coupé, or two-door Saloon? The Abbott body on Bentley MkVI B389DZ had quite conservative lines for 1950 and could be described as either. (Anton van Luijk via Klaus-Josef Rossfeldt)

With the top up, this Abbott four-light Drophead Coupé body looked both elegant and snug. The chassis is Bentley MkVI B495EW, which was delivered in May 1950. (Klaus-Josef Rossfeldt)

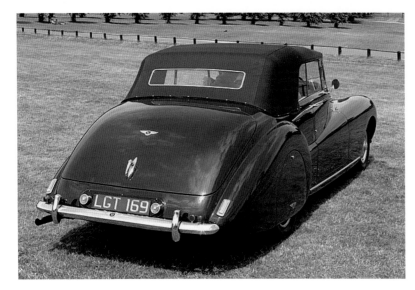

(WGC17), too, which was delivered in January 1950 and had lines that were very much in the idiom of the late 1940s, with the front and rear wings still quite separate volumes in the full-width body.

A further unique body left the Abbott works in May 1950, and this was an estate car on Bentley MkVI chassis B259FU. At the time, there were tax savings to be made in Britain on commercial vehicles, and with careful interpretation of the regulations it was possible to get such a body classified as a commercial type. Like many of its kind, the Abbott body was of wooden construction, in this case having no side windows at the rear but rather wooden panels where the windows would otherwise have been.

Much more interesting to the coachbuilder,

however, was an order that came in from Crewe itself during 1949. At the time, Rolls-Royce were evaluating ideas for coachwork designs that would draw on the new styles that were coming in during the later 1940s, and they asked Abbott to come up with a proposal. Quite why the company was selected for this job is not clear: although a well-respected coachbuilder it did not have a track record of radical designs or of special construction methods. Nevertheless, it was Abbott who constructed the experimental full-width Saloon body on a Bentley development chassis, numbered 8-B-VII. The car was always known as the Bentley Farnham, after the location of its coachbuilder.

The overall lines of the Bentley Farnham certainly anticipated the themes that would be adopted for the later Standard Steel bodies on Silver Cloud and Bentley S-type chassis. Of particular interest was its front end design, which had the wide, partially cowled style of grille seen on the Pinin Farina bodies for the Bentley Cresta project. From Ian Rimmer's *Rolls-Royce and Bentley Experimental Cars*, we know that the Rolls-Royce people considered some features of the coachwork and trim to be poorly designed. However, that should not necessarily reflect badly on the Abbott company: the car was, after all, an experimental model. Like so many of its kind, it was broken up when its experimental duties were over – and it remained unique.

The Bentley Farnham project went no further, but it was an important one for the Abbott company. It must have been while working on this body that they became aware of Crewe's plans for a high-performance Bentley chassis. This would of course become the Bentley

Continental, but in 1949 it was still very much under development. The Abbott people probably came to believe that their involvement in the Farnham project indicated they were highly regarded at Crewe, and they clearly anticipated a supply of those new high-speed chassis when they entered production.

To that end, designer Peter Woodgate drew up a particularly sleek and striking lightweight two-door saloon with a long and tapering boot. It is not at all surprising that this has frequently been misidentified as belonging to the R Type Continental chassis, because that is what it was originally intended to suit. Unfortunately for the Abbott company, Crewe had other plans, and all of the first Continental chassis would go to HJ Mulliner.

Nevertheless, Crewe and Abbott seem to have settled on a typically British compromise. Crewe did agree to supply the coachbuilder with standard Bentley R Type chassis which had the lower Continental radiator grille, more steeply raked steering column, 12/41 axle gearing and 120mph speedometer. Not only that, but they supplied the very first production R Type chassis (B2RT) to Farnham in 1952, and on that the coachbuilder constructed the first of its lightweight two-door saloons. The body design, number 3843, was certainly a success for Abbott, who took orders for a further 14 examples that were built over the next two years. These 14 "production" bodies, of which the last was delivered on B252YD in 1954, had some differences from the one on B2RT, with a different tail light design and a roofline lowered by an inch that made them look even sleeker.

Even so, it was a drophead coupé on the new Bentley R Type chassis that Abbott chose to display on their stand at Earls Court in 1952. B18RT was the second R Type chassis delivered to Farnham and its elegant coachwork followed very closely the lines that had been established for the earlier MkVI drophead coupés. Yet it remained unique. For the next two years, the only Abbott bodies for any chassis from Crewe would be those lightweight two-door saloons on the R Type chassis, and they would be its last.

ABURNSONS

Aburnsons (Coachbuilders) Ltd were at Lancing in West Sussex, and were responsible for the body on a single Bentley MkVI. They supposedly built a total of seven coach bodies for local operators, on Commer and Seddon chassis, and are believed to have been active between 1947 and 1956. In the early part of this period, they built a number of wooden utility bodies to meet current regulations (please see the entry for David Joel below for a fuller explanation of these).

The single body for a Bentley chassis was a wooden utility type with a sloping rear panel, mounted on MkVI chassis B384CF, which was delivered in January 1948. It no longer exists, although the chassis survives as the basis of a "special".

ALPE & SAUNDERS

Alpe & Saunders (Coachbuilders) Ltd was founded in Kew, then in Surrey but latterly considered south-west London, in 1937. The company had earlier been known as G Wylder & Co, and had been established as a coachbuilder in 1923.

Messrs Alpe and Saunders had put their names to a special body for an Austin 7 chassis in the late 1920s, but this had almost certainly been built for them under contract. They went on to specialise in hearse coachwork, and in the 1950s also built at least one "woody" shooting brake body on a 1929 Rolls-Royce Twenty chassis. The company continued in business until the mid-1960s.

There were four Alpe & Saunders hearse bodies on Rolls-Royce Silver Wraith chassis. The earliest of these was on WFC94 in September 1950. WGC55 and WME70 both followed in January 1952. The fourth one was the only hearse known to have been built on a long-wheelbase Silver Wraith, and was BLW21 in December 1953.

BAKER & SON

The name of Baker & Son crops up just once in connection with coachbuilding, and that is as the constructor of a Saloon body for Bentley MkVI chassis number B200CF. Absolutely nothing is known about the company except that it was very probably based in Bristol, and no pictures of the car have yet been found.

Chassis B200CF was ordered via Bristol Motors and was delivered to Charles Cruickshank Motors of Bristol. The completed car went to a Bristol resident in January 1950 and attracted a Bristol registration number.

The sole Bentley MkVI bodied by Aburnsons was a wooden utility type.

Although Coopers fitted this body to Silver Wraith WVA62, they can take no credit for its design. The body was a pre-war type built by HJ Mulliner and originally intended for a Rolls-Royce Wraith chassis.

COOPER

Cooper Motor Bodies (HF Cooper & Sons) was not a coachbuilder but purchased end-of-run bodies from the major London coachbuilders – no doubt for bargain prices – and fitted them to whatever chassis their customers brought to them. Freestone & Webb were certainly among their suppliers. Sometimes, modifications were needed to make these bodies fit a chassis for which they had never been intended. The company was based in Putney, in south-west London. It is known to have mounted bodywork on two post-war Rolls-Royce chassis and on one Bentley chassis. The two Rolls-Royce chassis were both Silver Wraiths. The earlier chassis was number WTA82, and the body fitted to it was a six-light saloon that in all probability was actually a Freestone & Webb body that had originally been intended for a Silver Wraith. (Freestone & Webb had six cancelled orders for their body design 3004 in 1948-1949, and the body that Cooper fitted was probably one of these.)

The later chassis was number WVA62, and the body that Coopers fitted to this was a rather upright razor-edged six-light saloon that was actually built by HJ Mulliner before the war and had originally been intended for a Rolls-Royce Wraith chassis. This chassis has a delivery date of August 1948.

The single Bentley MkVI that received Cooper's attentions was on chassis number B178EY. This was delivered in October 1949 and was recorded as having a fixed-head coupé body. The chances are that this body was another one built by Freestone & Webb and sold to the Cooper business. Ironically, it was replaced in 1952 by a six-light Saloon to Freestone & Webb's design 3046/C/F – and this time, the coachbuilders fitted it themselves.

DAVID JOEL

In late 1940s Britain, there were tax advantages to be had from driving a commercial vehicle. Regulations introduced to help the post-war economic recovery meant that commercial vehicles were both exempt from Purchase Tax and entitled to a greater ration of petrol than private cars. The quid pro quo was that they were limited to 30mph at all times.

Nevertheless, a number of small enterprises sprung up to build bodies which trod a fine line between the definitions of a commercial and a passenger-carrying vehicle. These were known as "utilities". Strictly speaking, they had to have a load-carrying floor that extended all the way from the front seats to the rear of the vehicle; they could not have a fixed rear seat (although they could have a folding or removable one); they had to have an internal capacity of at least 72 cu ft; and they had to have doors in the rear panel.

Many of these "utility" bodies – inspired by earlier shooting-brake designs – were built from wood to reduce costs further. Others had steel bodies with wooden facings. Many had just two doors, probably again to save costs. Some were fitted to older chassis whose bodies had deteriorated beyond economical repair during the war years, and a few brand-new chassis were also given similar bodywork.

David Joel Ltd was one of the companies that met demand for these money-saving bodies. Based at Tolworth in Surrey, just off the Kingston By-Pass, the company constructed a total of five utilities on new Bentley MkVI chassis in 1949. These are thought to have been the company's only products.

The David Joel estate bodies probably all had wooden panels over steel framework to give the impression of a typical utility style. It is not clear whether all of them had the same design of body. The first one (B382DA) was delivered in March 1949 and the last (B273EW) in December the same year. There are probably no survivors, although some of the chassis have subsequently been used as the basis of "specials". The David Joel body that was mounted on B110TN in 1953 by Freestone & Webb was almost certainly the one that the company had removed from B340EY and replaced with a saloon body to one of their stock designs.

Misleadingly parked outside the premises of Yorkshire coachbuilder Rippon Bros, Bentley MkVI B263DZ actually carries a shooting brake body built by David Joel in London. The registration number was issued in London in 1949, but the car belonged to the owner of a Yorkshire woollen mill.

This wooden shooting-brake body on Bentley MkVI B93FU was the only one of its kind constructed by the Belfast coachbuilder W Denby & Sons. (Real Car Co.)

DENBY

W Denby & Sons was a Belfast coachbuilder with premises on the Antrim Road. It built just two bodies on Rolls-Royce chassis before the Second World War, and after the war seems to have specialised in bodies for the funeral trade.

Denby built a pair of hearses on Rolls-Royce Silver Wraith chassis in 1949 and 1951 for a leading local firm of undertakers. The two hearses were on chassis numbers WCB14 and WHD33. In between them, the company also constructed a single wooden-bodied estate car on a Bentley MkVI chassis. This had chassis number B93FU, and was delivered in June 1950.

DOTTRIDGE

The firm of Dottrridge Brothers appears in Kelly's Post Office London Directory for 1891 as "wholesale undertaker's sundrymen, manufacturers and warehousemen". Among their other activities was renting out horse-drawn hearses from their premises in the Islington district of central London. More than 50 years later, the company also built a single hearse body on Rolls-Royce Silver Wraith chassis WAB55, and delivered it in July 1949 to a funeral business in Bradford.

DUNCAN

Ian Duncan was an aircraft engineer who set up Duncan Industries (Engineers) Ltd at North Walsham in Norfolk in 1946. He designed and produced an attractive two-door saloon body for Alvis chassis, having wooden frames made up by a local boatbuilder and covering these with alloy skin panels. A version of this body was also designed to suit the Healey chassis, and meanwhile Duncan designed his own small two-cylinder model that he called the Duncan Dragonfly. He later sold the design to Austin and went to work for that company when Duncan Industries folded.

Duncan Industries built just one body for a Bentley MkVI chassis, number B385DG. This was a drophead coupé with some visual similarities to the Alvis and Healey closed bodies, and it was delivered in November 1948. It still survives, in a collection in Portugal.

EADON

Alan Eadon purchased Bentley MkVI chassis B159BG in 1948, and had it delivered to his own company in Sheffield, the Eadon Engineering Co Ltd. The workshops there constructed a metal-panelled four-door shooting-brake body on it, with four windows on each side. This presumably enabled the car to qualify as a commercial vehicle and so avoid Purchase Tax (and obtain a larger petrol ration, as explained in the entry for David Joel, above).

EPPS BROS

Epps Bros was one of many small coachbuilders that sprang up in the years immediately after the Second World War. It was founded by three brothers in Penge, south-east London, and seems to have drawn most of its workforce from nearby coachbuilders James Young and Gurney Nutting. It was perhaps best known for drophead coupé bodies on Riley chassis but also constructed individual bodies on other makes of chassis. The company was closed down in 1949 after attempting to evade an embargo on shipping armoured vehicles to Israel.

Among the bodies it built was a single drophead coupé on a Rolls-Royce Silver Wraith chassis, WYA69. This was a very distinctive car, echoing to some degree the styling of a one-off Riley that was known to Epps employees as the "banana" car on account of its curvaceous shape. The Silver Wraith body was nevertheless much more elegant and attractive than that description suggests, and (until this author discovered a photograph proving its origins while researching Riley history) was often thought to have been by built by Franay.

The rakish lines on this Drophead Coupé by Epps remained unique – and their origin was incorrectly attributed for many years. (© N/K)

Some early post-war Freestone & Webb designs showed a Hooper influence, although there was always a distinctive touch somewhere. This is a Six-light Saloon built in 1947 to design 3004/A2, one of several variants of the basic 3004 design. It is on Silver Wraith chassis WVA21. The flash on the wheel spat is an unusual touch.

FREESTONE & WEBB

Freestone & Webb was the smallest of the five major British coachbuilders working with Rolls-Royce and Bentley chassis in the post-war period. Established in north London in 1923, the company immediately began building coachwork for Bentley chassis, later adding Rolls-Royce to its quite extensive portfolio of chassis makers. The company was best known for its sports saloon bodies, and during the 1930s pioneered razor-edge lines with its Brougham Saloon design. In that decade, Freestone & Webb had built coachwork for many makes other than Rolls-Royce and Bentley, but in the post-war era they were confined exclusively to those two marques with the exception of 18 limousine bodies on Daimler chassis in 1946-1950.

Post-war, Freestone & Webb was back in action before the end of 1945, and gradually built its business back up in the late 1940s. The company built sports saloons, six-light saloons and limousines on most Rolls-Royce and Bentley models, plus a few fixed-head coupés, and even constructed a "utility" estate body as well. However, only a small number of open bodies was built by the firm, and there were never any Freestone & Webb bodies on either the Bentley

Continental or the Rolls-Royce Phantom chassis.

VE Freestone had left the company before the war, and in late 1954 AJ Webb died. Very soon after that, negotiations began that would eventually see Freestone & Webb bought out by the Swain Group, which owned the HR Owen dealership chain. Meanwhile, the company took on the odd bizarre commission – a futuristic nine-seater limousine with glass roof in 1956 being a case in point – and went out with a bang by showing the so-called Honeymoon Express on its last stand at Earls Court in 1957. Built on a Silver Cloud chassis, this deliberately extravagant two-seater had a long rear deck, power-operated convertible roof, and pronounced American-style tail fins. It went down so well that the company picked up commissions for two more (one on a Bentley S Type) that they completed before closing for good in mid-1958.

In the first decade after the war, designs for Rolls-Royce and Bentley chassis were given separate numbers, even when they were closely similar. However, with the advent of the Silver Cloud and S Type, some body designs were available for both chassis types, and shared the same design numbers.

Saloons and Limousines
Getting started, 1946-1948
Freestone & Webb had been a pioneer of razor-edge styling in the 1930s, and so it was only to be expected that they would enter the post-war market with coachwork derived from the designs that they were building in 1938-1939. As soon as details of the post-war Rolls-Royce and Bentley chassis became available in 1946, the company began working up new designs to suit them.

However, their approach was understandably cautious, and the designs they drew up for the Silver Wraith (number 3004) and the MkVI (number 3010) were quite closely related. They were designed to be flexible,

---

HOW MANY BODIES?

The figures below have been calculated by chassis type. They should be considered as "probable" totals, because some bodies were built for stock as part of batch runs but have not been definitively associated with a chassis. Re-bodies are not included.

Rolls-Royce		Bentley	
Silver Wraith	120	MkVI	109
Silver Dawn	6	R Type	31
Silver Cloud	17	S Type	23
Total	**143**	**Total**	**163**

too, and over the next few years both designs would be adapted in several ways. It was Freestone & Webb practice to give one or more suffix letters or numbers to variants of a core design, and this is most easily understood by thinking in terms of design "families".

Both designs were four-light saloons, the razor-edge style being most obvious in the sharp edge to the roof above the shallow windscreen and in the lines of the tail. The door panels were slightly outswept at the bottom, and front and rear wings were joined by a low-down sweep that concealed the running-board area; both front and rear doors were rear-hinged.

By late 1947, design 3004 had been adapted as a six-light body, with rear quarter-lights borrowed from Hooper designs. This became 3004/A2. In this guise it became a Saloon Limousine with division as well, and although the basic exterior design remained relatively unadorned it was varied with different designs of rear wheel spat. During 1948, a four-light variant with division was offered as 3004/C, both examples built featuring twin side-mounted spare wheels.

The 3004 family remained available until 1950, further variants of this flexible design being 3004/A (five bodies, 1947-1948), 3004/A3 (one body, 1947), 3004/B (five bodies, 1948-1949), 3004/1 (one body, 1947) and 3004/2 (two six-light bodies, 1949). All had minor variations from the core designs, but all were readily recognisable as members of the 3004 family.

The evolution of the 3010 family was less complex. The first body delivered in 1947 was a 3010/C, followed immediately by a 3010/B and a pair of 3010/D variants, all in the same year. Between 1947 and 1948 there were eight bodies to design 3010/A, of which one (on B80BH in 1947) had an interesting rib running down the rear panel that divided the rear window into two sections. Different types of rear wheel spat and single-colour or two-tone paint schemes made for further variation between bodies.

Then early in 1948 came the 3010/E variant with six windows (and Hooper-like rearmost windows on each side) instead of four; seven of these were eventually built, the last in 1949.

The second generation, 1948-1952

The first ideas for replacing the 3010 family on the Bentley chassis became evident in early 1948, when a four-light design numbered 3038 appeared. It was recognisably from the same school of thought as the body it was expected to replace, however, the main differences being a more streamlined tail with a differently shaped boot, and a thicker waist moulding. This was a success, and 12 examples found buyers in 1948-1949.

Unlike other major coachbuilders, Freestone & Webb did not scramble to get new designs ready in time for the 1948 Earls Court Motor Show. Instead, they made a minor revision to existing designs, adding a scallop between rear wing and rear door that gave a neater boundary to the two-tone paintwork that was now increasingly being ordered. For the Bentley MkVI bodies, the change occurred mid-way through production of design 3010/E, and there was no new design number. For the Silver Wraith, however, it coincided with the arrival of six-light versions of design 3004. Most were built as 3004/A2 types, but there was a single Show special called 3004/A2/F on chassis WCB11.

Making sure that they had something spectacular to display alongside the eye-catching new designs that other coachbuilders might put forward at Earls Court, Freestone & Webb did prepare one other Show special. This was a saloon on a Bentley MkVI chassis, B445CD, and it was essentially similar to the 3010 family but with a six-light design where (for a change) the rearmost side windows were less obviously derived from Hooper designs than on other Freestone & Webb

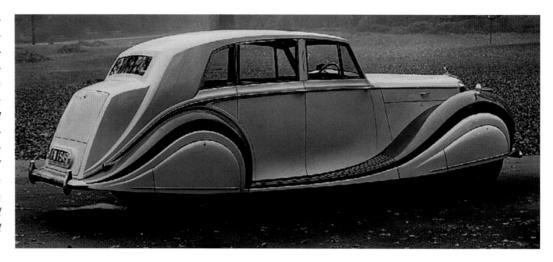

Trying for something eye-catching at the first post-war Earls Court Motor Show in 1948, Freestone & Webb borrowed an idea from French coachbuilders and added four wheel spats to this otherwise conventional Six-light Saloon on a Bentley MkVI chassis. Although design 3046, here presented in two shades of blue, earned repeat orders, the wheel spats were never seen again.

bodies. The most striking feature of this new design, number 3046, was that it had spats on all four wheels – an idea probably borrowed from French coachbuilders of the time. In two-tone blue with blue upholstery, it must have drawn the crowds.

There were no more examples made with those spats – and whether they were ever intended as anything other than a Show special is debatable – but design 3046 went on to have a distinguished career. There were four bodies to the core design in 1948-1949, 18 of the 3046/C variant between 1948 and 1952, and no fewer than 21 of the 3046/C/F type on Bentley MkVI chassis between 1948 and 1952. By then, the style was looking a little old-fashioned, but the customers seem to have loved it.

The 3004 family of designs were selling well on the Rolls-Royce Silver Wraith chassis, and so it was 1949 before Freestone & Webb came up with an alternative. The first examples of design 3047 were delivered that summer, and as usual there would be several variants. It

was pretty much a scaled-up version of design 3046 on the Bentley chassis, although the R100 headlights that were probably fitted to all those built added a degree of conservatism and formality to the mix. There were two examples of the 3047/B variant in 1949-1950, but only one example of each of the others: 3047, 3047/1, 3047/2 and 3047/2/A were all built in 1949 and all had divisions; and 3047/B/2 was built without one in 1949.

Right at the end of the decade, design 3050 for the Silver Wraith was the first of six variants of the same design, variously a six-light saloon with division, a limousine, or a plain saloon. The public announcement was at Earls Court in 1949, with the 3050/A/B variant on chassis WGC19, displaying conventional low wing lines but with the side scallop introduced in 1948 to improve the look of two-tone bodies and with the front doors now hinged at their leading edges. Four of these were built in 1949, in addition to the single example of a plain 3050. Further variants followed. There

This Six-light Saloon on Silver Wraith WHD72 in 1950 had design number 3047/B, but did not present any radically new ideas.

Not many Silver Wraith chassis were bodied as Coupés, but when Freestone & Webb built this one on chassis WOF54 in 1952, the result was extraordinarily attractive. Even so, the lines were conservative, and very much an adaptation of the coachbuilder's saloon designs.

were two examples of 3050/B, a saloon derivative, in 1950-1951, and then one each of 3050/A/C/E and 3050/A/D in 1951, both described as limousines. The last built was 3050/A/C, another singleton limousine, in 1952, making a total of 11 bodies in the 3050 family.

Raised wing lines, 1950-1956

Although older designs remained available from Freestone & Webb, the main news at Earls Court in 1950 was raised wing lines. Both the new Saloon design 3070 for the Silver Wraith and the new Saloon Coupé (3073) on the Bentley chassis had the same lines, with the front wing line now sweeping downwards across the doors to meet a spatted rear wing that followed the contours of the wheel. The razor edges had gone from these new designs, too, which seem to have been inspired by a Park Ward design (number 114) that was shown at Earls Court in 1949.

The trend continued at Earls Court in 1951, as more new designs made their bow. Front wings gained

deeper valances that were given interest by swages, and softer lines prevailed: the company itself took to describing the lines of its new six-light saloon design 3082 for the Bentley MkVI as having a "semi-razor-edge" style. This became a most successful design, with 21 examples ordered on the MkVI and R Type chassis between 1951 and 1954; there was also a single 3082/D on the R Type in 1952.

Even so, for the Silver Wraith chassis Freestone & Webb hedged their bets. New design 3091/A catered for the more traditional buyer, and was really a slightly softened 3070 with the older wing lines and boot; this was a six-light saloon with division of which five would be built, plus one 3091 without the division. Both had the latest swage lines. New design 3092 with full wings was then a mildly updated version of 3070, and this six-light saloon ended up looking quite similar to the HJ Mulliner lightweight designs of the time; the more modern design actually proved more popular, with seven orders plus (inevitably) a pair of 3092/A variants

Almost forbiddingly formal and, of course, essentially conservative were the lines of design 3074/A/B, a Limousine seen here on 1951 Silver Wraith chassis WME15.

Evolution at last… the raised wing line gave a more modern appearance to this Coupé body to design 3107 on Silver Wraith WVH6. The company was proud enough to display it at Earls Court in 1952, but only one other like it was made.

with a division. As for formal limousines, the new wing lines were clearly not considered appropriate, and the new design 3074/A/B (of which only two would be made) was a distinctly upright design with the older style of wing line that incorporated running-boards.

By 1953, the old razor-edge and semi-razor-edge designs were near the ends of their lives. They made a last appearance on Silver Wraith chassis as new Limousine and Touring Limousine designs. The Limousine had the older style of low-line wings but incorporating the latest swage lines, and was design 3110/A; just one was built, plus a single 3110/A/L variant. The Touring Limousine 3131/A had the higher wing lines with swages and was more successful; there would eventually be four variants and a total of 12 of all types was delivered up to 1956. But by then, new designs had come to the fore at Freestone & Webb.

The "Empress" designs, 1952-1958
Freestone & Webb have often been accused of copying the Hooper "Empress" style for their next new design, which appeared in prototype form on a Bentley MkVI chassis (B390MD) in July 1952. There

was unquestionably strong inspiration from that direction, although it has to be said that it was only a small step from some of the more recent Freestone & Webb designs to the shape that Osmond Rivers had drawn up for Hooper. Nevertheless, the Freestone & Webb "Empress", initially a six-light design numbered 3093/A, was rather sleeker than the Hooper original. It also had all its doors hinged at their forward edges, whereas the Hooper design had "clap-hands" doors. This led to a difference in the panel lines, and here the Freestone & Webb version was (at least initially) less satisfactory than the Hooper design, with a rather ugly shut line for the door just ahead of the rear wheel spat.

Just the one of these bodies was built on a MkVI chassis; ten more were mounted on Bentley R Type chassis, plus a further seven of a further evolved successor known as design 3093/A/L that arrived in summer 1954. The last of these, on chassis B390YD, was delivered in April 1955. Meanwhile, and somewhat inevitably, customers had started to ask for the same style of body on the Rolls-Royce Silver Dawn chassis – and as that had the same dimensions as the Bentley R Type, Freestone & Webb were easily able

It is not hard to see how Freestone & Webb made the transition from designs like the Coupé in the picture above to a shape that was almost a direct copy of the Hooper "Empress". The Freestone & Webb bodies always looked sleeker than the Hooper originals, although early ones had an awkward rear door shut line. This is design 3093/A on a 1953 Bentley R Type. (Frank Dale & Stepsons photograph)

to oblige. The Silver Dawn version emerged as design 3163 in April 1954, the first one to be delivered being on chassis SNF107. There were then four more of these, and the last of them was delivered in October 1955 on chassis STH55.

It was obvious that this style had considerable appeal, and the company's next move was to adapt it as a Touring Limousine body for the Rolls-Royce Silver Wraith chassis. Design number 3171/A duly appeared in the early summer of 1955 and two examples had already been sold before it appeared (on chassis ELW3) on the Freestone & Webb stand at Earls Court that October. The extra length of the Silver Wraith chassis unquestionably did the design a favour, and at the same time Freestone & Webb took the opportunity to tidy up the lines around the rear door, putting the body into production with a neat single panel line that echoed the design Hooper's "Empress" had used from the start. Nevertheless, the Freestone & Webb doors were still front-hinged. Design 3171/A was another palpable hit. There were ten more bodies to the original design between 1955 and 1957, and the last one (on chassis FLW94) flew the flag for Freestone & Webb at their last Earls Court appearance in October 1957. There were three other bodies derived from the same design, too: variant 3171 (presumably actually a first iteration of the design on the drawing-board) attracted two orders during 1955; and there was a single body to a variant known as 3171/M on chassis FLW76 in 1957.

Meanwhile, the new generation of chassis had entered production, and unsurprisingly Freestone & Webb adapted their successful design to suit these as

well. Bentley versions arrived first, as design 3199 in late 1955. Thirteen bodies were built to this design between then and 1958, and one example (on chassis B532EG) was on that final 1957 Earls Court stand. The Rolls-Royce equivalent, for the Silver Cloud, made its bow as design 3206 on chassis SWA56 in March 1956, and six more followed between then and February 1958. There was also a single example of 3206/A, an Earls Court "special" on SZB95 that was most attractively presented in Dark Green over Pastel Green with light green hide upholstery.

Inevitably, there was a very special variant for a very special customer, and in this case that customer was the wealthy socialite Nubar Gulbenkian. For him, Freestone & Webb created a two-door saloon using the "Empress" lines, and gave the design number 3193. This was unquestionably a success, and the single long door on each side made the body look even longer and sleeker than the Touring Limousine versions on the Silver Wraith. However, when chassis SWA42 was

Although Empress-like bodies proved very popular on all sizes of chassis, Freestone & Webb offered several other options in the early 1950s. This was their design 3192/A on the long wheelbase Silver Wraith, in this case DLW45 from 1955. It was the only example built of this Saloon with Division.

On the Rolls-Royce Silver Dawn chassis, the "Empress" design became number 3163. Here it is on chassis SNF107, showing very clearly the flat bumpers used on early variants. (RL GNZLZ/WikiMedia Commons)

The Empress-like style adapted well to the long-wheelbase Silver Wraith chassis, and one was a Freestone & Webb exhibit at Earls Court in 1954. It had body design 3171/A and was on chassis DLW44.

delivered to its new owner in January 1956, it would be the only one of its kind. Some would argue that it was the most elegant of all the Freestone & Webb "Empress" designs.

The Special Sports Saloon and its relatives, 1954-1958

The last new Freestone & Webb saloon design intended for quantity production made its debut in 1954 on a late Bentley R Type chassis. Design 3191 arrived in November 1954 on chassis B30YD as a six-light design with long and low lines that very much anticipated the sort of shapes that would become commonplace in the Silver Cloud and Bentley S era. The front wings now had headlights embedded in their leading edges, and at the rear was a most unusual and distinctive wing design. Each wing had a kick-up in its profile that provided a hint of the tail fins then becoming popular on American cars, and each wing stood separate from the boot sides, with a gap that

Individuality raised its head again with this design in 1954. Special Sports Saloon number 3191 was on a Bentley R Type chassis, and those wing lines would soon spread to other designs.

The Special Sports Saloon was modified a little to suit the new Bentley S Type chassis, and here it is on what is probably B23AP, an early 1956 chassis. The rear wings were separate from the boot on these bodies – a most unusual feature.

created three distinct volumes at the tail.

This design was later known as the Special Sports Saloon, but the name may not have been applied to the first two, which were on R Type chassis. As soon as Bentley S Type chassis became available, the design was adapted with longer rear doors to suit that and became 3191/A, of which the first example was delivered on chassis B23AP in January 1956. A version for the Rolls-Royce Silver Cloud could not be long in coming, and indeed it appeared a few months later as design 3194 on chassis SWA48, which was delivered in March.

It was about this time that modifications were introduced at the front end, where the headlamps looked rather conservative in comparison with the quite radically modern appearance of the tail. Bodies for both the Bentley and Rolls-Royce chassis began to appear with cowled headlamps – an idea perhaps borrowed from the latest Hooper designs – although it is not clear which came first. Design 3191/A attracted a total of seven orders, all of which were delivered during 1956, but only two examples of the Rolls-Royce version 3194 were built, both again during 1956. (To complicate matters, an eighth body on Bentley chassis was recorded as a 3191, but would logically have been a 3191/A.)

Even though production of the Special Sports Saloon bodies had ended several months earlier, Freestone & Webb revived the shape during 1957 and modified it to suit the new long-wheelbase Silver Cloud chassis. The "stretched" design with cowled headlamps in a triangular pressing on each front wing was generally known as a 3191, although a design drawing makes clear that the coachbuilder called it a 3191/LWB. It worked very well on the longer chassis, the first example (on ALC1) doing duty on the Freestone & Webb stand at Earls Court in 1957. But there would be only one more of these bodies, which was delivered on chassis ALC10 in February 1958.

The last chance saloons, 1956

Perhaps discouraged by the low take-up rate for the Rolls-Royce version of their Special Sports Saloon, Freestone & Webb quickly prepared another design for the standard-wheelbase Silver Cloud and Bentley S Type. Design 3224 – 3224/SC in Rolls-Royce form and 3224/1 for the Bentley – was ready in time for the 1956 Earls Court Show, at which the Bentley version was shown on chassis B354CK. The cowled headlamps were retained, but there was a much higher and less curvaceous wing line and the rear quarters were very much toned down. The distinctive gap between wing and boot seen on the Special Sports

Saloons disappeared in favour of a more conventional fin-like wing design that had some similarities to that on the later Koren designs from Park Ward.

The Rolls-Royce version of the design seems to have followed a few months after the Bentley, on chassis number SYB54 that was delivered in March 1957. But there were no repeat orders for either of them, and these two bodies remained unique.

Special orders and special bodies

Although the saloon and limousine designs that were built in quantity remained Freestone & Webb's bread and butter in the late 1940s and early 1950s, the company was always prepared to take on special commissions. Some of these attracted small numbers of repeat orders.

Coupés

The most numerous of these bodies were closed two-door types, variously described as fixed-head coupés and saloon coupés. There were 20 in all, spread over a variety of different designs that began in 1947 with 3014 on the Silver Wraith chassis. Very much a two-door version of the company's razor-edge saloons, this had shallow windows that gave a somewhat pre-war appearance, and there were no repeat orders.

In complete contrast, the more rounded lines of design 3027 (one in 1947) on the shorter Bentley MkVI chassis made for a very attractive design. This was followed later the same year by design 3029, a Saloon Coupé with rounded lines that was pillarless above the waist. Just one was built, but there were two of the mildly revised 3029/A (which incorporated the new-for-1949 side scallop) during 1949. A third

version, 3029/C, proved the most popular, but its features now included full chromed window frames; there were four of these between 1949 and 1951.

The rounded lines remained in favour for design 3030, a Saloon Coupé on the Bentley MkVI of which the first example was built in 1947 for actor Stewart Granger on chassis B288BH. This had distinctive pontoon-like wings with spats on the rear pair and dispensed with running-boards; it also had a distinctive curve in the waistline just behind the windscreen that allowed deeper side windows. A second example, to design 3030/A, followed in 1948.

The Freestone & Webb style had changed quite dramatically by the time of the next new design, which was Saloon Coupé 3073 in 1950. There were high wing lines with swages, rear wheel spats, and plenty of curves for this design on the Bentley MkVI that was also carried over for the R Type; four examples were delivered, the last in 1953. An older wing line returned for the next design on the Silver Wraith chassis, which was number 3087 and appeared in 1952. Like 3073, it incorporated the side scallop introduced in 1948; yet it was a more deliberately elegant design with cutaway spats that suited the larger chassis very well. Strangely, perhaps, only two were built, the second in 1953.

The last two coupé designs were both for Silver Wraith chassis, and both had high wing lines that swept down to meet spatted rear wheels. The earlier one, design 3107, was the more successful aesthetically, and combined a falling waistline with semi-razor-edge lines at the rear. Two were built, both in 1952. The second design was number 3183, of which just the one example was built in 1954. Here, the high wing line met the rear wing pressing quite high up – an idea

The so-called Honeymoon Express was Freestone & Webb's swansong, and a quite remarkable statement. Of the three made, only one was on a Bentley chassis, and this is it. The design was number 3243/B, the chassis number B377EK, and the coachbuilder's own records suggest that this was the very last body to be completed at Brentfield Road, the car being delivered in November 1958.

that would be repeated on the bizarre Silver Wraith limousine body to design 3222 built in 1956.

Limousines

Just one example of design 3190 was built in 1955, on Silver Wraith chassis DLW83. This was a formal limousine, deliberately conservative in appearance and distantly related to designs such as limousine 3110 but with the more modern wing lines of its touring limousine contemporary 3131.

In complete contrast was design 3222, a deliberately futuristic bespoke limousine with a glass roof. A single example was built in 1956, on Silver Wraith FLW26, and its looks have always been controversial.

Open bodies

Freestone & Webb were not particularly known for their open bodies, and these were very much in a minority in this period. There were in fact just eight of them, one an all-weather and the other seven drophead coupés.

The all-weather was built on a Silver Wraith chassis in 1947 to design 3005, and looked a little old-fashioned – not least, perhaps, because all-weather bodies in general were no longer in fashion. All four drophead bodies had concealed heads, achieved by stowing the folded top below a rather ugly flat pressing behind the passenger compartment. The first was on a Bentley MkVI in 1947 and had design number 3008, where the lower body was very similar to the fixed-head design 3030. New wing lines were in vogue by 1952, when design 3077 appeared, again on the MkVI chassis, and this body had strong similarities to the contemporary 3073 saloon coupé. There was just one 3077; a single 3077/A followed later in 1952 on a late MkVI chassis; and then the design was further modified to become 3077/A/P for the R Type, and just one example was delivered, in 1954.

Design number 3243 was not only Freestone

& Webb's last but also became one of their most famous. It was a two-door, two-seat drophead coupé, with tail fins in the then-current idiom, and when SED 179 appeared at the 1957 Earls Court Show, the press christened it the Honeymoon Express. One more example would be built on Silver Cloud chassis SGE270, in 1958; there would also be one on Bentley S Type chassis B377EK in 1957.

One-off saloons

For clients who wanted something different from the standard saloon designs, Freestone & Webb produced three individual bodies between 1947 and 1953. The first of these was on Bentley MkVI B63AJ, and design 3013 was really a 3010 modified with running-boards. In 1951, design 3081 on Silver Wraith chassis WLE27 was essentially a six-light 3050 saloon with division but with imitation wicker-work on the door panels. The last of these three was the most individual, and was design 3132, built on Bentley R Type chassis B382SR. With very rounded lines, this four-light saloon seems to have been heavily influenced by Park Ward designs.

Phantom rebodies

Perhaps strictly outside the coverage of this book are two individual bodies that the company built on pre-war Rolls-Royce Phantom III chassis. The earlier of the two was their first post-war body, commissioned by the flamboyant "Sir" John Gaul (who had no right to the title, which he used when living in France) and conceived as an equally flamboyant sedanca de ville. It had razor-edge lines and much of its exterior was copper-plated to contrast with the deep red coachwork. Freestone & Webb numbered the body design as 2100, closing off their pre-war sequence. It did well at the "concours d'élégance" events for which Gaul had bought it.

The second body had design 3089 and was built in 1952. It was a large four-light coupé with lines very much in the contemporary Freestone & Webb idiom, and in fact only the wire wheels and set-back radiator gave it away on first glance as a pre-war chassis.

Utility

As explained in the entry for David Joel, the vogue for wooden utility or shooting-brake bodies came about as a reaction to tax regulations in the UK. Nevertheless, Freestone & Webb fielded a request for such a body from overseas, and constructed it on Rolls-Royce Silver Wraith chassis LWHD73 in 1950, to their design 3068. It was well-proportioned, but there were no repeat orders.

GURNEY NUTTING

J Gurney Nutting & Co Ltd was one of the most highly respected British coachbuilders of the 1930s, having been established in 1918. A fire at the original Croydon premises in 1923 prompted a move to fashionable Chelsea, closer to their customer base. The company began to use Weymann construction to reduce the weight of its bodies and, most importantly, took on AF McNeil from the Cunard coachbuilding company as chief designer.

McNeil had an unerring eye for graceful and elegant lines, and his designs kept Gurney Nutting in the forefront of British coachbuilding through the inter-war years. Head-hunted by London dealer Jack Barclay to take over at James Young (which Barclay had bought in 1937) towards the end of the 1930s, McNeil was replaced by his protégé, John Blatchley – who after the war would become head of Crewe's own body styling division.

In 1945, the company was renamed Gurney Nutting Ltd as it was in turn absorbed by Jack Barclay, and the works moved to Merton. It turned to building coach bodies as an additional source of income, and from 1948 the Merton works was exclusively devoted to that. Car body building continued at the James Young works in Bromley, although Gurney Nutting had its last Motor Show stand in 1948, and the final car bodies were built in 1950. Coach body building continued at Merton until the company closed at the end of 1953.

Sedanca Coupés (1947-1950)

While other coachbuilders depended on saloons and limousines for their bread and butter in the post-1945 era, Gurney Nutting did not. All of its bodies for Rolls-Royce and Bentley chassis were two-door types, the best known probably being the sedanca coupés on Bentley MkVI chassis that were delivered between 1947 and 1950. This design was later continued by James Young.

The first of the sedanca coupé bodies was delivered on chassis B175AJ in October 1947, and three

more followed, the last being delivered in February 1950. These had a straightforward but superbly proportioned design that was known by the James Young design number of C15. That same number was also used for a further development of the design that appeared about a year later, the earliest delivery being of B296CF in November 1948 – which may have been on the company's Earls Court Show stand that year. This further development had the beautiful and highly distinctive "teardrop" style, in which the otherwise blind rear quarters had a teardrop-shaped window. There were again four of these, and the last one, on chassis B214EY, was also delivered in February 1950.

Drophead Coupés (1948-1950)

Gurney Nutting came to the Rolls-Royce Silver Wraith chassis quite late on, with the result that probably all of its bodies for those models were actually built at the James Young premises. Seven (a figure that is challenged) were Drophead Coupés, and all of them had design number WR20, which was actually a two-door derivative of James Young's WR18 saloon design. This was introduced at the 1948 Motor Show, when there was one example on the Rolls-Royce stand and a second on Gurney Nutting's own stand. Most of the seven examples built had a flat boot, but with WCB50 in 1949 came an alternative and far more elegant curved boot. A curious feature of these bodies

There were four of these lovely "teardrop" Sedanca Coupé bodies on Bentley MkVI chassis between 1948 and 1950. The design was by John Blatchley, who had trained under AF McNeil and would later take over as head of body styling at Rolls-Royce itself. (©Anton van Luijk/ WikiMedia Commons)

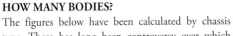

HOW MANY BODIES?

The figures below have been calculated by chassis type. There has long been controversy over which post-war bodies were sold as Gurney Nutting types and which as James Young, and as a result these figures may differ from those published elsewhere.

Rolls-Royce		Bentley	
Silver Wraith	12	MkVI	8

The lines work just as well from this angle. The Sedanca Coupé body on Bentley MkVI B320LFV has the C15 design without the "teardrop" feature, and was the last of four to this design. It was delivered in February 1950. (Klaus-Josef Rossfeldt)

was that the semaphore arms for the turn signals were embedded in the door, below the quarter-light. The last example was on chassis WGC76, which was delivered in July 1950.

Fixed-head Coupés (1949-1950)

There were also probably two fixed-head coupés for Rolls-Royce Silver Wraith chassis, WDC8 dating from August 1949 and again a derivative of the James Young WR18 saloon. The flat boot was accompanied by dummy hood irons, and the semaphore arms were accommodated behind the doors, a far neater solution than that adopted for the drophead coupés. This body was later converted into a sedanca coupé. The second example was on chassis WDC100 and was delivered in March 1950.

HARWOOD

Very little information is available about Harwood Coachworks of Great Yarmouth, who built a single six-light saloon body on Rolls-Royce Silver Wraith chassis WYA75. The car was delivered in August 1950. It would be fair to say that the coachbuilder struggled to get the proportions right on this body, which incorporated elements of the fashionable semi-razor-edge style but ended up looking very heavy and slightly ungainly.

HJ MULLINER

The London coachbuilder HJ Mulliner, with headquarters in Chiswick, was considered to be one of Britain's top exponents of the art. It had been founded in 1900 by a distant relative of the Mulliner family of Northampton, but there were no business links with any of the other Mulliner coachbuilding companies of the time.

HJ Mulliner built its first bodies on Bentley chassis in 1923, and its first for a Rolls-Royce chassis five years later. It developed strong connections with both chassis makers, and during the 1930s built on few other makes of chassis. Those it did clothe were from other top-quality manufacturers.

Generally, customers made their way to HJ Mulliner for a body that was beautifully proportioned, somewhat conventional, and ultimately discreet. In the post-war era, this coachbuilder built a lion's share of the bespoke coachwork on Rolls-Royce and Bentley chassis – over 500 bodies for the Silver Wraith, for example, and more than 300 for the MkVI.

Despite their conventional appearance, HJ Mulliner bodies were also innovative, the most notable example perhaps being the all-aluminium Lightweight designs that began to appear in 1950. The company was clearly highly respected at Crewe, too, becoming involved in the development of the special fastback bodies for the original Bentley Continental and gaining the contract for their construction as well. It was also HJ Mulliner who built the coachwork on no fewer than nine of the 18 ultra-exclusive Rolls-Royce Phantom IV chassis between 1950 and 1956.

Nevertheless, the company could not avoid feeling the effects of the decline in the coachbuilding trade during the 1950s. By the end of the decade it was clear that its position was becoming unsustainable, and in 1959 it made an approach to Rolls-Royce. The chassis maker took control of this old-established coachbuilder, and in 1961 merged it with its Park Ward coachbuilding subsidiary to create HJ Mulliner, Park Ward Ltd.

HJ Mulliner found a comfortable niche in the market for its Sedanca de Ville bodies in the late 1940s. This one is unidentified but dates from 1949 and appears to have design 7153.

HOW MANY BODIES?			
The figures below have been calculated by chassis type.			
Rolls-Royce		**Bentley**	
SIlver Wraith	335	R Type	67
Silver Wraith LWB	182	Continental	193
Silver Dawn	3	Silver Cloud	45
S Type	43	S Continental	218
S Cloud LWB	2	Silver Cloud II	107
S2	15	S2 Continental	221
S Cloud II LWB	1		
Phantom IV	9		
Phantom V	9		
Total	**693**	**Total**	**1058**

Bodies attributed to Mulliner, Park Ward are not included here; please see the separate entry for that coachbuilder. The Silver Cloud and Bentley S figures include the drophead coupé conversions of the standard steel coachwork. The two Silver Cloud LWB bodies were estate conversions for coachbuilder Harold Radford; there were two similar bodies among those on the standard-wheelbase Silver Cloud, and all four are discussed further in the entry for Radford.

Sedancas de Ville, 1947-1954

While there was still demand for Sedanca de Ville coachwork, HJ Mulliner catered for it with a will. The coachbuilder's earliest post-war bodies were Sedanca de Ville types, and by being fairly quick off the mark the company was able to establish its position in the market for this type of coachwork and hold onto it. Most were on the short-wheelbase Rolls-Royce Silver Wraith chassis; for a sedanca on the smaller Bentley MkVI, most customers turned to Gurney Nutting (or later, James Young), although HJ Mulliner did build one such car in 1948. A characteristic of the HJ Mulliner designs was an all-metal sedanca extension.

The company's earliest Sedanca de Ville design was number 7019 for the Silver Wraith, with a razor-edge style that was readily recognisable as a cousin of the touring limousine (design 7062) that followed soon after it. All four doors were rear-hinged, and there were occasional seats in the rear. There were 13 examples of this body, of which the earliest was delivered in January 1947 on chassis WTA29 and the last in September that year on WTA1.

Before the last of these sedanca bodies had been delivered, a new design began to appear. This was number 7055, the earliest examples of which date from spring 1947. In truth, there was very little difference between this "new" design and its predecessor. The first example delivered was on chassis WTA64 in May 1947, and the last of a probable 61 was on WHD93 in October 1950. There were nevertheless at least 62 chassis involved: the body originally mounted on WDC76 was later transferred to chassis WHD49 when that chassis was new in 1950.

There was yet a third Sedanca de Ville design in this period, and design 7042 overlapped with the production of both 7019 and 7055. But only four examples were delivered between March 1948 (WZB3) and January 1950 (WGC38). Visually similar to the two mainstream designs 7019 and 7055, this one had its front doors hinged at their leading edges and no occasional seats.

The single example of design 7045, on WHD35 in July 1950, brought no surprises, and then from autumn 1950, HJ Mulliner focussed on another new Sedanca de Ville design, which was introduced at the Earls Court Motor Show with number 7120. This one was a rather formal-looking machine with fairly conservative lines. Deliveries to customers began in December 1950 with chassis number LWLE16, and the last example (on WVH93) was not delivered until April 1954, and there were probably 18 of these bodies altogether.

Paradoxically, design 7153 had appeared before 7120, being introduced on the HJ Mulliner stand at Earls Court in 1948 on chassis WCB17. Nine more examples were built, eight of them in 1949-1950 but the last (on WSG31) not being delivered until September 1952. A variant on WFC99, with Hooper-style quarter-lights, was on the Rolls-Royce stand at Earls Court in 1949, and the only left-hand-drive example (LWHD12) appeared at the New York Show in March 1950.

There were also two one-off Sedanca de Ville designs on the Silver Wraith chassis in 1949 and 1953. The earlier one was number 7144, and it was delivered on chassis WDC23 in January 1949. The other was delivered in May 1953 and had number 7334; it was delivered on chassis LWVH90.

Last but not least, a Sedanca Coupé body (the distinction is a fine one) was built on Bentley MkVI chassis B382CF, delivered in July 1948. The body had sweeping wing lines of traditional HJ Mulliner style with twin side-mounted spare wheels, and the rear section had a drophead configuration that has led to the erroneous description of this car as a three-position Drophead Coupé.

Touring Limousines, 1947-1958

Touring Limousines followed very quickly after the first Sedanca de Ville bodies in 1947, and quickly became HJ Mulliner's core business. The majority were built on Rolls-Royce Silver Wraith chassis, both on the original 127-inch wheelbase chassis and on the long-wheelbase type from 1953. Just two Touring limousines were built on Bentley MkVI chassis in 1951-1952.

The primary designs on the short-wheelbase Silver Wraith were the four-light 7062 that later became design 7118, and the six-light design 7249 that replaced it in 1950. There were 85 examples of this second design, which was later modified to suit the long-wheelbase chassis, becoming number 7356; 78 of these were then built.

What might be called the first-generation Touring Limousine body appeared in 1947 as design number 7062, a semi-razor-edge four-light type with cutaway rear wheel spats, and although its lines were understandably based on pre-war HJ Mulliner bodies, they set the style for all the early post-war ones. Many were delivered with two-tone paintwork, and this could be arranged in several different ways; typically the lighter colour was applied above the waist moulding, or only on the side panels.

There were probably 77 of these bodies, delivered between October 1947 (WTA69) and September 1950 (WHD75). At least six were built without

This second-generation Touring Limousine body was delivered on Silver Wraith chassis LWVH114 in November 1953, and shows the full wing lines of the time. Both rear wheel spats and razor-edge lines nevertheless remain in evidence. (©Mr.choppers/WikiMedia Commons)

divisions as Saloons, and some were simply described as Limousines, which probably only indicates that HJ Mulliner were prepared to modify the design to meet the customer's requirements. Four examples of design 7062 were displayed at overseas Motor Shows. WAB61 was at Paris in 1948, WDC3 at the Melbourne Show that year, WDC10 was at Brussels in 1949, and WDC30 was at Geneva that year.

Worth noting is that there were also two one-off Touring Limousine designs on the Silver Wraith chassis in 1947-1948. The earlier one had design number 7081 and was delivered in September 1947 on chassis number WVA36. The second one had an earlier design number, 7043, and was delivered on chassis number WAB19 in October 1948. This one might not quite have been a one-off: the "long Limousine" body delivered in chassis WGC45 in December 1949 has also been tentatively identified as a 7043.

Design 7062 was replaced for the 1950 season by design 7118, although there were no apparent changes between the two and design 7118 was fairly short-lived. The first example (on chassis WGC29) was delivered in November 1949; most of the rest had 1950 delivery

dates but the last of 21 bodies (on WME61) was not completed until July 1951. The actual descriptions of these bodies varied: some were described as Saloons with a division, and at least two as plain Saloons.

It was in 1950 that the second-generation Touring Limousine body made its debut as design 7249, on chassis WHD89 at that year's Earls Court show. Design 7249 was a six-light style, the rearmost side windows leaving no room for the companion sets with mirrors that had featured on the earlier bodies. Nevertheless, some examples would be built with smaller windows so that companion sets could be installed. These bodies all had a higher front wing line than those they replaced, and there were different arrangements at the rear: the boot now had a self-supporting lid that was hinged at the top, and the spare wheel was stowed within it rather than in a separate compartment below the boot floor. Free-standing R100 headlamps were still the norm, but some bodies were ordered with smaller built-in headlamps.

Only one of the 77 bodies to this design was recorded as a Saloon (ie without a division), and that was on chassis WLE8 in 1951. One example (on WME49) was HJ Mulliner's exhibit at the Festival of Britain in 1951, and another (probably WOF30) was on the company's stand at Earls Court later that year. The design remained available until the end of short-wheelbase Silver Wraith production, the final delivery being on chassis WVH107 in December 1953, although the last numerically was on LWVH114 a month earlier.

When the long-wheelbase Silver Wraith became available, there was a change of policy at HJ Mulliner. Instead of a single mainstream design, the company offered two different styles from the beginning in autumn 1953. Just as was the case for the six-light saloons on Bentley MkVI chassis from 1950, there was one ultra-modern Lightweight type (which is described below), and a conservative style as the alternative. The conservative design, number 7356, was the stronger seller, and a probable total of 76 were sold up to the end of Silver Wraith production in 1958.

Design 7356 was introduced at Earls Court in October 1953 by chassis number LBLW53 on the coachbuilder's own stand. Not surprisingly, it was a derivative of design 7249 on the earlier short-wheelbase Silver Wraith, extended with longer rear doors and updated by omitting the rear-wheel spats. It was also closely related visually to design 7358, the Limousine introduced at the same time, but had a larger boot and slightly less room inside the body to fit its Touring Limousine role. All the first cars had free-standing R100 headlamps, but from September 1956 the headlamps were smaller, built-in units.

Examples of design 7356 appeared twice more at Earls Court, when DLW46 was on the Rolls-Royce stand in 1954 and ELW14 appeared on the coachbuilder's own stand in 1955. The last one was delivered in February 1959 on chassis LHLW52, which was numerically the final Silver Wraith chassis. The body originally on DLW10 was transferred to HLW7 when that chassis was delivered new in May 1958.

The two Touring Limousines on Bentley MkVI chassis were both individual designs. The earlier one was delivered in June 1951 and was a six-light body with a spare wheel mounted in each front wing alongside the bonnet. This one was to design number 7261. The later car had design number 7290 and was delivered in April 1952 on chassis number B289MB.

Limousines, 1947-1962

Full Limousines, as distinct from Touring Limousines, also figured in the HJ Mulliner repertoire, and among them were some very distinctive designs. They were all on Rolls-Royce chassis, predominantly Silver Wraiths of both lengths but latterly also on the Phantom V.

Although the first post-war HJ Mulliner Limousine was delivered in October 1947, there was only one example of design 7082, which was built on chassis number WTA74. Design 7127 also produced only one example, on chassis WAB27 in September 1948. This rather formal-looking body came with rear wheel spats and was described as a "long Limousine", presumably indicating that HJ Milliner had done their best to make plenty of room in the body despite the inadequate wheelbase length of the early Silver Wraith!

It was not until 1949 that the construction of Limousine coachwork got under way more seriously at Chiswick, and the first example of design 7171 (on chassis WFC25) was delivered that October to the Duchess of Kent. This was a very formal and upright

As newer designs became popular for Saloon and two-door bodies, so Limousines retained the conservative lines of the 1940s. This one was on the HJ Mulliner stand at Earls Court in 1951. It was on a Rolls-Royce Silver Wraith chassis, but the chassis number is unidentified.

Those conservative lines were very much in evidence on design 7171, of which this was the first example, delivered to HRH the Duchess of Kent in April 1949. The chassis was a Silver Wraith, number WFC25.

development of design 7171 appeared in late 1951 as number 7258. Very similar to its parent design, this was drawn up to meet a special order for seven examples from the hire car company Godfrey Davis, Ltd. Not only were there seats for up to seven passengers, but there was a sunroof over the rear compartment, a built-in roof rack for luggage, and to make more room in the boot the Godfrey Davis cars had the spare wheel mounted pre-war-style alongside the left-hand side of the bonnet. Five more of these bodies were also built for other customers, and the last example of design 7258 was delivered in November 1951, on chassis LWME59.

A new Limousine design followed for the long-wheelbase Silver Wraith as number 7276, a seven-passenger design that was specially drawn up for it. Few other coachbuilders sold many Limousines during the currency of the A-series chassis, but HJ Mulliner delivered a total of 46 examples to this design between January 1952 (when the first example, on ALW1, was delivered) and April 1954 (BLW41). At least three became Show cars: LALW22 was displayed at the Toronto Show in 1952; LALW34 was at Earls Court later that year; and ALW44 was shown at Geneva in 1953.

There was also a single example of a variant derived from 7276, which was delivered in December 1952 on chassis number LALW27. The main difference

This rear view of the Limousine body on the Duchess of Kent's Silver Wraith Limousine shows that the old-style small boot was retained – but, just in case, a boot rack was added as well!

seven-passenger body, of which 13 examples would eventually be delivered before the last pair (WME93 and WME95) in November 1951. A variant was also delivered as design 7280 in February 1952 on chassis number LWOF35, the sole example built having a roof rack – probably inspired by a similar feature on the special Limousines to design 7258 (see below). One way or another, it appears that the purchaser asked for it because he considered the boot was too small!

Meanwhile, there were two examples of design 7221 during 1951, both on left-hand-drive chassis – LWME31 and LWME34 – before a further

The later Limousine design, 7358, was conservative and yet very stylish when introduced in 1953. Touring Limousine 7356 used the same lines with minor adjustments to permit a larger boot.

Not a lot had changed in the style of the HJ Mulliner Limousine body for the Rolls-Royce Silver Wraith chassis by the time this one was delivered in 1957, on FLW7. The earlier lines had simply been adapted to the longer wheelbase that became standard from late 1952, and (from September 1956) the headlamps were built into the coachwork rather than free-standing.

HJ Mulliner's first Limousine design (7276) for the long-wheelbase Silver Wraith was a major success for the company. This side view is of an unidentified example.

Touring Limousine design 7356 is seen here in its earlier form, on a 1956 Silver Wraith with free-standing R100 headlamps. (©el.guy08_11/WikiMedia Commons)

HJ Mulliner's original Limousine design for the Phantom V had wing lines that were more recognisably their own, but the company's absorption by Rolls-Royce resulted in this modified design that incorporated Park Ward wing lines and other features. This is on chassis 5AS93, one of just two with right-hand drive built to design 7516, and it was displayed at Earls Court in 1960.

between this body (to design 7310) and the "standard" design 7276 appears to have been a more upright rear panel that gave a more formal look to the body.

The discreet, smooth HJ Mulliner lines were in evidence on no fewer than four Limousine bodies built on the Rolls-Royce Phantom IV chassis, too. By their very nature these were bespoke designs, although Spain's General Franco ordered two of design 7181, which were delivered in June (4AF14) and July (4AF16) 1952. Both were armour-plated. The other two were a single Special Limousine with design 7162 that went to HRH Princess Elizabeth on chassis 4AF2 in July 1950, and a single seven-passenger Limousine with design 7368 for her younger sister HRH Princess Margaret that was delivered on chassis 4BP7 in July 1954.

By the time the Rolls-Royce Phantom V chassis

became available, HJ Mulliner's days as an independent coachbuilder were very nearly over, but the company did build a total of nine Limousine bodies for the new chassis, to two different but related designs.

The original HJ Mulliner design was numbered 7515 but the only example built was on chassis 5LAS3, which was displayed on the coachbuilder's stand at Earls Court in 1959. Its wing lines were very much charactristic of HJ Mulliner designs of the period. The merger with Park Ward that year prompted a redesign that incorporated Park Ward features and new wing lines, and the result was the heavily modified design 7516. The first example of this, on chassis 5AS93, appeared on the Rolls-Royce stand at Earls Court in 1960. There were then seven more examples, all but one with left-hand drive, and the last HJ Mulliner Phantom V was delivered in January 1962.

This Drophead Coupé was one of only two that HJ Mulliner built on the Rolls-Royce Silver Dawn chassis. This one was completed in 1952, and the overall lines of the body are typical of the company designs at the time. The rear window shape earned for this style the nickname of "Jensen hood", an analogy with the shape that Jensen used on their later 541 coupé.

Drophead coupés, 1947-1962

HJ Mulliner's drophead coupés were not a major element in its post-war output. They were primarily for the smaller chassis, the Bentley MkVI and R Type and the Rolls-Royce Silver Dawn, but the company did build a single example for the Rolls-Royce Silver Wraith as well.

A fully disappearing head was a characteristic of all the company's drophead coupé designs for the MkVI Bentley. A metal tonneau panel closed over the folded hood, and this particularly neat feature was copied with varying degrees of success by other coachbuilders. There were three individual designs in 1947-1948, with slightly angular rears and cutaway wheel spats, before a settled design appeared at the 1948 Earls Court Motor Show.

The three early designs were numbers 7008 (one example, on B42AK, delivered in August 1947), 7075 (one example, on B19AJ, delivered in October 1947), and 7088 (again one example, on B273DG, delivered in October 1948).

The definitive early MkVI Drophead Coupé design was then introduced at the Earls Court Show in 1948

as number 7121, the show car having chassis number B451CD. It was followed by three more cars in 1949 and then after an interval of nearly two years by a fifth and last example in July 1951. From mid-1949 there was a further evolution of the same design numbered 7171/A, the first example being delivered that June on chassis number B409DZ. There were then two more in late 1949, and then the final example was delivered in June 1950.

There was then a pause in the production of drophead coupé bodies at Chiswick, although February 1950 also brought the sole example of such a body that HJ Mulliner built on the Silver Wraith chassis. This was very much a special order, to design number 7175/A, and was on chassis number WGC48. It was built to special order for the American wife of a British industrialist, with deliberate echoes of French styling of the day. The two-seat body was originally intended to have a dickey seat, but the design was changed before completion and a bar was fitted, together with a full picnic set in the boot.

When a new Drophead Coupé design appeared in summer 1952, it was based on the Lightweight body construction principles – and the examples built on Bentley MkVI, Bentley R Type, and Rolls-Royce Silver Dawn chassis are described in the section on the Lightweight designs below. But once again, these bodies represented just a small proportion of the total built at Chiswick.

Very much outside the mainstream was a single Drophead Coupé for the Shah of Persia on the huge Rolls-Royce Phantom IV chassis. This was quite unlike other HJ Mulliner drophead coupés, with very much more rounded lines. Despite the length of the vehicle, design 7205 (delivered in December 1951 on chassis 4AF6) had impeccable proportions that were a testimony to the skills available at HJ Mulliner's Chiswick headquarters.

There was only ever one HJ Mulliner Drophead Coupé on the Silver Wraith chassis, and this is it. WGC48 was new in early 1950. (Mr.choppers/WikiMedia Commons)

Design 7504, the "beheaded" Silver Cloud, was a masterful adaptation of the standard steel coachwork for the Silver Cloud. This one is on a Silver Cloud II chassis, LSWC730, and was new in October 1960. (Simon Clay)

On design 7504, even the rather bulky hood looked perfectly in place when folded down onto the body. This is LSWC730 again. (Simon Clay)

The bench front seat in the Mulliner Drophead Coupé was of course the same as in the standard-steel Saloons, although the door cards were different because the doors were considerably longer. (Simon Clay)

HJ Mulliner took a renewed interest in Drophead Coupé bodies during the Silver Cloud era, developing a very handsome design that was quite clearly related to their two-door Saloon design for the Bentley Continental chassis (see below). There were 22 of these bodies to design 7410 on the Silver Cloud chassis, plus 12 on the Bentley chassis, when the design was known as a 7509. There were variations on the design as well. One car (SKG33) had the tail fins fashionable at the time and one was built without the quarter-light, becoming design 7415 on LSWA106 with a further variant (7415/A) on LSGE466. There was a handful of other one-off designs from 1956, including the rather strange 7405 on Silver Cloud LSWA62, which had lines more appropriate to the late 1940s and an externally mounted spare wheel on the tail. Design 7413 (on LSWA104 in 1958) was very similar.

However, all these were superseded by design 7504, which was introduced at the New York Auto Show in April 1959. This became by far the most numerous of the HJ Mulliner Drophead Coupé designs for the Silver Cloud and is often known as the "beheaded" design, as it was an extensive conversion of the standard production four-door Saloon body to produce a most elegant two-door drophead model. The initial pair of bodies had in fact been converted by Park Ward, but under Rolls-Royce the production contract was allocated to HJ Mulliner.

Twelve of the 7504 bodies were built on the six-cylinder Silver Cloud and a further 107 on the Silver Cloud II, the latter as a batch between late 1959 and June 1962, when the last one was delivered. There were also two on the six-cylinder Bentley chassis (as design 7492) and 15 more on Bentley S2 chassis. The design was then taken over by the combined Mulliner, Park Ward organisation and re-numbered as their 2007 for the Silver Cloud III. Many examples had electric windows and power operation for the convertible hood, both of which were optional extras.

Special mention must nonetheless be made of a single four-door Cabriolet (as it was called) to design 7484 that was delivered in June 1961 on a long-wheelbase Silver Cloud chassis, LLCB16. This most elegant body had the familiar lines established during the days of the six-cylinder Clouds and S Types, and the design was carried over to the Silver Cloud III, for which it became Mulliner, Park Ward's design 2033.

Fixed-head Coupés, 1947 and 1957

HJ Mulliner built a special one-off coupé body for Captain RG McLeod, the Australian-born owner of a London tool manufacturing company. McLeod had some very firm views about car bodywork and had ordered some special bodies to his own design from HJ Mulliner on Derby Bentley chassis in the 1930s. He returned to the same coachbuilder after the war to have a special body constructed on a Bentley MkVI chassis, and the completed car was delivered to him in March 1947.

The chassis number was B22AK, and the chassis frame was shortened by nine inches to reduce the rear overhang (McLeod thought a luggage boot was wasteful of space). The body had an angular four-light design, similar to those on his pre-war Bentleys. In the meantime, he had been using a (modified) Citroën Light 15 and had taken a liking to its front wing design, and so he had the same style incorporated into the body for the Bentley.

There was just one more Fixed-head Coupé, and that was a special order on Silver Cloud chassis LSED91 in 1957. The design number was 7458, which was in all important respects a fixed-roof version of the popular 7410 Drophead Coupé.

Saloons, 1947-1954

It was simple enough to remove the division from a touring limousine design and call it a saloon, and HJ Mulliner did so more than once. Nevertheless, the company also drew up some dedicated saloon designs, a few of them for the Silver Wraith chassis but more for the Bentley MkVI and R Type, and for the Rolls-Royce Silver Dawn.

There were not large numbers of saloon bodies for the short-wheelbase Silver Wraith, the earliest being to design 7064 on chassis WVA12 in May 1947. The company then displayed a four-light Saloon with Division at the Paris Show in October 1947. Outwardly, the body on WVA30 was very similar to the rather formal design 7127 Limousine on WAB27, but it incorporated the pre-war HJ Mulliner feature of High-Vision perspex panels above the driving

compartment. This design, of which the number is unknown, seems not to have attracted any orders.

By August 1948, design 7135 had become available, and the earliest of these was on chassis WAB2. However, customers who wanted a saloon body did not generally need a chassis as long as that of the Silver Wraith, and the last HJ Mulliner saloon on the short-wheelbase type was delivered in August 1949 on WFC83. This had design number 7118, of which a probable total of six were built that year.

Nevertheless, two customers ordered saloon bodies on the long-wheelbase Silver Wraith chassis, both in 1954. Presumably they wanted the extra legroom for some reason. The earlier of these bodies was on LBLW45 and was delivered in February that year as a one-off four-light Saloon to design 7338. The later one was on DLW30 and was essentially a version of the Touring Limousine design 7356 but without a division.

HJ Mulliner displayed this Saloon body on Rolls-Royce Silver Wraith chassis WVA30 at the Paris Salon in 1947. Its formal lines were essentially pre-war in style, although enclosed running-boards and rear wheel spats were newly fashionable at the time. Just visible in this picture are the clear panels of the "High Vision" feature above the driving compartment, another carry-over from pre-war HJ Mulliner designs.

For the Bentley MkVI chassis, Saloon design 7059/C proved very popular. Though quite plain in typical 1940s fashion, it had an element of panache about it. This one, on chassis B177AJ, was new in October 1947. (Charles01/WikiMedia Commons)

Saloon design 7220 was an accomplished shape that sold well, and it is easy to see why from these photographs. This example is on Bentley MkVI B127NY, which was delivered in June 1952. (Klaus-Josef Rossfeldt)

On the smaller chassis types, six-light saloons were more HJ Mulliner's style than four-light types, perhaps not least because the "standard steel" body from Crewe was a four-light design and six-light designs gave the coachbuilder greater opportunity to create something different. There were only three four-light Saloon bodies on early Bentley MkVI chassis, all of them with traditional styles, and HJ Mulliner built no more four-light saloons apart from the six "New Look" cars (see below) that represented a not wholly successful leap into the unknown.

Two of those three early chassis had bodies of essentially pre-war design, and one of them has been described as a leftover from the Bentley MkV programme that was aborted in 1940. (HJ Mulliner's only MkV had a six-light body that was supposedly completed after the war.) When there was a delay in completing the first standardised steel body for the MkVI, Crewe called on HJ Mulliner to provide a body for the first experimental chassis, 1-B-VI. 1-B-VI was renumbered as B256AK in May 1952 and sold on. A second body of very similar design went onto the second production MkVI chassis, B4AK – a 1946 chassis although not actually delivered until 1952. This is the body that was supposedly left over from the MkV programme.

Both bodies have front wings that sweep low across the doors, and both have cutaway rear-wheel spats that were fairly typical of HJ Mulliner designs. Of interest is that they also both have the same triangular feature behind the rear door as was found on the standard post-war saloon body, and a very similar boot shape as well. The third body was built on B379BG and was delivered in September 1948. It did not prompt any repeat orders.

The four-light saloons were small beer compared to the six-light types, and the company's four most successful designs accounted for no fewer than 266 bodies on the MkVI chassis. More followed on the R Type. The main designs in this period were an updated pre-war style with sweeping wings, and the deliberately more modern Lightweight type of 1950 that is discussed elsewhere. Each of the major designs also gave rise to minor variations.

HJ Mulliner's first six-light saloon design for the MkVI chassis was also its most successful, and 125 examples of number 7059/C were delivered in just over three years between April 1947 and mid-1950. This design combined a sporting air with a degree of formality, featuring traditional sweeping wing lines and rear wheels with cutaway spats.

Reasoning that there was no point in spoiling a successful product, the coachbuilder essentially updated the earlier design in autumn 1949 as design 7220. This became another strong seller, of which 63 examples were delivered on MkVI chassis, the last in 1953. It was also carried over for the R Type chassis, on which a further 27 examples were built between 1952 and 1954, so making no fewer than 90 bodies of this design.

Straddling the production of six-light saloons 7059/C and 7220 was a third design that appeared in mid-1950. Design 7122 was really a cautious update of 7059/C that on most examples did away with the earlier design's rear wheel spats to give a less formal air. Why it was needed gives some insight into the coachbuilder's thinking at the time. As 7122 appeared alongside the new Lightweight design, HJ Mulliner probably wanted customers with more traditional tastes to feel that they were being offered something new and were not being obliged to settle for the more modern and more costly new shape. Design 7122 was another success: 36 examples were built up to the start of 1952, by which time its job had presumably been done.

There was also a handful of individual designs, all of them probably no more than variants of the long-running 7059/C and 7220 designs and all on Bentley MkVI chassis. Design number 7103 covered a pair of bodies delivered in the first half of 1948, on chassis numbered B83BG and B192CF. There was

then a single example of design 7111 in June 1948 on B267BG. The design number of the six-light body delivered on B124FV in March 1950 is not known, and there was also just one body recorded as having design 7248/A. This was on chassis number B132JO that was delivered in February 1951.

If the Silver Wraith chassis was longer than was needed for a saloon design, then the 12ft 1in wheelbase of the Phantom IV (a foot longer than a long-wheelbase Silver Wraith) was even more so. Nevertheless, when the Sultan of Kuwait asked for three saloon bodies on Phantom IV chassis, that was exactly what he got. The earliest one was delivered in July 1951 on chassis 4AF8 and had a six-light design, number 7206. Four years later came the other two, both with design 7376, which was very similar to the earlier one. They were on chassis 4CS2 (delivered in November 1955) and 4CS4 (delivered in August 1955).

The HJ Mulliner coachbuilt Saloons for the Silver Cloud and S Type chassis all shared their wing lines and boot shapes with the coachbuilder's other mid-1950s designs for these chassis. There was a six-light Saloon – oddly, with rear-hinged rear doors, which were unusual except for Limousines by this date – numbered 7401 for the Bentley, and 27 examples were built. The Rolls-Royce version, of which there were just four, was number 7412. On later examples of both types, the bottoms of the sills were turned under the body, in contrast to the earlier style where they were turned outwards. These designs were often known as All-metal Saloons and of course continued the design principles seen earlier on the Lightweight bodies. They were nevertheless discontinued in 1957 in favour of the Flying Spur, which was only made available on the Bentley Continental chassis.

Experimental saloons, 1948-1949

Like the other major coachbuilders in Britain, HJ Mulliner recognised the importance of the 1948 Earls Court Motor Show – the first one since 1938 – as a showcase for their wares. So they developed a striking New Look design (which had their number 7163) as an illustration of their ability to keep up with the times.

Unfortunately, they chose to base their new Four-light Saloon on the "bathtub" shape of the latest Hudson models. They were not alone in this, and James Young displayed a body of similar inspiration at the same Motor Show. If the design was certainly modern, it also lacked the grace and elegance usually expected from HJ Mulliner. The Show car, B335CD, was followed by five others during 1949, but the design had run its course before the end of that year.

HJ Mulliner's "lightweight" construction was above all associated with this style of saloon coachwork, pictured here on Bentley MkVI B355GT, new in October 1950. The extended tail demanded a rear chassis extension, which was made by the coachbuilder.

"Lightweight" construction was pioneered on a small number of fastback bodies to design 7210, like this one on Bentley MkVI B359EW, which was delivered in May 1950. Despite the superficial similarities, there is a world of difference between this design and the fastback design for the later Continental chassis. (Klaus-Josef Rossfeldt)

The Lightweight bodies, 1949-1958

HJ Mulliner's Technical Director, Stanley Watts, and the company's managing director, Arthur Johnstone, were keenly interested in the way some Italian coachbuilders were using tubular steel body frames to reduce weight. During 1949, Watts developed a new form of lightweight body construction, which used aluminium alloy panels on extruded aluminium framing made by Reynolds Metals. From the beginning, this form of construction was formidably expensive as compared to the composite (wood and metal) type that was then commonplace, but it certainly did produce coachwork that was both strong and light.

HJ Mulliner introduced it at the Earls Court Motor Show in 1949 on a new fastback saloon coupé design for Bentley MkVI chassis, the show car being B9EW. Although only three bodies to design 7210 were made in 1949-1950, the new method of construction quickly attracted attention at Crewe, and would soon gain HJ Mulliner the contract to build the coachwork for the first Bentley Continentals. Meanwhile, the company gradually introduced its new construction methods on a range of different coachwork.

The fastback shape of saloon coupé 7210 made this design unusual, but it was in some respects a little awkward. It also had a perspex section at the front of the roof, continuing an idea from HJ Mulliner's pre-war High Vision bodies. Perhaps for structural reasons, it had a vee-shaped windscreen, and that same feature (discreet though it was) would reappear on the famous Mulliner Lightweight that the company showed on its stand at Earls Court in 1950. This was on a Bentley MkVI chassis, believed to have been B371GT.

Design 7243 was a six-light saloon, a deliberately more modern design with curvaceous lines that offered something quite new and anticipated the design trends of the mid-1950s. It has often been described as the main influence on the design of the standard bodies on the later Rolls-Royce Silver Cloud. Notably, it had a huge luggage boot – far larger than was available on a standard MkVI – thanks to the familiar coachbuilder's trick of extending the car behind the rear wheels. These advanced all-aluminium bodies were formidably expensive, and a Mulliner Lightweight cost nearly 40% more than a Standard Steel MkVI Bentley. Nevertheless, a total of 41 examples were built on MkVI chassis, the last on B479NY in August 1952.

So successful was the Mulliner Lightweight that it was carried over for the Bentley R Type as well, where a further 34 were built in 1952-1954, and for the Rolls-Royce Silver Dawn – although there was only one of these, which was delivered in 1955 on the very last Silver Dawn chassis of all, numbered LSVJ133. In addition, there were two variants, of which the first had design number 7342 and was built as a single example on MkVI chassis B215LH, delivered in January 1952. The other was design 7270, which was specially modified with a shortened boot to suit the wishes of Captain RG McLeod, the long-standing HJ Mulliner customer who had some very

The styling pioneered by the "lightweight" bodies also carried over to this attractive Saloon Coupé, built in late 1951 to design 7260 on Bentley MkVI chassis B34MD.

clear ideas of his own on car styling. This one was built on MkVI B50MD in 1952, and that its lines worked so well was a tribute to the coachbuilding skills deployed at HJ Mulliner.

The curvaceous lines of the Mulliner Lightweight saloons accompanied lightweight construction on a number of other bodies as well. There were two saloon coupé designs, the first being number 7264, of which just one was delivered, on Bentley MkVI chassis B75KL in May 1951. This was followed by the rather more successful 7260, that number suggesting it may have been earlier in conception, of which either three or four were built on MkVI chassis between late 1951 and early April 1952, and a further three on R Type chassis. Design 7260 had a smaller boot than 7264, with longer rear quarter-windows and greater rear-seat legroom.

There were some lightweight Drophead Coupés, too. Four had design 7259, beginning with Bentley MkVI B275MB, which was delivered in July 1952 and was followed by three further examples on the R Type chassis. There were then two different designs for the Rolls-Royce Silver Dawn. Design 7296 was a two-light style with a wraparound rear window that has sometimes been called a "Jensen-style" window. It was on chassis number SHD50. The four-light version of this design, without the wraparound rear window, became design 7297 and was built on chassis LSLE31 in 1953; like the earlier body, it remained unique.

Largest of all the Mulliner Lightweight designs, however, was a Touring Limousine for the long-wheelbase Rolls-Royce Silver Wraith that was numbered 7348. Briefly known as the All-Metal Sports Limousine on its introduction at Earls Court in late 1953, this scaling-up of the saloon design worked well enough to sell 20 examples in five years, the last one being delivered in November 1958 on chassis number FLW29.

The new mainstream Limousine body made its appearance in late 1953 as number 7358, and was a slightly longer relative of the latest 7356 Touring Limousine design. There were 30 of these bodies between December 1953 (when BLW56 was delivered) and July 1960, when LGLW23 was delivered with a special variant of the body that had blind rear quarters. Other deliveries had nevertheless ended in December 1958 with the completion of four examples for the Commonwealth of Australia. These four (HLW45, HLW46, HLW48 and HLW50) were purchased specially for a Royal Tour.

Inevitably, perhaps, there was also a variant of the 7358 design, and the single example of design 7493 was delivered to an American customer in December

The body design may have been "lightweight", but there was no attempt to skimp on expected levels of luxury, as this 1952 Saloon body shows.

1958 on Silver Wraith chassis LHLW36. Essentially the same as 7358 up to waist level, it had a raised roof and much deeper glass, as if for formal parade duties.

Cabriolets and Landaulettes, 1951-1953

Parade cars were a rarity by the early 1950s, and HJ Mulliner fielded orders for just six examples. Five of them were on Silver Wraith chassis, and the sixth was a Phantom IV. All of them went overseas, and all but one were for the use of foreign dignitaries or Her Majesty's representatives. The sixth was for a leading musician of the day.

The earliest of these cars was a Landaulette with design number 7254 which was delivered in April 1951 on chassis number WLE31 and was the only example on the short-wheelbase Silver Wraith chassis. There were then no more until 1953, by which time the long-wheelbase Silver Wraith was available. Two further Laundaulettes were then built, with design 7281, which was essentially similar to the Limousine design numbered 7249 on the short-wheelbase chassis. The first example was on chassis ALW32 and was delivered in January 1953 to the Governor of the Gold Coast. The second was on BLW10 and was delivered in August 1953 to the Sultan of Trengganu, in Malaysia.

The two Silver Wraith Cabriolets each had a different design. The earlier body had design 7311 and was built on chassis LALW29 for the President of Brazil. This was a four-door car with a division and wide running-boards. It was delivered in March 1953. The second parade Cabriolet was delivered in November 1953 and was a special order for Marshal

Still quite breathtakingly beautiful, especially with the spats envisaged in the original design, is the HJ Mulliner fastback body for the R Type Continental. This one has chassis number BC5C and was delivered in October 1953. (Simon Clay)

Tito of Yugoslavia. This was another four-door body with a division and seats for seven occupants, but it had a more modern wing-line without running-boards. It had body design number 7347 and was built on chassis number LBLW37.

It was General Franco's request that his new parade Cabriolet should be armour-plated that persuaded Rolls-Royce to build it on a Phantom IV chassis rather than a Silver Wraith. HJ Mulliner gained the contract for the coachwork, and their design 7183 shared its wing lines and other panelwork below the waistline with saloon design 7181, also for the General. The single example of this body was built on chassis 4AF18 and was delivered in March 1952.

Continental fastbacks, 1952-1960

John Blatchley's masterfully delicious two-door fastback body design was used for all the Bentley Continental chassis built between 1952 and 1954, and for a high proportion of the later R Type Continental chassis as well. Aficionados still argue about whether its shape could have been inspired, consciously or unconsciously, by the very similar one on the 1949 Cadillac Series 62 Coupé. Others prefer to see its origins in the earlier all-metal fastback Saloon Coupé body by HJ Mulliner, design 7210 on the Bentley MkVI chassis.

One way or another, the Blatchley design was turned into reality with the aid of HJ Mulliner, whose latest lightweight construction methods enabled

The remarkable shape of the standard HJ Mulliner fastback body gave the Continental chassis the distinctive identity that its manufacturers wanted for it in the early 1950s. (Simon Clay)

the completed car to weigh some 10% less than the equivalent standard saloon. There were 192 examples of this body, which had design number 7277. Some had rear wheel spats and others did not, and there were multiple more minor variations because these bodies were built strictly to order. There were also two bodies with more major differences from the standard design.

One variant was delivered in January 1954 on chassis BC4C, and was a special order with a curved rear panel and reshaped boot lid to suit. The second was a special order for HJ Mulliner's long-term customer RG McLeod, and was his third special body on a post-war Bentley chassis. Built on Continental chassis BC50D and delivered in July 1955 as one of the last examples of the breed, it retained the distinctive fastback shape of the standard design but also incorporated McLeod's wish for a reduced rear overhang.

The longer wheelbase of the new Bentley S Type Continental demanded a redesign of the body, and HJ Mulliner took the opportunity to make some more comprehensive revisions at the same time. Although design 7400 was readily recognisable as a relative of the original "fastback" saloon, its differences began with a new front wing line that now ran parallel with the waist line. This wing line was higher than before and ran straight through to the rear, where the wing now had a swage line of its own. There were 119 examples of design 7400 on the six-cylinder Continental chassis, of which just 22 had left-hand drive.

During 1957, HJ Mulliner introduced the Flying Spur body for the Continental chassis (see below), and its front wing lines were added to the fastback saloon body, which now became design 7466. The sidelights were now in the wing tops, the swage lines were higher up, and the wheel arches were slightly flared as well,

In contrast to the streamlined shape of the coachwork, the interior of the Mulliner Continental body was old-school in its approach. The figured wood trim was of the highest quality, but the door trims, seats, and dashboard layout were quite plain in the way expected of sporting machinery at the time. (Simon Clay)

Despite the tapering roofline, there was plenty of room for passengers in the rear. This is BC5C again. (Simon Clay)

Delivered a month before BC5C, this is BC3C, which does not have the wheel spats. The design remains extremely graceful. (Simon Clay)

Proudly signed by the coachbuilder… this is the sill plate of BC3C. (Simon Clay)

and these elements of the design were used for the last 20 two-door bodies on the S1 Continental (four with left-hand drive). The fastback designs were then discontinued as the six-cylinder Continental chassis went out of production. There was, though, just one more, which was built to special order for shipping magnate Aristotle Onassis on an early Continental S2, BC41LAR, in 1960. Essentially to design 7466 with the Flying Spur-type wings, this design was numbered 7519 and also appears to have had a painted radiator shell from new.

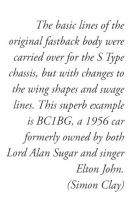

The basic lines of the original fastback body were carried over for the S Type chassis, but with changes to the wing shapes and swage lines. This superb example is BC1BG, a 1956 car formerly owned by both Lord Alan Sugar and singer Elton John. (Simon Clay)

Every line at the front of body design 7400 seems to be a perfect fit for a car of the S Type Continental's stature.
(Simon Clay)

Two-door Saloons, 1956

Alongside the fastback bodies for the Continental chassis, HJ Mulliner also offered a two-door Sports Saloon design for the standard chassis, which became design number 7407. Just two were built on Bentley chassis in 1956. Their wing lines were broadly similar to those of the Saloon bodies to design 7401, and to the Drophead Coupés of design 7410, and a large rear side window made for a light and airy interior and an attractive side view. The rear window was in three sections, joined by slim vertical pillars.

The number-plate area on the S Type Continental fastback is quite different from its equivalent on the R Type, and would influence similar designs on later HJ Mulliner coachwork.
(Simon Clay)

A comparison of the rear view of BC1BG with the rear view of the fastback R Type Continental reveals that the newer car had much larger tail light units.
(Simon Clay)

By this stage, there was no longer any pretence that this was a lightweight design: the S Type Continental was simply a fast and luxurious grand tourer.
(Simon Clay)

The rear seat was shaped for two occupants. Even the longer wheelbase of the S Type could not restore all the extra legroom lost to thicker and plusher front seats.
(Simon Clay)

The Flying Spur, 1957-1963

Luxurious though the fastback saloon body on the Continental chassis may have been, the overall concept was not quite ideal for a fast touring car designed to cover long distances. The boot was not ideally shaped, and access to the rear seats was awkward. It was HJ Mulliner who first had the courage to point this out to the Crewe management, and it was HJ Mulliner who gained permission in 1957 to build the first four-door body on the Continental chassis. Other coachbuilders scrambled to get agreement for their own four-door designs.

The new body, to design number 7443, was given the romantic-sounding name of Flying Spur. This came from Arthur Talbot Johnstone, HJ Mulliner's managing director, and the flying spur was the heraldic device of his family. Drawn up by chief designer George Moseley, the Flying Spur was exceptionally well-proportioned, replacing the fastback style by a three-box shape with a larger boot. With a raised rear roofline, there was more room in the back and of course the extra pair of doors gave much easier access for rear seat passengers. A six-light configuration helped to balance the side elevation to perfection, and the wing lines were higher than those of the fastback bodies. Moreover, HJ Mulliner managed to keep their weight the same as that of their two-door bodies on the Continental chassis.

The first Flying Spur body appeared on chassis BC90BT in May 1957, and the design became a major success. No fewer than 54 examples were built on the S Type Continental chassis, and a further 14 examples were built of a modified design 7443/B, which had

a four-light passenger compartment. There were also two examples of what was called "Mod 2", where the swivelling rear quarter-light was separate from the rear door. This allowed a slimmer rear pillar than on the four-light body while still leaving room for a vanity set on the inside. Both examples were built for a customer called Van Gerbig and this special design was known within HJ Mulliner by his name; strangely, however, he actually rejected both cars before taking delivery.

The basic lines of the Flying Spur were carried over to the S2 Continental chassis in 1959 and then to the S3 Continental in 1963, by which time it had become a product of Crewe's HJ Mulliner, Park Ward coachbuilding division (see below). There were 113

The Flying Spur design on Bentley S Type Continental chassis was named after the heraldic device of the coachbuilder's managing directors. This four-door Saloon allowed buyers to combine the performance benefits of the Continental chassis with a body that provided dignified access to the rear seat.

The Flying Spur had an absolute mastery of line that combined the sleekness expected of a Continental with four-door practicality. This superb 1962 example is on S2 Continental chassis BC35LCZ. (Simon Clay)

The contrasting edging to the wood sections lends a special appeal to the interior of this S2 Flying Spur. (Simon Clay)

The Flying Spur remained available into the V8 era, too, and this 1963 example on an S2 Continental chassis would have remained fully contemporary in the first half of the 1960s.

examples of the standard Flying Spur design for the S2 Continental, which had design number 7508. These bodies had a deeper boot lid that gave a lower loading height than on design 7443, and they also had a slightly shorter radiator shell that required the bonnet to slope downwards gently at the front.

Not every customer wanted the six-light design; a few asked for blind rear quarter-panels that gave the rear-seat occupants greater privacy. So HJ Mulliner also developed a four-light version of the Flying Spur design during the S2 era, calling it design 7508/D and building a probable total of 15. This continued into the S3 era, when two more examples were built.

Once again, the Flying Spur offered top-quality comfort in the rear seats. (Simon Clay)

The lines of the two-door four-light Saloon for the Continental chassis are quite clearly related to those of the Flying Spur. This one is on S2 Continental chassis BC25BY, and was delivered in 1961. (Simon Clay)

The booted Continental bodies, 1958-1963

Lack of boot space was a problem of which some buyers of the fastback Continental bodies complained, and during 1958 HJ Mulliner resolved to do something about it. The result was design 7500, the Continental Special, which made its debut at that year's Earls Court Show. Apart from having a proper projecting boot and altered roofline to suit, this design was affected by the vogue for copying American designs that had reached its zenith (some would say "nadir") in Freestone & Webb's

This is an example of the first two-door four-light bodies made for the V8-engined Bentley S2 Continental in 1959.

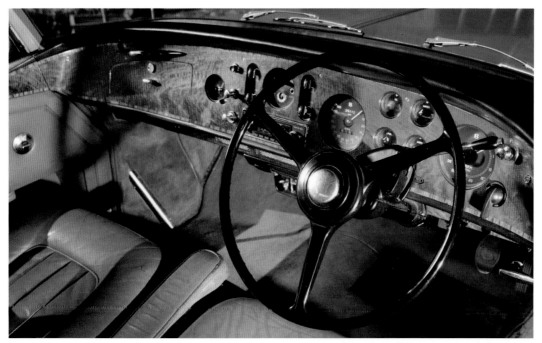

Shared with the Flying Spur, this slim design of tail light is generally called the "cathedral" style today. (Simon Clay)

Honeymoon Express a year earlier. The Continental Special had a very odd front end design, with the sidelights in angled projections over otherwise curved wing fronts, and quite prominent tail-fins on what was otherwise still recognisably an HJ Mulliner two-door body. Nine were built, of which just one had left-hand drive. In later years, some owners had the fins removed and the rear end of their cars reworked to suit.

HJ Mulliner clearly detected customer resistance early on, and modified the design to dispense with the fins and incorporate a more conventional front end. The result looked very much like design 7407 on the standard S Type chassis. Just one example of this redesigned body, which was still called design 7500, was built on chassis BC27GN in 1959. Aesthetically, this was a major success, and so HJ Mulliner carried it over for the S2 Continental chassis that followed a few months later, and gave it the new design number of 7514. It became the coachbuilder's standard two-door design for the S2 Continental, and was later modified with the four-headlamp front end for the S3 Continental chassis as well, when it became a product of the Mulliner, Park Ward division (see below). No fewer than 74 examples were built, of which 26 were on left-hand drive chassis.

Inevitably, perhaps, there was one special-order variant of design 7514, and that was ordered by RG McLeod and was built on S2 Continental chassis BC106AR. It may well have been the final body built

Seen on the two-door Continental body, this door handle shows the design characteristic of HJ Mulliner. (Simon Clay)

solely by HJ Mulliner, and was completed in 1960. As was his wont, McLeod had asked for the boot and rear overhang to be shortened, changes which rather undermined the balance of the original design.

The estate bodies (1959)

When Harold Radford (see separate entry) drew up an estate conversion for the Silver Cloud in 1959, he lacked the resources to build the bodies himself. So the contract went to HJ Mulliner. There were two bodies on the standard-wheelbase chassis (to design 7506) and two on the long-wheelbase chassis (to design 7503). There is more about these bodies in the entry for Radford.

HOLLAND

The sole body attributed to JA Holland of Southport was a Drophead Coupé built on Bentley MkVI chassis B289BG and delivered in November 1947. JA Holland was Jack Holland of the confectioners, which became the world's largest toffee and caramel makers in the 1960s. It appears that he also had some interests in the motor trade in the Southport area, and it is likely that one of those actually constructed the body for his Bentley. No pictures of the car have yet been discovered.

HOOPER

Hooper, "the Royal coachbuilder", held a Royal warrant continuously from 1830 until its closure in 1959. Founded in London early in the 19th century as Adams & Hooper, it was acknowledged as one of the foremost coachbuilders by the end of the century, and was among the first British companies to build a motor car body, in 1896.

In the 1920s and 1930s, the Hooper company was very highly regarded for its top-quality coachwork, which was typically quite formal in design and was always expensive enough to be the choice only of the very wealthy. Hooper became closely associated with both Rolls-Royce and Daimler chassis – the latter at the time being the favourite of the British Royal family. The company expanded to meet increasing demand, and by 1937 was operating three factories. A year later it also absorbed its former rival, Barker & Co.

During the war, Hooper was taken over by BSA (Birmingham Small Arms), who also owned Daimler. As Daimler chassis were then the Royal favourite, the alliance was a fortunate one and probably increased public esteem for the company. Despite the threats to the coachbuilding trade in the late 1940s, Hooper emerged triumphant, thanks in no small measure to the alliance with Daimler and to the talents of its chief

designer, Osmond Rivers. The esteem in which the company was held can be measured by the fact that it was commissioned to build the coachwork on no fewer then seven of the 17 "heads-of-state-only" Rolls-Royce Phantom IV chassis built for sale.

It was Osmond Rivers who was responsible for the company's most recognisable post-war design, which was introduced in 1949 on a Rolls-Royce Silver Wraith chassis as the New Look but became popularly known as the Empress Line after it featured on a Daimler Empress show chassis in 1952. Hooper went on to develop it to suit both Rolls-Royce and Bentley chassis in the 1950s, and it also had a major influence on one of Freestone & Webb's most popular designs of the time. Nevertheless, the descendants of some of the company's older styles remained available for those customers who found the Empress style a little too unconventional.

Although the Hooper reputation remained very much intact at the end of the 1950s, the company realised that the end was near when they learned that the next new Rolls-Royce model would not have a separate chassis. So the coachbuilding operation closed down – although the name remained alive for a few more years as a service organisation that looked after the cars of former customers.

The Teviot touring saloons, 1946-1953

Hooper's first post-war coachwork on the Silver Wraith chassis was a Touring Saloon that had the semi-razor-edge lines typical of its times. But it also introduced a new and highly distinctive Hooper feature – a rear quarter-light with a drooping, nearly triangular rear corner. This was not yet the Teviot design, but its very similar replacement in 1948 was, and with periodic revisions this saw the company through until 1953. Thereafter, the Hooper Touring Saloon design was a version of Osmond Rivers' New Look, familiarly known today as the Empress.

Hooper's characteristic post-war rear quarter-light shape is very obvious on this picture of a Touring Limousine to design 8034. The chassis is a Rolls-Royce Silver Wraith, in fact WTA2, which was the third prototype, completed in September 1946.

HOW MANY BODIES?			
The figures below have been calculated by chassis type.			
Rolls-Royce		Bentley	
Silver Wraith	323	MkVI	61
S Wraith LWB	146	R Type	42
Silver Dawn	12	S Type	45
Silver Cloud	41	S Type LWB	7
Silver Cloud LWB	13	S Continental	6
Phantom IV	7	S2 Continental	1
Phantom V	2		
Total	**544**	**Total**	**161**

The original Teviot design was introduced in 1948 and was derived from the earlier design 8034. Dating from February 1949 (although the registration number is later), this is a Saloon to Teviot design 8122. Both doors were rear-hinged on these bodies. The chassis is a Rolls-Royce Silver Wraith, WDC55. The car was pictured parked on a steep hill, and the photographer has squared it up, so making the building in the background appear tilted.

For 1950, a revised version of the Teviot appeared, and the "Teviot II" or design 8235 illustrated here was readily recognised by a forward-hinged front door and a higher wingline with concealed running-boards. This 1950 example is on a Rolls-Royce Silver Wraith chassis.

While the Teviot family had begun as a Touring Saloon, it was not long before it was adapted as a Saloon (without the division, see below). Over the years, there would be both six-light and four-light versions of the design, and versions with both external R100 headlamps and the smaller built-in style.

The first of these body designs, often called the "pre-Teviot" because the name had not yet been applied, had number 8034. The first example was commissioned by Rolls-Royce Ltd and was delivered in May 1946 on the very first experimental Silver Wraith chassis (1-SW-1). It was a six-light design that brought no surprises at the time, except for the distinctive rear quarter-window shape already mentioned. All the doors on these bodies were hinged at the rear, and the lower door panels were gracefully outswept to cover the running-boards.

The first customer bodies to this design were delivered in February 1947, all of them an inch longer than that first example, and over the next 18 months or so a further 65 Silver Wraith chassis were bodied as 8034 touring limousines. The last of these was delivered in September 1948, by which time design 8098 – the first Hooper Teviot – was already in production as its replacement. Nevertheless, there were also three more bodies to a variant design, 8034A, which were delivered between December 1948 and March 1949.

The Teviot proper, in its first incarnation, gradually took over from the original 8034 Touring Saloon during 1948. The first example was on chassis WVA38 in October 1947, but quantity build had begun by February or March 1948. All these bodies were equipped with a division, and their front doors were hinged on the centre pillar. There was also a Saloon derivative of the design, without a division, numbered 8122 (see below).

There were around 112 examples of the first Teviot design, Teviot I, the calculation being mildly

complicated by the fact that the body from WZB5 was transferred onto LWLE22 when the latter chassis was new in 1951. The last example was delivered in January 1950, by which time the Teviot II replacement had already been announced.

Teviot II was introduced in November 1949 with design number 8235, just too late for that year's Earls Court Motor Show. Very similar to Teviot I, its front doors were nevertheless now hinged at the front, and the running-boards had disappeared. The first car, WGC18, had swaging on the wings like the Teviot I, but later cars did not. There were 11 examples in all (the total is disputed), the last one being delivered on chassis LWHD62 in February 1951. Like Teviot I, Teviot II had composite construction, with a wooden body frame and alloy panels. It was replaced by Teviot III.

The third version of the Teviot Touring Limousine body was introduced at the Earls Court Show in 1950, with an example on Silver Wraith chassis WHD91 displayed on the Rolls-Royce stand. It had body design number 8283. Visual differences from the Teviot II included smaller rear quarter windows, but there were more important differences under the

This was the Teviot design on a Bentley MkVI chassis, in this case B8LHR, delivered in November 1950 to a customer in the USA. In this guise, the design had number 8111/A. (Klaus-Josef Rossfeldt)

This was the first of Hooper's Limousine designs for the long-wheelbase Rolls-Royce Silver Wraith, a typically formal shape that had design number 8330.

skin. Osmond Rivers had visited the USA earlier in the year and had picked up the idea of all-metal construction there, and the Teviot III body was made entirely of aluminium alloy.

Teviot III appeared twice more on the Rolls-Royce stand at Earls Court, on chassis WOF12 in 1951 and WVH9 in 1952. Examples were also exhibited at Paris in 1952 (WVH16) and at Brussels in January 1953 (LWVH15), and there was a noticeable increase in the number of these bodies on left-hand-drive chassis after that. Exactly 50 Teviot III bodies were built, the last one being delivered in October 1953 on the last (numerically) of the short-wheelbase Silver Wraith chassis, LWVH116.

Limousines, 1946-1958

Hooper built Limousine bodies on Rolls-Royce Silver Wraith chassis of both lengths, and was also responsible for five Limousine bodies on the Phantom IV chassis in the first half of the 1950s.

The company's Limousine coachwork for the Silver Wraith chassis tended to be rather stiff-backed and conservative in appearance, which was doubtless what the customers expected of it. The fact that the original short-wheelbase chassis was not really long enough for

a full Limousine body did not deter customers from requesting such designs, and the earliest was delivered to HRH the Princess Royal in December 1946 on chassis WTA14. This had design number 8056 and was rather plain, in the manner of the day, with a pronounced waist moulding that ran around the rear of the body above the boot.

That waist moulding was changed for one that fell away above the rear wing on design 8134, but the overall body shape was otherwise very similar when WYA71 was delivered with this design around 18 months later. When design 8195 arrived in 1949, it was clearly from the same school of thought, and this time attracted a clutch of orders. There was a single body to Limousine design 9347 in 1947, but it was the long-wheelbase Silver Wraith chassis that provided the platform that Hooper needed.

The earliest Hooper Limousine design for the long-wheelbase Silver Wraith was design 8330, which made its debut on chassis ALW37 on the Rolls-Royce company stand at the 1952 Earls Court Show. This was an essentially conservative but beautifully balanced shape that remained available for two years, the last of 19 examples being delivered in October 1954 on chassis DLW71. An example was displayed on chassis ALW40 at the 1953 Geneva Show.

Design 8330 evolved into design 8400, of which the first (BLW97) was delivered in May 1954, although the design was first shown on the Rolls-Royce stand at Earls Court that October on chassis DLW47. The last of 14 examples was delivered in September 1956 on chassis FLW6. There had meanwhile been attempts to create a limousine design from the Empress lines (see the section below on Empress bodies), but these had not been wholly successful.

The final evolution of Hooper's more conservative Limousine style was then number 8460 and was introduced on the Rolls-Royce stand at Earls Court in 1956 on chassis number FLW17. Other examples had been built earlier, the first being on chassis ELW70 in July that year. Most of the 17 examples made had the built-in headlamps that became the norm in September 1956. All those built had much smaller wheel spats than had been fitted to design 8400, which this one otherwise resembled. Hooper were clearly proud of this design, and it appeared twice more at Earls Court. FLW90 was shown on the Rolls-Royce stand in 1957, and HLW20 showed it on the Hooper stand in 1958. It was, however, the last design of its kind.

The five Limousine bodies on Phantom IV chassis were built between 1951 and 1956, and each one had a different and bespoke design. The earliest design was numbered 8292 and was a typically formal body with

side-mounted spare wheels which made no attempt to conceal its size. This one was mounted on chassis number 4AF10 for the Duke Of Gloucester, and was delivered in September 1951.

Next in the sequence of Hooper designs was 8307, actually delivered before the single example of 8292 in July 1951 and on chassis number 4AF12. Broadly similar to the earlier body, it nevertheless had typical Hooper-style rear quarter-lights, wheel spats and concealed spare wheel stowage. It went to Ernest Hives, the managing director of Rolls-Royce, on his elevation to the peerage as Baron Hives. However, Hives appears to have used it only rarely, and in 1954 the car was sold to HRH Princess Marina, the Duchess of Kent.

Two more Hooper Limousines were delivered in March 1953. Chassis number 4BP1 carried a body to design number 8361, which had sweeping wing lines and a distinctive bright lower body finisher with a small peak in the centre of the rear wheel spat. This car was delivered to King Faisal II of Iraq. On 4BP3, body design 8370 was a touring limousine for which the latest "Empress" lines had been very successfully scaled up, complete with characteristic Hooper rear quarter-light. This car was built for the Prince Regent of Iraq, nephew of the King.

The last of the Hooper limousines for the Phantom IV was mounted on the last of those chassis built, number 4CS6. The body design number was 8425, which in practice was visually very similar indeed to design 8361 delivered in 1953 to King Faisal on 4BP1. It was ordered by the Shah of Persia and was delivered in October 1956.

Saloons, 1947-1953

Hooper's initial Saloon design for the Rolls-Royce Silver Wraith chassis came in two guises, as a plain Saloon or as a Touring Saloon with a division.

Although the Touring Saloon was actually made first (see design 8034, above), the Saloon was not far behind and the first example, on chassis WTA28, was delivered in March 1947. There were 15 examples altogether of design 8060, the last being on chassis WZB17 delivered in May 1948. Two more bodies were subsequently built to a variant of the design known as 8060A, on chassis WCB61 and WDC1, the latter being delivered in January 1949.

Saloon design 8122 for the Silver Wraith appeared in March 1948, but added nothing really new to the Hooper repertoire. It was simply a version of the Teviot I design (number 8098) that dispensed with the division, and was the replacement for Saloon design 8060. Either 10 or 11 examples of this attractive body were built, the last one being delivered in September 1950.

Under pressure to deliver something new for the 1948 Earls Court Motor Show, Osmond Rivers came up with design 8181 for Hooper, and the first example was displayed at the Show on Silver Wraith chassis WCB57. Not only was the shape new, with wing lines that swept almost all the way to the rear

The wheel spats are different, and the bonnet release handles are of a later type, but otherwise not much distinguishes this 8400 Limousine from the earlier 8330 body.

The rear-wheel spats and free-standing headlamps were anachronisms in 1956, when this Limousine body was delivered to the Shah of Persia, but there is no denying the overall elegance of the design. The chassis is the last Rolls-Royce Phantom IV built, number 4CS6.

of the body and fully spatted rear wheels, but Rivers was clearly trying to make the rear seat as wide as possible by making maximum use of the body width. It was, though, unhappily rotund – which Rivers later admitted was because he expected a reaction against razor-edge designs. His prediction turned out to be premature.

Design 8181 – and similar ones on Daimler chassis – was an important stage in the evolution of what became the Empress design. It did not quite achieve its aim of using the full width of the rear body to the benefit of the seat, because a shallow pressing for the falling waistline still ate into the space available. It also suffered from a rounded boot shape that made the body look slightly ungainly. Nevertheless, six more examples were ordered after the prototype had been shown at Earls Court, and all were delivered within the next 12 months, the last on chassis WGC52.

Earls Court in 1949 then brought another step towards the Empress design, with body design 8234 on Silver Wraith chassis WGC16. This Saloon body retained the overall approach of the previous year's 8181 design but added razor-edge lines and a much more pleasing boot shape. It remained the only one of its kind, but the full-blown Empress designs (see below) began to appear not long afterwards.

Hooper built 10 bodies on the long-wheelbase Silver Wraith chassis that were described as Saloons. In all cases except for one, they were based on contemporary Touring Limousine designs, with the division omitted. The most numerous of these Saloon designs was 8409, of which seven examples were built between April 1954 (CLW2) and March 1956 (ELW51). The "parent" design was Touring Limousine 8390.

Saloon bodies were understandably more common on the smaller chassis, and Hooper delivered a good number on the Bentley MkVI and R Type chassis between 1948 and 1949. Most of these were four-light designs, but there were also three six-light bodies.

The best seller among the four-light designs on Bentley chassis was number 8111, of which the first example was delivered in March 1948. The last of 25 to the original design was delivered in February 1950, but a slightly modified version of the design remained available as number 8111/A. This was the Bentley version of the Teviot, an elegant, conservative design with the same outswept lower body panels as on the Drophead Coupé design (8100) that had become available around six months earlier. One example (B120DA) was on the Hooper stand at the 1948 Earls Court Show.

There were some minor variations on this design

which had individual design numbers. Almost certainly a variant of 8111 was 8113, although there are no known pictures of the only example, delivered in April 1948 on chassis B85BG. Design 8117 was essentially an 8111 with large R100 headlamps, and there was just one example delivered in July 1948 on chassis B102CF. Then there was a single 8197, actually an 8111 with a division, delivered in May 1949 on chassis B448DA.

Design 8111 was also the basis of Hooper's six-light saloon for the Bentley chassis in the late 1940s, design number 8139. Unsurprisingly, the fifth and sixth lights had the characteristic Hooper shape. Two examples were built, and were delivered in March and April 1948 respectively. The second, B288CF, had R100 headlamps and an electrically-operated driver's window. A later six-light design, 8222, was displayed on the Hooper stand at the 1949 Earls Court Motor Show, but the body on B193EW remained a one-off.

From 1951, Hooper focussed on new Saloon designs with the Empress styling, and those later designs are discussed below. Nevertheless, there were two further "traditional" Saloon designs on the Silver Wraith chassis, both introduced that year and both lasting until 1953. The first was design 8303, of which 10 examples were delivered, and the second was 8317, of which there were just four.

Drophead Coupés, 1947-1958

Hooper was not a major builder of Drophead Coupé bodies in the post-1945 era, and its bodies of this configuration can be counted on the fingers of one hand. The earliest were three built to design 8100 for the Bentley MkVI chassis. Of these, the first (on B11AJ) was delivered in October 1947 and the last (on B407DZ) in June 1949. These bodies pioneered the wing lines and overall shape that were also seen on the slightly later four-light Saloon design, 8111, but a unique feature of the drophead design was a cutaway section between rear seat back and boot which allowed the hood to sit low down on the body when folded.

Two more Drophead Coupé bodies were built in 1953, one with lines derived from the Empress style (see below) and the other to design 8372 on Silver Wraith chassis WVH37. This was an elegant but unexceptional body, and the completed car was shown at Geneva in 1953. There were then no more Drophead Coupés from Hooper until 1958, when design 8530 was built on a Silver Cloud chassis (LSGE252) for King Faisal II of Iraq. This had some similarities to the contemporary Hooper design for the Bentley Continental chassis, but was unfortunately not one of the company's more accomplished designs.

Sedanca designs, 1947-1952

Sedanca designs formed only a small part of the Hooper repertoire in post-war years, but when asked the company was more than capable of stepping up to the mark. One early special commission on a Rolls-Royce Silver Wraith chassis is discussed in the sidebar about the Nubar Gulbenkian cars. Otherwise, there were single examples on the short-wheelbase Silver Wraith and the Phantom IV, and two on the Bentley MkVI chassis, in this case described as Sedanca Coupés rather than Sedanca de Ville types.

The earliest of the Hooper Sedanca de Ville designs was a unique body to design 8057 on Silver Wraith chassis WTA71, delivered in January 1947. The Gulbenkian car followed shortly after that, but the next bodies to be completed were the two on Bentley MkVI chassis in 1949. Both had design 8172 and both were delivered to overseas royalty, the first to the Prince Regent of Iraq in February and the second to the Maharaja of Mysore in December 1949. Although the Sedanca Coupé was no longer a common style in Britain, the two bodies very successfully combined the traditional elegance of such styles with a more modern design that incorporated spatted rear wheels. They were on chassis B175CD and B47EW.

The last Hooper sedanca design was numbered 8293 and was for the Rolls-Royce Phantom IV chassis. Delivered to the Aga Khan in May 1952, the single body was built on chassis number 4AF20 and its overall lines were similar to those of the Hooper Limousine body on 4BP1. The car was painted in dark green with a light green relief line on each side.

Touring Limousines, 1949-1958

Not every Touring Limousine by Hooper had one of the Teviot designs or one of the Empress designs, even though these were the mainstream types. There were other designs on Silver Wraith chassis of both lengths, and also on the Silver Cloud. Nevertheless, many of these were derivatives of designs for other body types.

On the short-wheelbase Silver Wraith, there were Touring Limousines in 1949 to designs 8090 (WFC44) and 8193 (WDC9 and WDC67). In 1952 there was a single 8333 on long-wheelbase Silver Wraith ALW10, and then in 1958 there was a single 8411 on ELW82. This was really an 8390 Touring Limousine modified to incorporate blind rear quarters.

Derivative of other designs in the mid-1950s were Silver Wraith designs 8422 and 8500. Design 8422 was a variant of the conservative Limousine design 8400, and was a four-light body featuring blind rear quarters and no spats on the rear wheels. The

two examples delivered were on chassis DLW133 in April 1955 and LELW86 in September 1956. Then design 8500 which was introduced on the Hooper stand at Earls Court in 1957 on chassis FLW99, drew its inspiration from Limousine 8460 (itself part of the same design lineage as 8400), having built-in headlamps as standard. A notable feature was that the rear wheel spat had the same design as the contemporary evolution of the Empress designs. Six examples of 8500 were delivered in 1957-1958. There was also a single 8502 Touring Limousine, delivered in August 1958 on chassis LFLW92.

On the Silver Cloud chassis, Hooper adapted Sports Saloon design 8435 to make Touring Limousine design 8444 by adding a division, and built four examples. The equivalent design for the Bentley S Type chassis had number 8443, of which there were two.

Landaulettes, 1949-1958

Landaulettes were ordered only as ceremonial or parade cars, and Hooper built just one on the short-wheelbase Silver Wraith chassis, three more on the long-wheelbase chassis, and a single example on the Phantom IV chassis.

The short-wheelbase Silver Wraith had chassis WGC1 and was delivered in September 1949 to the

This is the late Touring Limousine design number 8500, seen on Silver Wraith FLW99, the car that introduced it on the Hooper stand at Earls Court in 1957. The built-in headlamps were standard for the Silver Wraith by this stage, but the design of the rear wheel spat was very much a late Hooper feature.

There was a sense that Hooper had lost their way on some of their mid-1950s designs, and there is a certain awkwardness about this Touring Limousine body to design 8516, especially around the rear. The body was on a late Rolls-Royce Silver Wraith chassis, number GLW14, and the completed car was delivered in April 1958.

The Hooper elegance was there again on this Landaulette body to design 8445. Landaulettes of any kind were rarely ordered by 1956, when this one was delivered on Rolls-Royce Silver Wraith chassis ELW55, but it had special duties to perform for His Excellency the Governor-General of Nigeria.

UK War Department. It had body design 8178, of which only the one example was built.

The three Landaulettes on long-wheelbase Silver Wraith chassis all had very much the same body design, although the first one (to design 8403) had free-standing R100 headlamps and the later two (to design 8445) had built-in headlamps. The lines of design 8403 broadly followed those of Hooper's Limousine design 8400 below the waist, and above that came a higher roof with deeper windows and, of course, the folding leather landaulette rear section.

The single example of this body was built on chassis number BLW92 and was delivered in June 1954 to the Governor of Singapore. The wood trim was made of oiled teak, because that was considered to be resistant to the termites prevalent in the Singapore region. The original upholstery is said to have been in Rexine plastic for the same reason – although that story has not been verified because the original coachbuilder's file for the car has been lost.

The later two cars, to design 8445, were hard to distinguish from the earlier body without seeing the headlamps. The earlier of them was delivered to the Governor-General of Nigeria in May 1956 on chassis ELW55, and the second one went to the Governor of Western Nigeria in December 1958 on chassis HLW35.

In between these two groups of Silver Wraiths came the unique Landaulette on a Phantom IV chassis, 4BP5. This had design number 8399 and was delivered to Her Majesty the Queen in May 1954. It was built with the project name of Jubilee, was finished in the Royal colours of Claret and Black, and was a rather austere-looking body that shared its lines with some of Hooper's upright formal Limousines of the period.

A van body, 1950

Bentley MkVI chassis B439EW had the distinction of being the only one ever to be bodied for commercial use. Scottish jeweller Donald Henderson ordered a van body for it from Hooper, to transport goods around his chain of jewellery shops. The idea made sense: high-class jewellery was matched by a high-class van. Delivered in January 1950, B439EW was sold on after five years and was converted to an estate car. It has since disappeared.

The "Empress" bodies, 1950-1958

In the late 1940s, Hooper's chief designer, Osmond Rivers, recognised that the latest all-enveloping "pontoon" style bodies on mass-produced cars were able to offer more interior room than was available in a coachbuilt car of similar size. While James Young and Park Ward experimented with full pontoon shapes during 1948 (and not very successfully), his response was to develop what he called the New Look, a ground-breaking design that is often claimed to have been first seen on a Daimler chassis.

In fact, several of the elements that contributed to the New Look were in evidence as early as October 1947 on a special one-off design for the wealthy socialite Nubar Gulbenkian built on a Rolls-Royce Silver Wraith chassis (see sidebar). Much closer to the style that would be built in volume was design 8234, on Silver Wraith WGC16 that was displayed at Earls Court in 1949. So although the new design entered the popular imagination with the name of Empress that was given to the Daimler chassis that later carried it, its key elements had already been seen on these one-off Silver Wraith models.

The most striking characteristic of the Hooper New Look coachwork was its elimination of the rear wings as separate volumes. Instead, the front wings swept right back to the base of the tail, and a particularly smooth line was achieved by using full spats over the rear wheels. Without the need for separate rear wings, the full width of the body could be devoted to the passenger cabin. The sweeping lines contrasted most effectively with some razor-edge styling elements to create a genuinely distinctive design.

Demand quickly arose for versions of this style to suit Rolls-Royce and Bentley chassis, and they rapidly became an important part of the Hooper repertoire. It was also built on Daimler chassis up to 1958, and for most of its life was available as a stylish alternative

The successor to the Teviot design as Hooper's big seller was the one that became known as the Empress – although Hooper initially called it their New Look. This is a 1953 example on a Rolls-Royce Silver Wraith chassis. Hooper still favoured a rear-opening rear door, which made for neat lines in that area of the body.

Hooper tended to favour large slabs of wood for the garnish rails on the doors, where other coachbuilders sought more subtle shapes. This is the rear interior of an Empress body, appropriately laid out with refreshments.

Despite the modern-looking exterior, the interior of the Empress body was distinctly conservative, as the dashboard of the 1953 car shows.

to Hooper's more conventional designs. The basic shape was also picked up by Freestone & Webb, who perhaps understood its potential better than Hooper and developed the concept to admirable effect.

The first Empress derivative to be constructed in volume on a Crewe-built chassis was actually a two-door, four-light design (number 8282) for the Bentley MkVI chassis. This is sometimes called a Sports Saloon. The first of seven examples was delivered in November 1950, and the design was then carried over for the R Type chassis as well, on which three more were built with the same design number. A four-door saloon style followed as design 8294 from April 1951, and no fewer than 14 examples of this were ordered on the MkVI chassis; this design was then also carried over for the R Type that followed, where a total of 39 examples provided ample proof of its popularity.

The Empress lines were first seen on a Rolls-Royce chassis in 1952, on an early long-wheelbase Silver Wraith (ALW11) for Nubar Gulbenkian. This time, they were used to impressive effect on an open body (with design 8335), which was called an All-weather but was really a large four-door cabriolet. The headlamps were blended into the wing fronts under curved glass, in the style seen on the "Docker Daimler" show cars of the time. By special agreement, this car was displayed at the 1953 Geneva Show, and it was very noticeable how well the extra length of the Silver Wraith chassis and the squarer lines of the Rolls-Royce radiator grille suited the Empress lines.

By then, Hooper had already scaled the Empress lines up even further to construct a single example of a Touring Limousine (design 8370) on the long Rolls-Royce Phantom IV chassis. Built for the Prince Regent of Iraq, this was delivered in March 1953 on chassis 4BP3. A single Limousine body to design 8381 on chassis BLW15 delivered in July 1953 perhaps showed that the flowing lines of the Empress styling were not most effectively deployed on an upright and formal body, but Hooper already had a Touring Limousine design in hand, and design 8390 worked much better. The first example was delivered on export chassis LBLW14 in June 1953, and the design caught on: the last of around 50 of these bodies was delivered in December 1956 on chassis FLW24, and the total included several with minor differences from "standard" to suit the individual preference of the client.

Nevertheless, there was still demand for the Empress styling on the smaller chassis from Crewe, and in 1954-1955 Hooper built 12 Saloon bodies on the Rolls-Royce Silver Dawn chassis. The design

was numbered 8401, but it was essentially a Rolls-Royce version of 8294 that had been pioneered on the Bentley MkVI chassis. The earliest example (on chassis SNF105) was delivered in April 1954, and the last (on SUJ4) in April 1955. The body on LSOG98 has been described as a Limousine, but is recorded as having the same design 8401 as the others.

Meanwhile, the mid-1950s brought more large Empress-style bodies for the Silver Wraith chassis. A second attempt to blend the Empress styling with limousine proportions and formality resulted in design number 8420, which was a most elegant motor car even though its uprightness was somehow at odds with the sweeping lines. Nevertheless, just one example was built, on chassis number DLW98, and was delivered in June 1955. There were two Saloons in 1957 with design 8456, which had built-in headlamps rather than the free-standing R100 types of design 8409. These were on chassis FLW57 (delivered in February 1957) and LFLW69 (delivered in June 1957). FLW57 had occasional rear seats like the Touring Limousines, but no division.

Built-in headlamps also featured on the latest version of the Touring Limousine design, which was introduced as number 8455 on the Hooper stand at the 1956 Earls Court Show on chassis number FLW5. In other respects, the design was simply an evolution of the successful number 8390, with an additional chrome strip on the wings. A total of eight examples were delivered, the last one in October 1957 on LFLW93. By then, the original Empress lines had been superseded by an evolution of the shape.

All-weathers, 1952-1959

The description of "all-weather" tends to suggest a four-door convertible with rather crude weather protection, but all the Hooper examples on the long-wheelbase Silver Wraith chassis were far grander than that. Four of the five were built as parade cars, and the fifth – actually the earliest – was an extremely elegant example that used the company's Empress lines as its basis. Built in 1952, this car was delivered to Nubar Gulbenkian (see sidebar opposite).

The other four All-weather bodies from Hooper were all delivered in 1959. Just one was built to design 8537, as a parade car for HM King Paul of the Hellenes. Built on chassis LHLW44 and delivered in March 1959, the car had sweeping wing-lines reminiscent of the Empress style but without any trace of razor-edges. It also featured a detachable Perspex roof for use in inclement weather when it was important for the occupants of the car to be seen during a parade.

The last All-weather design was numbered 8548, and three were constructed, all of them destined for parade duties. The design featured Hooper's then-current cowled headlamps. The first two were ordered specially for the Royal Tour of Australia in 1959, and were on chassis numbers HLW47 and HLW49, being delivered in March and April 1959 respectively. The third car was on LHLW51 and was delivered to the Emperor of Ethiopia in April 1959.

The "evolved Empress", 1956-1959

In the mid-1950s, Hooper produced a further evolution of the Empress style for the new Rolls-Royce Silver Cloud and Bentley S Type chassis. The evolution brought a much more rounded look and a very long boot that offered much more space than the one in the sloping tail of the earlier Empress designs. Cowled headlamps were a further new feature, affecting the profile of the wing fronts, although the wing lines once again swept elegantly across the doors to meet the rear wheel spats low down on the body sides. Opinions about the success of this late redesign is divided.

On the Bentley S Type chassis, the strongest-selling design with these revised lines was numbered 8430, and the 39 examples on Bentley chassis were accompanied by just two for the Silver Cloud. The strongest seller on the Rolls-Royce chassis (with 18 examples) was numbered 8435, which its makers described as a Sports Saloon. On the Bentley S Type chassis there were four Saloons to design 8497,

which was modified for 1958 with a cutout in each wheel spat that continued the wing line and then swept upwards. A single example of its Silver Cloud counterpart, numbered 8506, was built.

Then as the Silver Wraith was joined by the long-wheelbase Silver Cloud, so Hooper adapted the Empress lines yet again, producing a Touring Limousine as design 8504 for the Silver Cloud. There were nine examples of this, but the cowled headlamps were clearly not to every customer's taste, and so design 8523 was developed, with conventional built-in headlamps between wings and radiator; there were four of these on long-wheelbase Silver Cloud chassis and two more on Bentley chassis. A four-light version of this, which a surviving publicity picture confusingly calls design 8585, became the only Hooper body for the long-wheelbase Silver Cloud II, and was displayed at Earls Court in 1959 on chassis LLCA1.

Three more designs were developed for the long-wheelbase Bentley, all recognisably in the Hooper style of the day. Three were Saloons to design 8524 in 1958-1959; one was a Touring Limousine to design 8525 in 1959; and one was a Saloon with Division to design 8559 in 1959.

Other late Empress designs were one-offs: an 8516 Touring Limousine on Silver Wraith GLW14 in April 1958, and a two-door 8546 Saloon on long-wheelbase Silver Cloud chassis BLC35 in April 1959, which was a derivative of Saloon design 8504. There was also a single Fixed-head Coupé in 1959 on Silver

---

THE GULBENKIAN CARS

Nubar Gulbenkian was the flamboyant socialite son of the oil magnate Calouste Gulbenkian and was one of the wealthiest men in the world. He had a liking for cars that got noticed, and ordered four special bodies from Hooper on Rolls-Royce Silver Wraith chassis between 1947 and 1956.

The earliest of these has always been the most controversial, and was a Sedanca de Ville delivered in October 1947 on chassis WTA62. The controversy has tended to focus on its front end, where the Rolls-Royce radiator was concealed behind a curved grille and the headlights were blended into the wing fronts under streamlined covers. The spats on all four wheels, probably inspired by French coachbuilders such as Figoni & Falaschi, were another controversial element – although they were the height of avant-garde fashion at the time.

Nevertheless, this body had no separate wing volumes at the rear, and its full width was made available for the rear seat in exactly the same way that Osmond Rivers would design the later New Look or "Empress" bodies. The body was initially drawn up with Hooper's design number 8141, but was later amended as 8152.

That first Gulbenkian body was on a short-wheelbase Silver Wraith,

but the three that followed were all on the long-wheelbase version of that chassis. All of them also had styling that was based on the Empress lines. The earliest of them (see main text) was an open body on ALW11 in 1952. The second was another Sedanca de Ville, which was delivered in August 1953 on chassis number ALW47. This remained the only example ever built to design 8359, but it was a most successful adaptation of the Empress styling, featuring the cowled lamps that would later become a regular Hooper feature. Snakeskin was used to trim the interior elements that would otherwise have been in wood.

The third body on the long-wheelbase Silver Wraith chassis was a Saloon, this time to design 8449 and once again unique. It was delivered in July 1956 on chassis number LELW74. Although the overall lines were those of the "evolved Empress" bodies, the unique feature of this four-door Saloon was a Perspex roof section. The car was intended for use in the south of France, and there was an electrically operated fabric inner blind to help keep the interior cool. The dashboard and other areas normally finished in wood were trimmed in leather, as on Gulbenkian's other cars, and there was a second speedometer in the rear compartment.

Cloud chassis LSLG78, clearly converted from a standard steel saloon and with rather awkward rear side windows. Some authorities claim this as design number 8585 (which, as noted above, has also been associated with a special four-light body for the Silver Cloud II)

Cowled headlamps and tail lamps were regular Hooper features by the time this Sports Saloon body was built in 1959. The chassis is a Bentley S2 Continental, number BC1AR, and this was the only Hooper body on such a chassis. It was also the very last body that Hooper ever built. The car was displayed on the Hooper stand at the 1959 Earls Court Motor Show. (Simon Clay)

Continental bodies, 1959

Hooper were late in building coachwork for the Continental chassis, perhaps because their reputation for rather grand coachwork seemed not to mesh with the need for lightweight designs on the original chassis. Nevertheless, as the original lightweight and performance aims were gradually submerged by customer taste for a grand touring

car that was simply stylish, so customers began to ask whether Hooper could clothe the latest S Type Continental chassis.

HJ Mulliner had already obtained permission from the factory to build a four-door saloon for the Continental chassis (which became the Flying Spur), and Hooper's Osmond Rivers followed suit with a

very distinctive four-door Sports Saloon body, of which six examples were built, just one of which had left-hand drive. Design number 8512 had the cowled front and rear lamps that were typical of the company's later 1950s designs, and had a most unusual side elevation in which the doors reached to the lower extremities of the body and no separate sill was visible on the outside.

The same design was carried over for the S2 Continental chassis, now re-numbered 8570. There was only ever one of these, which was built on the first of the breed, number BC1AR. The car was displayed on the coachbuilder's stand at the 1959 Earls Court Show, and carried the last body ever to be built by Hooper.

The Phantom V bodies, 1958-1959

Hooper built just two bodies for the Rolls-Royce Phantom V chassis, one for a prototype car and the other on a production chassis. Both had the same Limousine design, number 8569, which was quite different from the mainstream Phantom designs, with more contemporary detailing that incorporated

the cowled headlamps then characteristic of Hooper designs and also the company's favoured rear end treatment with flattened tops to the rear wheelarches.

The first of these bodies was built for Phantom V prototype 44EX, which first ran in January 1958. This body later spent some time on chassis 45EX before being refitted to the original chassis and then sold. The second was on production chassis 5AS19 and was built for the 1959 Earls Court show. Rolls-Royce gave it the honour of space on their own stand, but of course by that time the Hooper coachbuilding activities were all but over.

J CAIRNS

Absolutely nothing is known for certain about this Edinburgh coachbuilder, who constructed an unidentified "Special Body" on a Rolls-Royce Silver Wraith chassis in 1950. The chassis number was WHD65, and no photographs have yet been found to indicate what the Special Body was. The car was delivered in August 1950 but has since disappeared without trace.

The interior of the Sports Saloon on BC1AR has some refreshingly individual touches, such as the fabric-covered sections outboard of the central instrument panel. (Simon Clay)

Pictured in surroundings typical of London in the mid-1940s, this Bentley MkVI is one of two Saloon Coupés to design WR16. The razor-edge lines have a pre-war feel to them, and the design of the wings and spats is very much of its time.

JAMES YOUNG

Founded as a carriage works in 1863, when James Young took over an older, established business and renamed it after himself, this major coachbuilder was located at Bromley in Kent. It bodied its first Bentley chassis in 1921 and later progressed to Rolls-Royce as well. In 1937, the company was bought by the London Rolls-Royce dealer Jack Barclay, and at the same time the hugely talented AF McNeil was recruited from Gurney Nutting to become its chief designer. There was a certain irony in the fact that Jack Barclay also bought Gurney Nutting in 1947, merging its business with that of James Young.

This coachbuilder's first post-war designs were a Saloon Coupé (WR16) and Saloon (WR17) for the Rolls-Royce Silver Wraith, and their overall lines were very similar to those of the bodies that James Young had built for the pre-war Rolls-Royce Wraith – which of course had a wheelbase that was nine inches longer than the post-war Silver Wraith. However, the company abandoned these early razor-edge styles fairly quickly, and got into its stride with Saloon (C11) and Saloon Coupé (C10) styles for the Bentley MkVI during 1948. It went on to provide coachwork for most of the major models from both Bentley and Rolls-Royce, but there were never any James Young bodies for the R Type Continental or for the standard-wheelbase Silver Cloud II, Bentley S2 and S3 models.

Some James Young designs of the late 1940s and early 1950s had a bloated, overbodied look to them, and there were some unhappy experiments with slab-sided bodies that were supposedly inspired by

Design C10M saw James Young trying to create something ultra-modern for the 1948 Earls Court Show, complete with painted grille surround. The show car was on Bentley MkVI B495CD, but it was not a great success. This rear view shows the car many years later, and after a repaint in sober black. The rear view was arguably more attractive than the front. (Anton van Luijk/WikiMedia Commons)

the American Hudson. Quite heavy-looking rear wings remained a characteristic of many designs and can help to distinguish a James Young body from the products of other coachbuilders, as can the square push-buttons for the exterior door handles that were introduced in 1950. However, by the time of the Silver Clouds and S Types in the mid-1950s, James Young had regained its form and began to turn out some very attractive bodies, typically rather

HOW MANY BODIES?
The figures below have been calculated by chassis type.

Rolls-Royce		Bentley	
Silver Wraith	105	MkVI	221
S Wraith LWB	100	R Type	67
Silver Dawn	11	S Type	34
Silver Cloud LWB	17	S Type LWB	5
S Cloud II LWB	38	S Continental	16
Silver Cloud III	26	S2 Continental	36
S Cloud III LWB	42	S3 Continental	20
Phantom V	196		
Total	**535**	**Total**	**399**

The Saloon Coupé on R Type chassis was much more attractive from the side, with subtle use of swage lines to relieve what might otherwise have been an uncomfortably slab-sided look.

By the time of this Bentley R Type chassis in 1953, James Young had created a new look, but the front end of this Saloon Coupé body was not particularly happy.

The front compartment of the Saloon Coupé was attractively finished, but there was an air of sobriety about it too.

softer and more rounded in form than the standard factory equivalents. Among its masterpieces were the PV22 Limousine for the Phantom V chassis and the similar SCT100 Limousine for the V8-engined Clouds and S Types.

James Young was the last of the "big five" British coachbuilders to remain in business, still independent of Rolls-Royce, but the arrival of monocoque construction in the mid-1960s at Crewe brought matters to a head, and McNeil's

DESIGN NUMBERS

James Young used a complex series of codes for its designs, always adding a letter prefix to the number (usually to identify the intended chassis type) and sometimes adding a suffix as well. The meanings of the prefixes were usually fairly clear, but those of the suffixes were less so.

B	Bentley S Type
B2	Bentley S2
B3	Bentley S3
C	Bentley VI, Bentley R Type or Rolls-Royce Silver Dawn
CT	Bentley Continental
CV	Bentley Continental S2 or S3
E	Probably indicated "External"; used only for Saloon Coupé design E10, which originated outside the company
PV	Rolls-Royce Phantom V
SC	Rolls-Royce Silver Cloud
SCT	Rolls-Royce Silver Cloud LWB
SCV	Rolls-Royce Silver Cloud (the V may indicate "Variant")
SW	Rolls-Royce Silver Wraith (only for design SW10)
WR	Rolls-Royce Silver Wraith
WRM	Rolls-Royce Silver Wraith, long-wheelbase

A and **B** suffixes were used rather inconsistently to indicate variants of a design, as on C10AM and C10BM, C20SAD, C20SDB and PV22MB. The A suffix was commonly used on its own to indicate that a division was fitted to a design that otherwise did not have one, as in WR25A.

The suffix **M** was used only for designs C10M, C10AM, C10BM and PV22SDM, and may have indicated something like "modern" or "modernised".

The suffix **N** was used only on design C10N, perhaps to indicate that it was a step further on from C10M.

The suffix **S** was used for the Touring Limousine version of design WRM 31 (WRM31S), to indicate a Limousine model (WRM35S), and also for the Saloon version of PV22 (PV22S).

The suffix **SD** was used both to distinguish C-prefix bodies for the Rolls-Royce Silver Dawn (eg C20SD) and to indicate a Sedanca de Ville version of another design (eg PV22SD).

death in 1965 may have been the final straw. A batch of two-door saloons bravely adapted from the four-door monocoques of the Rolls-Royce Silver Shadow and the Bentley T Series made clear that the scope for James Young's craftsmanship was very limited, and the company built its last bodies in 1968, on the Phantom V chassis.

Drophead Coupés

James Young was not a major builder of Drophead Coupé coachwork, although the company did build a handful of bodies on the Bentley MkVI and on the six-cylinder Rolls-Royce Silver Cloud chassis. There were two basic designs, the C23 for the MkVI and the SC20 for the Silver Cloud; there was also a special two-seater variant of the SC20, again for the Silver Cloud.

C23 (MkVI, 1949-1951)

All three Drophead Coupé bodies by James Young on the MkVI chassis had Design C23. This was a three-position type with pleasant but conventional lines, and appears to have been very costly – which probably explains why so few were built. The first two examples were delivered in February 1949 but the third customer did not receive his until January 1951, supposedly after nearly two years' wait!

SC15VL (Silver Cloud, 1958-1959)

The SC20 design was a two-door derivative of the SC10 Saloon that had been introduced in 1955. The first variant was a Two-door Saloon that arrived in 1957, and the design was later developed to create both Drophead Coupés and Sedanca Coupés (see below for these other variants).

The Drophead Coupé was a late arrival, and there were two variants of it. One was called SC15VL (those suffix letters have not yet been satisfactorily decoded), and the other, perhaps more logically, was called SC25. There were just two examples of SC15VL, which were built in 1958-1959, on Silver Cloud chassis LSGE448 and LSHF169.

James Young had resolved its front end design problems by the time of the C20 family of Saloon designs for the Silver Dawn chassis. This is a 1954 example, which in many ways anticipates the standard-steel design for the Silver Cloud and Bentley S models, although that rear wing style could only have come from James Young.

SC25 (Silver Cloud, 1958-1959)

The other Drophead Coupé variant of the SC20 was a two-seater, of which just one example was built. This was on chassis number LSJF202 and was delivered in May 1959.

Limousines

Probably well aware that the original Rolls-Royce Silver Wraith was too short to accommodate a proper seven-passenger Limousine body, James Young avoided using the term for any of its designs on this chassis, and customers who wanted a limousine were offered what the company called a Saloon with Division. The suggestion that James Young did not do Limousines may well have discouraged buyers from approaching the company for a Limousine body even after the long-wheelbase Silver Wraith had become available, and its first example was not built until 1956, some five years later.

Designs for the long-wheelbase Silver Wraith sufficed until 1959, when James Young introduced a new Limousine design for the latest V8-engined Bentley S2 in long-wheelbase form.

WRM35S (Silver Wraith, 1956-1959)

James Young's first post-war Limousine design was numbered WRM35S and was for the long-wheelbase Silver Wraith chassis. Unsurprisingly, the shape followed the main lines of the contemporary WRM31 Saloon, but with a lengthened passenger compartment. The first of 15 examples was delivered in March 1956 on chassis LELW39, and the car was formally introduced at the Earls Court Show later that year, when FLW14 did the honours. The last body was mounted on LHLW43, which was delivered in March 1959.

WRM54 (Silver Wraith, 1956)

There was a single example of Limousine design WRM54 on long-wheelbase Silver Wraith LELW76. It was delivered in April 1956.

WR50 (Silver Wraith, 1959)

A single example of the WR50 Limousine design was built on Silver Wraith chassis number LHLW4 and was delivered in March 1959. Although sharing the superstructure of the WRM35S, it had a flat rear panel without the standard protruding boot, free-standing headlamps instead of the built-in units of the WRM35S, and modified wing-lines that permitted side-mounted spare wheels. The WR50 designation seems anomalous; logically, it should have been a WRM50.

PV15 (Phantom V, 1959-1965)

For the new Rolls-Royce Phantom V chassis, AF McNeil developed a pair of related and superbly elegant designs: PV15 was for a Limousine and PV22 (see below) was for a Touring Limousine, and both designs were adapted to make Sedanca de Ville bodies as well.

It was a PV22 that introduced the new shape at Earls Court in 1959, but the first PV15 was delivered in December that year, on chassis 5AS17. The main external difference was that the PV15 Limousine had a more upright rear panel to give extra room in the passenger cabin. This was a proper seven-seat Limousine body, with a forward-facing pair of occasional rear seats to make the number up to seven when needed. Early examples had a single-headlight design but those on the VA and later series chassis from September 1962 had the twin-headlamp design of the contemporary Silver Cloud III. A total of 34 of these bodies were built, the last one numerically being 5VD93 in 1965. A minor adjustment to the design then produced its successor, the PV16 Limousine.

PV10 (Phantom V, 1960)

Just one body was built to design PV10 (sometimes called PV10M) on the Phantom V chassis in 1960. This was essentially similar to the PV15 but had a special roof and boot. It was on chassis number 5AT48.

PV16 (Phantom V, 1965-1967)

Design PV16 replaced PV15 in late 1965 as James Young's seven-passenger Limousine for the Phantom V. It was visually the same as its predecessor, except for an angular Hooper-style rear quarter-window on each side; the same modification turned the related PV22 Touring Limousine into a PV23 at the same time. Just five examples were built, the first on chassis 5VE47 and the last on 5VF73. Only one (5LVF41) had left-hand drive.

Saloons

A high proportion of the special coachwork that James Young built between 1945 and 1967 was Saloon designs. The WR17 Saloon for the Rolls-Royce Silver Wraith was one of the company's first two post-war designs, and it was followed by designs for the Bentley MkVI and the R Type, as well as for the Rolls-Royce Silver Dawn – which were the only James Young bodies on this chassis. There were Saloon bodies for the long-wheelbase Silver Wraith and then for all three series of Silver Cloud and Bentley S chassis. James Young also built four-door Saloons for the Bentley S Continentals of all three series, and a pair of rather special bodies for the Rolls-Royce Phantom V as well.

WR17, WR17M, and WR17MA (Silver Wraith, 1947-1948)

Very slim window pillars were a characteristic of both pre-war and post-war four-light Saloon bodies from James Young. The obvious visual difference between the post-war WR17 design and its pre-war equivalent was that the front wing of the newer design swept across the door panel. The first WR17 was probably on chassis WTA34 and was delivered in December 1947, although it was later converted into an All-weather body. This original design was built until mid-1948, and was used for 34 Silver Wraith chassis before giving way to the updated design WR18. Eight of these bodies were built with a division as WR17A, beginning probably with WTA53 delivered in November 1947 – before the first "standard" WR17.

There was also a WR17M design, which had some quite radical differences from the original WR17. There were 11 of these, of which three were completed with a division and the designation WR17MA.

C11 (MkVI, 1947-1950)

James Young's first post-war bodies for the Bentley MkVI were four-light Saloons to Design C11, of which the first examples were delivered in the summer and autumn of 1947. These were neat but conservative, with razor-edge styling, rear-hinged back doors, cutaway rear spats and slim chromed window frames.

B345CD displayed the body on the coachbuilder's stand at Earls Court in 1948, by which time the C10 Saloon Coupé was already proving popular, and no fewer than 49 examples were delivered between July 1947 and June 1950. Thereafter, the James Young Saloon offering for the MkVI was a more curvaceous six-light design, number C12.

WR18 (Silver Wraith, 1948-1951)

The second volume-built James Young Saloon design on the Rolls-Royce Silver Wraith chassis was the WR18, which appeared in 1948 and brought a slightly more modern appearance than the WR17 it

James Young's PV22 Limousine design for the Rolls-Royce Phantom V chassis was exceptionally attractive, and it gave rise to a rare Sedanca de Ville variant, PV22SD. This is one of those rare bodies, with the sedanca roof in place, built in 1961 on chassis 5AT76. The lines of the rear panel are quite different from those of the parent Limousine. (Rex Gray/WikiMedia Commons)

This rear view is fairly typical of James Young bodies in the first half of the 1950s. The body is a C12 Saloon, on a very late Bentley R Type chassis, number B3ZX, which was delivered to its first owner in spring 1955. (Anton von Luijk/ WikiMedia Commons)

replaced. It was introduced on the James Young stand at the 1948 Earls Court show, on Silver Wraith chassis WCB20. A further 22 were built, the last examples being delivered in March 1951 on chassis numbers WME9 and WME18. Of those 22, no fewer than 13 were actually to design number WR18A and featured a division.

C12 (MkVI & R Type, 1950-1953)

At the 1950 Earls Court Show, James Young introduced a new Saloon design for the Bentley MkVI to replace the C11 design that dated back to 1947. The new C12 style displayed on chassis B361GT was not only more curvaceous, with swaged wings and a clear family resemblance to the new C10BM Saloon Coupé that appeared at the same Show; it also had six side windows instead of four. No fewer than 36 examples were delivered on the MkVI chassis, the last one in September 1952, and design C12 was carried over to the Bentley R Type chassis as well, for which six more were built in 1952 and 1953.

WR19 (Silver Wraith, 1951-1953)

The third of the volume-built Saloon designs for the Silver Wraith was the WR19, which appeared in the autumn of 1951. Though visually related to its predecessors, this was a much more handsome design, with a raised wing line, swage lines on the wings, and a more steeply raked rear panel. WMW69 was the first example delivered, in November 1951, and WVH99 was the last one, in July 1953. There were six altogether, plus one example with a division (to design WR19A) on WOF71 in April 1952.

C14 (R Type, 1952-1953)

There was another new six-light Saloon design for the Bentley R Type, which was introduced on chassis B36RT at the 1952 Earls Court show. This design incorporated new wing lines, with the descending line from the front meeting the leading edge of the rear wings quite high up in a gentle curve. Horizontal air intakes below the headlamps were another feature. Six examples were built.

C20 (R Type, 1952-1955)

The C20 family of designs were four-light Saloons drawn up for the Bentley R Type and contemporary Rolls-Royce Silver Dawn chassis. The designation C20 itself was used for the R Type version of the design, and ran throughout the production life of that chassis. There were 28 examples of it.

WRM30 (Silver Wraith, 1953-1954)

Design WRM30 was the first James Young Saloon for the long-wheelbase Silver Wraith chassis. It was introduced in 1953 while the WR26 Saloon with Division design was still current on the short-wheelbase Silver Wraith, and inevitably it inherited a good deal from the lines of that. These bodies had

The first James Young Saloon design for the long-wheelbase Silver Wraith chassis was numbered WRM30, and its lines were typical of the company's products when this one was delivered on chassis BLW65 in 1954. (Simon Clay)

The WRM30 was a Saloon, but its proportions could easily be mistaken for those of a Limousine. The double swage lines lend character to the side elevation here. (Simon Clay)

Once again, those rear wings could only have come from James Young. The tail lights were tiny, even by the standards of 1954. (Simon Clay)

The front compartment of the WRM30 Saloon shows the combination of pleated backrests and plain cushions that was common at the time. The piping lends its own attraction to the interior. (Simon Clay)

The rear seat of the WRM30 saloon was positively opulent. Note the delightfully ornate pull handle on the door. (Simon Clay)

Although this was a Saloon body, it had a half-height division that contained pull-down picnic tables and compartments for stowing such items as drinking glasses. (Simon Clay)

a distinctive twin swage line on both front and rear wings. The first example was on chassis BLW43 and was displayed at the Paris Salon in 1953, and the last one was on DLW146 and was delivered in June 1955. A total of 30 bodies were built to design WRM30 – although that total is another one that is disputed – and among them were at least seven of the WRM30A variant with a division. There was one more Show appearance, when DLW41 was displayed at the Paris Salon in 1954.

C20SD (Silver Dawn, 1954-1955), C20ASD (1954) and C20SDB (1954)

The Rolls-Royce Silver Dawn version of the C20 Saloon design was known as the C20SD type, and was the only design that James Young built for the "small" Rolls-Royce, variants apart. The original design was quite modern in appearance and presaged the lines of the factory offering for the later Silver Cloud, but it was more upright and awkward with a rather square boot line. Nine of these bodies were made, the earliest being delivered on chassis SNF27 in January 1954 and the last one on STH97 in July 1955.

There was one example of a minor C20 variant known as C20ASD. This was built on chassis SPG101 and was delivered in September 1954. A second variant was C20SDB, which had a more attractively curved boot line and reshaped rear wings to suit. The sole example was built on chassis number SOG42 and was delivered in August 1954.

WRM31 (Silver Wraith, 1955-1959), WRM31A, and WRM31ST (1957)

The WRM30 Saloon design for the long-wheelbase Silver Wraith chassis was updated in summer 1955 to become a WRM31, notably having a less fussy single swage line on each wing. It remained available until the end of Silver Wraith production. The first example delivered was on DLW153, in June 1955; the last of 46 (yet another disputed total) was on HLW34 in January 1959. Seven of those had a division and were therefore strictly WRM31A types. Some later bodies had slightly modified rear wings to take the light units associated with the Silver Cloud saloons. Four examples appeared at Motor Shows. These were LELW1 at Paris in 1955, FLW12 at Earls Court in 1956, FLW74 at Geneva in 1957, and FLW82 at Earls Court in 1957.

There was also a single example of a variant called WRM31ST, those last two letters reflecting the surname of the customer (Strauss). This was distinguished by headlamps built into the tops of the front wings and was on chassis FLW73. It was delivered in July 1957.

SC10 (Silver Cloud, 1955-1958)
and B10 (S Type, 1955-1958)

The new design prefix SC indicated the Silver Cloud chassis from Rolls-Royce, and the first James Young design for that chassis was numbered SC10, a Saloon introduced at the 1955 Earls Court Show on chassis SWA52. The overall outline was very similar to that of the standard steel saloon, but the all-aluminium James Young body was more rounded, with a full-length swage line which followed the wing contours and, of course, the coachbuilder's favoured square push-buttons for the door handles. Early examples had some very noticeable fins on the otherwise rounded rear wings, but on the later bodies these were reduced to almost nothing. There were 25 SC10 bodies, and the last example was delivered in July 1958 on chassis SXA133. There was also a one-off SC10S variant in 1956 (on SXA129) with a modified front end design that added protruding headlamps to the wing fronts.

There was a version of this design for the Bentley S Type chassis, too, designated B10. It was essentially the same as the SC10, and early examples had the same fins on the tops of the rear wings. A total of 26 examples of this body were built at Bromley, plus a single example of variant B10R, delivered in 1957 on chassis B63BC.

SC12 (Silver Cloud, 1957-1959)
and B12 (S Type, 1957-1959)

James Young's first design for the long-wheelbase Silver Cloud was numbered SC12, and it was really a lengthened version of the SC10, offered on the standard-wheelbase Silver Cloud. Some of these bodies were built with a division. ALC2 introduced the design at Earls Court in 1957, and ALC3 promoted it at the same year's Paris Salon. BLC15 then did the job at Earls Court in 1958. The last of the 17 examples of this body was on chassis CLC14

and was displayed at the Geneva Show in 1959; some examples were described as Touring Limousines. The SC12 design was carried over for the Silver Cloud II chassis as number SCT12.

The Bentley equivalent of the SC12 body for the long-wheelbase Rolls-Royce Silver Cloud was known as the B12, and the only differences lay in the bonnet panels and the motifs. There were five bodies to this design in 1958-1959, which was briefly continued as design B2.12 for the S2 chassis.

SCT100 (Silver Cloud II & III LWB, 1959-1965),
B2.100 (S2 LWB, 1959-1962) and
B3.100 (S3 LWB, 1962-1965)

The SCT100 design for the long-wheelbase Rolls-Royce Silver Cloud II chassis was cleverly conceived to satisfy two different requirements. On the one hand it was not too large to work as a particularly spacious Saloon, with individual front seats, no division, and no occasional seats in the rear. On the other hand it was large enough to work as a Touring Limousine, fitted with a bench front seat, division, and inward-facing occasional seats in the rear. Although the Saloon versions were by far the more common, the design's familiar nickname of "Baby Phantom" tends to associate it more with the idea of a Touring Limousine.

SCT100 was indeed a "baby Phantom". It was introduced at the Earls Court show in 1959 and was quite clearly derived from the PV22 Touring Limousine design for the Rolls-Royce Phantom V that was making its Earls Court debut at the same time. There are those who would argue that the version for the rather shorter Silver Cloud chassis was actually more attractive. SCT100 combined much of the grace and presence of the larger PV22 design with a considerably lower cost. The Earls Court show car was a Saloon version on long-wheelbase Silver Cloud II chassis LCA2, and a further 32 with the SCT100 Saloon specification were built before production of that chassis ended in 1962. One example (LLCC2)

James Young maintained distinctive wing lines, especially at the rear of this Saloon body on the Bentley S Type. In common with other coachbuilders at the time, the company added discreet fins at the rear. This is a 1957 body to design B10. (Anton von Luijk/ WikiMedia Commons)

The four-door Saloon body introduced on the six-cylinder S Type chassis was carried over to the S2 Continental, of which this is an example. The treatment of the body's lower edges is nevertheless quite different from that on the earlier body pictured.

was built with R100 headlamps and rear quarter-lights of reduced size to give more privacy to the rear-seat occupants. Another (LCB49) was built jointly in 1961 by James Young and FLM Panelcraft, a small but active west London coachbuilder.

It should come as no surprise that James Young fielded orders for a version on the Bentley S2 long-wheelbase chassis as well, giving this one the name of B2.100; there were just two of these built as Saloons, plus a further three Touring Limousines (see below).

For the third generation of the Silver Cloud chassis, James Young continued to offer the SCT100 design, changing it to accept the twin headlamps associated with these later models. For the long-wheelbase Bentley S3, the design number changed to B3.100, and eight examples were built. The revised design was introduced at Earls Court in 1962 on Silver Cloud III chassis CAL3, and the last of 30 Saloon versions of SCT100 on that model chassis was CFL15, delivered in October 1965.

There were also nine Touring Limousine versions of the third-generation design on the Silver Cloud III chassis, which was introduced at the 1962 Paris Salon on chassis LCAL1. There was then a right-hand-drive example at Earls Court in 1963, and another left-hand-drive car on LCDL81 did the honours at the 1964 Paris Salon. The last of the nine was delivered in October 1965 on chassis CFL15. Some of the B3.100 bodies on Bentley chassis were also configured as Touring Limousines.

CV100 (S2 & S3 Continental, 1959-1965) and SCV100 (Silver Cloud III, 1963-1965)

After HJ Mulliner were granted permission to build four-door bodies for the Bentley Continental chassis and came up with the Flying Spur design, James Young followed suit. Their four-door, six-light Sports Saloon for the Continental appeared in 1959 for the S2 Continental and was called the CV100 – although the design is very often misleadingly described as a "James Young Flying Spur". The CV100 body had full-length swage lines and the characteristic James Young square push-buttons on the door handles, both of which make it easy to distinguish from the otherwise quite similar Flying Spur.

There were 36 CV100 bodies on the S2 Continental chassis (six with left-hand drive), and the design remained available for the S3 Continental, suitably modified with a four-headlamp front end. There were 18 examples on the later chassis, only one with left-hand drive. Then at the Earls Court Show in autumn 1963, design CV100 was joined by a version called SCV100 that was for the newly available Rolls-Royce Silver Cloud III chassis with more raked steering column. The SCV100 bodies brought a minor change in that their door handles were now blended into a bright side moulding that extended along the full width of each door, but by 1965 this distinction between CV100 and SCV100 had blurred and the bodies for Bentley chassis also had the side moulding.

The first of the SCV100 bodies was built on chassis

The four-door Saloon body introduced on the six-cylinder S Type chassis was carried over to the S2 Continental, of which this is a 1962 example, on chassis BC105AR. (Simon Clay)

The rear view of BC105AR shows quite clearly how the treatment of the body's lower edges had evolved from the original body for the six-cylinder S Type Continental chassis. (Simon Clay)

Here is the four-door Saloon on an S3 Continental chassis, the paired headlamps adding their own distinction to the front end design. This is a 1965 example. (Charles01/WikiMedia Commons)

James Young's four-door Saloon body for the Continental chassis provided plenty of legroom for rear-seat passengers. (Simon Clay)

The square push-button and ornate handle shape were carried over to the boot lid as well. (Simon Clay)

The boot was of course trimmed to match the interior, and was rather more capacious than it looks in this picture. (Simon Clay)

BC105AR has a fabric sunroof, which permits this view of the most attractive dashboard with its figured wood veneer. (Simon Clay)

This is one of James Young's beautifully ornate door handles with its distinctive square push-button, on BC105AR. (Simon Clay)

Here, the coachbuilder's use of sharp creases in combination with curved lines becomes very apparent. (Simon Clay)

James Young's four-door Saloon body was carried over to the S3 Continental chassis as well, and is seen here on a 1965 example, BC46XW. The paired headlamps add their own distinction to the front end design. (Simon Clay)

The rear seat of the S3 Continental remains as inviting as ever. This car does not have the ornate door pulls seen on the S2 Continental pictured earlier. (Simon Clay)

Some coachbuilders used quite ornate sill or body plates, but James Young preferred simplicity. (Simon Clay)

From this angle, the main differences between the S2 Continental and S3 Continental chassis with the four-door Saloon body are the over-riders, which are smaller and neater on this later car. (Simon Clay)

The standard steel S3 had split front seats instead of a bench, and the James Young Saloon for the Continental evolved in the same way. (Simon Clay)

SEV121 in 1963, and the last of 20 examples built was delivered in December 1965 on chassis CSC115B, the one on CSC117B having been delivered the previous month. The basic lines of the CV100 and SCV100 bodies were also adapted to make two-door variants called CV150 and SCV150 (see below).

SCT12 (Silver Cloud II LWB, 1961-1962) and B2.12 (S2 LWB, 1959-1960)

The only other design by James Young for the long-wheelbase Silver Cloud II chassis was a four-door Saloon, with design number SCT12 and clearly a continuation of the earlier SC12. Just two examples were built, on chassis LCB81 in 1961 and on LCD19 in 1962. A small number of the Bentley equivalent numbered B2.12 was also built, the last in 1960.

Saloons with Division

Reacting to demand for formal coachwork with a division, James Young were very honest about the relative lack of space afforded by the Silver Wraith chassis in its original short-wheelbase form. So they offered a Saloon with Division rather than pretending it was a full Limousine. This started off in 1950 as a WR25 and was then given the later raised wing lines from late 1952 to become the WR26. These bodies were constructed for the original Silver Wraith chassis between 1950 and 1953, and there was a later reprise of the idea – this time for the long-wheelbase Silver Wraith chassis on which a proper Limousine would become available – as the SW10 in 1955.

WR25 (Silver Wraith, 1950-1952)

The first of these designs materialised in 1950 as number WR25, with a degree of formality about it that clearly hinted at the Limousine its buyers probably wanted. The first of 27 examples was shown at Earls Court that year on chassis number WHD96, and the last was probably delivered in autumn 1952 on chassis WSG71. The appeal to Limousine customers was certainly successful, because no fewer than 13 of these bodies – just under half – were built as design WR25A with a division.

WR26 (Silver Wraith, 1952-1953)

Saloon with Division design WR25 gave way to WR26 in late 1952, and the first example was delivered in November on Silver Wraith chassis WVH8. The overall shape was similar to the superseded design, but the front wing line was higher and ran across the doors to meet the rear wing quite high up, while the lines of the boot were also raised. This revised design last only until summer 1953, when the last of 11 examples was delivered on chassis WVH72 that July.

SW10 (Silver Wraith, 1955-1958)

Not quite ready with their planned Limousine design for the long-wheelbase Silver Wraith (which became WRM35S in 1956), James Young introduced another Saloon with Division in 1955. This had the SW10 designation, and four examples were built, all with left-hand drive. The first was on chassis LDLW115 and was delivered in June 1955; the last was delivered in December 1958 and was on chassis LHLW28.

Saloon Coupés

The Saloon Coupé had been a James Young speciality before the 1939-1945 war, and the company continued to build such coachwork into the 1960s. Saloon Coupé bodies were always on the shorter chassis, whereas a two-door Saloon (see below) might be on a long-wheelbase chassis. So there were Saloon Coupés for the short-wheelbase Rolls-Royce Silver Wraith, for the Bentley MkVI and R Type chassis, and for the standard-wheelbase Rolls-Royce Silver Cloud.

WR16 (Silver Wraith, 1947)

The WR16 Saloon Coupé for the Rolls-Royce Silver Wraith chassis was actually the first James Young design to appear after the war, and unsurprisingly its lines were closely related to those of the WR17 Saloon that appeared soon afterwards. Only three examples were built, the first on chassis WTA22 in June 1947, the second on WTA58 that August, and the third on WTA79, which was delivered in February 1948.

C10 (MkVI, 1948-1951)

The C10 Saloon Coupé for the Bentley MkVI chassis shared many of its features with the contemporary C11 four-light Saloon, and the body number suggests that it may well have preceded that on the James Young drawing-boards. Nevertheless, the first examples were not delivered until July 1948 – even though the very first was actually on the very first production Bentley MkVI chassis, which must by then have been well over 18 months old. Deliveries of C10 bodies had mostly ended by February 1949, although there were a couple of late deliveries in 1950 and early 1951. There were 52 bodies to this design, which evolved into a variant called C10N in 1950.

C10M (MkVI, 1948-1949)

James Young's attempts to create a new style for the 1948 Earls Court Show inevitably included a Saloon Coupé on the Bentley MkVI chassis. The first example of design C10M was on B495CD and was displayed on the company's show stand, but it was not one of James Young's best. Perhaps the M in the designation stood for "modernised" rather than "modified", but one way or the other its slab sides and full rear wheel spats were probably inspired by the 1948 "step-down" Hudson.

The large bumpers and vee-windscreen did not help the overall appearance, and the show car attracted orders for only two copies, of which both were delivered in late 1949.

C10AM (MkVI, 1949-1950)

Undeterred by the relative failure of the overly modernistic C10M design, James Young introduced a much more attractive new Saloon Coupé design at the 1949 Earls Court Show. The rounded styling of design C10AM instantly made the earlier razor-edge designs appear old-fashioned, and the body shape was nicely balanced by a longer boot which the coachbuilder was able to achieve by extending the rear chassis rails. The first example, on B131EW, was the Show car in October 1949, and the last of 16 examples was delivered about a year later.

C10N (MkVI, 1950)

Design C10N was a variant of the basic C10 razor-edged Saloon Coupé, with detail modifications. There were 12 examples, all delivered between January and September 1950.

C10BM (MkVI, 1950-1954)

Design C10BM replaced C10AM at the 1950 Earls Court Show. Essentially the same shape, it looked more different than it really was thanks to the addition of swage lines on the wings. There were two Show cars: B347GT was on the Bentley Motors stand and B375GT was on the James Young stand. Both featured a bench front seat but only B375GT had electric windows, and not all the 30 examples built on MkVI chassis had these features. The last ones were built in late 1952, the final car not being delivered until January 1953, and the body design remained available for the R Type Bentley. Three further examples were built over the next two years.

C17 (MkVI, 1951-1954)

The James Young Saloon Coupé was updated yet again at the 1951 Earls Court Show, this time with a raised wing line and the new designation of C17. The Show car was on Bentley MkVI chassis B48MD. The last of eight examples on the MkVI was delivered in August 1952, but the design was retained for the Bentley R Type chassis, and four further examples were built.

C18 (R Type, 1952-1955)

Saloon Coupé design C17 became a C18 for the 1953 season, and the first example (on Bentley R Type B30RT) was shown at Earls Court in 1952. There were 12 of these bodies, which had their sidelights back on the wing tops and horizontal grilles below the headlamps and sidelights. Further identifying features were flared wheelarches and a more strongly defined leading edge to the rear wing. One of the 12 built, on chassis B125SP, had special modifications to meet its purchaser's requirements, and the final example (on B316YD) was delivered in January 1955.

E10 (MkVI, 1952)

Robert Miesegaes, the head of long-standing Bentley dealer Dex Automobiles, arranged for James Young to build a Saloon Coupé to a design he had commissioned from a Frenchman, Pierre Brandone. There was not much James Young about the body on Bentley MkVI chassis number B196MD except perhaps the quality of construction. What James Young called design E10 was completed and delivered in April 1952. It dispensed with the Bentley radiator surround (although it retained the grille bars) and was overall a rather unhappy and bulbous looking creation. The single example has now been lost.

B10S (S Type, 1956)

Design B10S was a very distinctive Saloon Coupé, of which four examples were built on Bentley S Type chassis in 1956. Though related to the contemporary B10 Saloon in profile, these bodies had a front end with headlamps set into the wing fronts and auxiliary lamps carried in round cut-outs in the front panel.

B20SR (S Type, 1956-1957)

The B20SR Saloon Coupé appears to have been an evolution of the B10S design, although the two types were very similar and shared the same distinctive front end design. There were three of these bodies, the first (on chassis B352CK) being shown at Earls Court in 1956; B207CM followed in 1957, and B120FG was displayed at the Geneva Show in 1957.

SC20 (Silver Cloud, 1957-1959)

James Young's initial four-door SC10 Saloon design for the Rolls-Royce Silver Cloud chassis developed into a two-door Saloon Coupé called SC20. Just two examples were made, on Silver Cloud chassis numbered LSDD44 and LSHF111. They were delivered in 1957 and 1959 respectively.

Sedancas

The absorption of Gurney Nutting in 1945 brought James Young a small-selling Sedanca Coupé design for the Bentley MkVI chassis that was nevertheless an acknowledged classic. From 1947, it entered the James Young repertoire with the design number of C15 – although the question of whether early examples should actually be attributed to Gurney Nutting is still debated. The C15 design remained available into 1950, but from 1949 James Young had developed a replacement that they called the C16 design. It was considerably less attractive but sold rather better in two years of availability.

The C15 and C16 designs were Sedanca Coupés, following the Gurney Nutting designation. For the Rolls-Royce Silver Wraith, however, the rather grander designation of Sedanca de Ville was used. Even so, there were few of these, and James Young seems to have been content to leave the field open to HJ Mulliner for several years after the war. The earliest was built in 1950, and there were just two on the short-wheelbase chassis; three more, with an extended version of the same body design, were built on the long-wheelbase Silver Wraith.

For the Rolls-Royce Silver Cloud chassis, James

Young reverted to the Sedanca Coupé name, but for the large and grand Phantom V that followed, this style of coachwork was once again called a Sedanca de Ville. Interestingly, design drawings exist for at least three other Sedanca designs intended for the Silver Cloud chassis, and these are numbered SC22D, SC60 and SCT100SD. A forward rake to the centre pillar (as on SC22D) appears to have merited the description Sedanca Coupé; a straight pillar brought the name Sedanca de Ville.

C15 (MkVI, 1948-1949)

The C15 design for the Bentley MkVI had of course originated with Gurney Nutting, and James Young had no reason to alter it. The Bromley company put its name to three examples with the original plain sides to the roof, the first being delivered in July 1948 and the last two in December 1949. There was also a single example of the "teardrop" variant, still classified as a C15 in the James Young scheme of things. This was delivered in March 1950 on chassis number B374EY.

C16 (MkVI, 1949-1951)

James Young's own Sedanca Coupé design for the Bentley MkVI was announced at the 1949 Earls Court Show as their design C16, and unsurprisingly had quite a lot in common with the contemporary C10AM Saloon Coupé. The obligatory sliding "de ville" head was present, but the rear quarters had large conventional fixed windows. B195EW introduced the design at Earls Court and seven examples were built in all. Most had been delivered by September 1950 but B176LLJ was ordered as a second example by the American owner of B255LFU and was not delivered until October 1951.

WR27 (Silver Wraith, 1950-1953)

There were just two Sedanca de Ville bodies from James Young on the short-wheelbase Rolls-Royce Silver Wraith chassis, and both probably had design WR27, which was essentially a contemporary Saloon design adapted to the Sedanca configuration. The first one, for which the design number is not certain, was delivered in November 1950 on chassis number WHD82, and the second on LWVH41 in May 1953.

C14F (R Type, 1953-1954)

Design C14F brought the new wing lines of the design C14 Saloon to a Sedanca Coupé design for the Bentley R Type chassis. A raked pillar at the front of the closed rear compartment was an attractive distinguishing feature. Eight of these bodies were built, all on right-hand-drive chassis.

C19S (R Type, 1953)

There was a single Sedanca Coupé to design C19S, derived from design C18 and on Bentley R Type chassis B55LSP.

WRM27 (Silver Wraith, 1955-1956)

For the long-wheelbase Silver Wraith, the earlier design WR27 was adapted to make design WRM27. The family resemblance remained, and with its sedanca roof in place, a WRM27 body could be mistaken at a distance for the contemporary WRM31 Limousine. It became another rarity, and just three examples were built, starting with LDLW 105 in May 1955 and ending with LELW72 in June 1956. Between these two came ELW44, which was displayed at the 1956 Geneva Show.

SC23 (Silver Cloud, 1958-1959)

Like the Drophead Coupé derivative of the SC20 two-door design for the six-cylinder Rolls-Royce Silver Cloud, the Sedanca Coupé was a late arrival. Just two examples were built, both of them on left-hand-drive chassis. These were numbered LSFE99 (delivered in July 1958) and LSJF112 (delivered in April 1959).

PV15 (Phantom V, 1965)

The PV15 design was for a seven-seat Limousine on the Rolls-Royce Phantom V chassis and was introduced in 1959. It lent itself very well to adaptation as a Sedanca de Ville, and the very last example built, on chassis 5VE21 in 1965, had that configuration. The car was displayed at that year's Earls Court Show. The body remained unique, but the principle of adapting a Limousine body as a Sedanca de Ville would be adopted again later.

PV22SD (Phantom V, 1960-1967)
and PV22SDM (1965)

Touring Limousine design PV22 for the Phantom V chassis lent itself well to adaptation as a Sedanca de Ville, and nine examples were built. The first was delivered in October 1960, on chassis 5AS95, and the last in 1967 on 5VF161. Within those nine there were variations. So 5LVA105 in 1963 was built without rear quarter-windows and with dummy landau irons; 5VE1 from 1965 was a PV22SDM, with modifications to the lines of the roof and boot, and specially shaped rear quarter-windows; and the final example, 5VF161 from 1967, had PV23-style rear quarter-lights.

PV23SD (Phantom V, 1966-1967)

Just as the PV22 Touring Limousine design gave rise to the PV22SD Sedanca de Ville, so its PV23 successor

gave rise to a PV23SD. Supposedly two examples were built, one in 1966 (on 5VF27) and one in 1967.

Touring Limousines

Theoretically, a Touring Limousine offered much the same space as a Limousine but had a larger luggage boot. Probably reflecting the same honesty that prevented them from giving the Limousine name to their Saloon with Division, James Young did not offer a Touring Limousine body for the short-wheelbase Rolls-Royce Silver Wraith chassis – although they did build a single one to special order in 1947. The company was then very late into the market for Touring Limousine bodies, building its first on a long-wheelbase Silver Wraith chassis in 1956 – the year when it produced its first post-war Limousine style.

Only a handful of Touring Limousine bodies were built at Bromley before the coachbuilder developed a new design for the long-wheelbase V8 Rolls-Royce Silver Cloud II. In addition, a few examples of Saloon design SC12 on the long-wheelbase six-cylinder Silver Cloud were described as Touring Limousines, and some examples of the SCT100 Saloon and related Bentley versions were built as Touring Limousines (see above).

WRM31S (Silver Wraith, 1956-1957)

As was the case with its seven-passenger Limousine bodies, James Young was very late into the market with a Touring Limousine. Design WRM31S was an adaptation of its contemporary Saloon design WRM31 (see above) on the long-wheelbase Silver Wraith chassis, but it came too late to attract any business. Only one was made, on chassis FLW73 in July 1957.

SC179 (Silver Cloud III LWB, 1964)

Design SCT100 spawned a variant with Hooper-style rear quarter-lights, but only one example of design SC179 appears to have been built. This was on long-wheelbase Silver Cloud III chassis LCFL39 and was delivered in October 1964.

PV22 (Phantom V, 1959-1965) and PV22MB (1960)

Design PV22 appeared at Earls Court in 1959 and introduced the new James Young approach to bodies for the longer chassis. This was the Touring Limousine version of the PV15 design for the Rolls-Royce Phantom V chassis, its more raked rear panel giving it even greater elegance. It was a great success, and a probable total of 106 examples was built before the PV22 gave way to its mildly altered PV23 successor in 1965. Like other designs in production when Rolls-Royce introduced twin headlamps across its range, the PV22 was modified in September 1962, and chassis 5VA7 introduced the revised design at Earls Court that year. One body was built to design PV22MB on 5LAS25 in 1960, with some modifications.

There were also two PV22S Saloon variants of the design, described above. Some authorities also ascribe the PV22 design number to the PV55 design (see below).

PV23 (Phantom V, 1965-1967)

Design PV23 was introduced in late 1965 as an updated version of the PV22 Touring Limousine. It was visually unchanged except for the angular Hooper-style rear quarter-lights. The first PV23 was shown at Earls Court in 1965, on chassis 5LVE23. James Young

James Young's SCT100 design, the so-called "baby Phantom", was perhaps the pinnacle of their coachbuilding work in the 1960s. This is a 1965 example, on long-wheelbase Silver Cloud chassis CEL41. (Simon Clay)

The lines of the SCT100 design worked extremely well from the rear, too, with just a trace of razor-edge in the rear panel. (Simon Clay)

The "baby Phantom" offered plenty of lounging room for the rear-seat occupants but, of course, did not have the occasional seats fitted to the full-size Limousine bodies on Phantom V chassis. (Simon Clay)

probably completed 35 examples and 5VF165 became the last James Young Phantom of all, completed in October 1967.

There were also probably two PV23SD Sedanca de Ville variants of the design (see above).

PV55 (Phantom V, 1962)

Definitions become blurred with James Young's design PV55 – which some authorities believe carried the PV22 designation. Although it might more appropriately have been called a Saloon Coupé in the great James Young tradition, this remarkable design for the Phantom V chassis was actually described as a two-door Touring Limousine. The lines of the lower body were clearly those of the parent PV22 Touring Limousine, but the boot and rear roof were redesigned to suit the new body style and the glasshouse was redesigned as a four-light type. Two examples were built, both with left-hand drive, on chassis 5LBV69 in 1961 and 5LBX76 the following year.

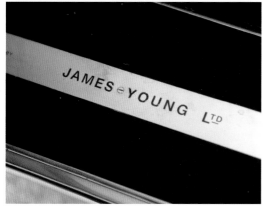

Once again, discretion was the name of the James Young game. (Simon Clay)

PV65 (Phantom V, 1966)

Design PV65 on the Phantom V chassis was another Touring Limousine created from the PV22 shape by eliminating the projecting boot to give a smooth rear panel, and by omitting the rear quarter-windows. The only example was built in 1966, on chassis 5LVF25.

Two-door Saloons

Nomenclature causes problems here, and exactly what distinguished a James Young two-door Saloon from one of the company's Saloon Coupés is hard to define. A Saloon Coupé was typically more rakish than a two-door Saloon, except of course on the Continental chassis.

Two-door Saloons entered the James Young repertoire in 1957, when there was a one-off body for the long-wheelbase Rolls-Royce Silver Wraith and a start to quantity manufacture of a two-door for the Silver Cloud chassis. James Young also developed a pair of two-door designs for the Bentley S Type, one for the standard chassis and one for the Continental (there had been no bodies for the earlier R Type Continental). Variants of these later designs remained available until the end of separate-chassis production at Crewe.

WRM12 (Silver Wraith, 1957)

Just one example of design WRM12 was built. This Two-door Saloon was for the long-wheelbase Rolls-Royce Silver Wraith chassis, and was built on chassis LFLW59. It was delivered in March 1957.

The front seats are divided – this is after all a Silver Cloud III – and in this case were ordered with cloth upholstery. The style of the door cards is typical of James Young. (Simon Clay)

The James Young PV22 Limousine body for the Phantom V chassis was a classic design and was visually closely related to the SCT100 "baby Phantom" shown on page 113. This 1965 example, on chassis 5LVA55, was delivered in March 1963 to Elvis Presley. (Simon Clay)

This rear view of the PV22 Limousine shows the close similarity to the slightly smaller SCT100 design. (Simon Clay)

SC20 (Silver Cloud, 1957-1959)

As explained elsewhere, the SC20 series of designs were two-door derivatives of the SC10 four-door Saloon for the Rolls-Royce Silver Cloud chassis. The most numerous of these variants was the two-door Saloon, of which six were built between March 1957, when the first example was delivered on chassis number SZB205 (the one on SZB203 was delivered later that year). Two were on left-hand drive chassis, LSDD44 in April 1957 and the last one, LSHF11, in February 1959.

PV22S (Phantom V, 1963-1966)

The PV22 Limousine design was adapted to make a Saloon by omitting the division, and two examples were built. These were on Phantom V chassis 5LVA53 in 1963 and 5LVE29 in 1966.

SCT200 (Silver Cloud III, 1964-1965)

The two-door variant of four-door Saloon design SCT100 for the long-wheelbase Silver Cloud III chassis was designated SCT200. Just two examples were built, on chassis numbers LCDL1 (for King Hassan II of Morocco, delivered in April 1964) and on CFL19 (for a UK owner, delivered in January 1965). The right-hand-drive car differed from the earlier example in having Hooper-style rear quarter-lights.

B10 (S Type, 1956-1959) and B10R (1957)

The James Young Two-door Saloon for the standard six-cylinder Bentley S Type chassis was a very elegant design that was quite similar in overall outline to the standard steel saloon of the time. The two doors apart, its most obvious distinguishing feature was the swage line that ran the full length of each side, following

Cloth upholstery throughout was specified for this PV22, which was originally finished in dark blue but was repainted at the request of its original owner. (Simon Clay)

Provenance – and who would re-upholster a worn seat like this one, on which not only Elvis Presley but probably many other celebrities once sat? (Simon Clay)

The division in this PV22 Limousine contained both drop-down tables and a useful centre cupboard, which in this case opens to reveal the luxury (for the 1960s) of an in-car telephone. (Simon Clay)

This is the discreet body number on a James Young creation, in this case on the four-door Saloon built for Bentley S2 Continental chassis number BC8CZ. (Klaus-Josef Rossfeldt)

three had left-hand drive. They were visually similar to the two-door body for the Continental that was offered by Park Ward, and had several similarities to the James Young two-door Saloon to design B10 on the standard S Type chassis as well. By comparison with the Park Ward body, the continuous swage line running from front to rear was an obvious difference, and a closer look would reveal the painted window pillar behind the door and James Young's characteristic square door press-buttons. By comparison with the James Young body on the standard Bentley chassis, the main differences were narrower rear window pillars that gave a more sporting look, and a straighter swage line that did not follow the contours of the wing pressings slavishly.

CV150 (Continental S2 & S3, 1960-1965) and SCV150 (Silver Cloud III, 1964-1966)

The CV100 and SCV100 four-door Sports Saloons were further developed to produce two-door variants that were known as CV150 and SCV150. The CV150 became available on Bentley S2 Continental chassis, on which four examples were built; just one had left-hand drive. In effect, these were the replacements for the earlier CT29 design on the six-cylinder Continental chassis. There was also a single CV150M variant, on BC27AR, with headlamps mounted on the wing fronts and different rear end details. The standard CV150 design remained available for the S3 Continental, and two more examples were built on this chassis, both with right-hand drive.

The body became available as an SCV150 at Earls Court in 1964, where it was displayed on Silver Cloud III chassis LSGT609C. There were six of these SCV150 types in all, the last one (on CSC101B) being delivered in January 1966.

JOHN JACKSON

John Jackson & Sons of Dunfermline in Fife was primarily a commercial body builder. In the 1920s it constructed bus bodies for various Scottish operators, and subsequently moved into commercial vehicle bodywork. The company built just one body on a car chassis from Crewe, and that was a wooden-bodied estate on Bentley R Type B76SR, which was delivered in July 1953. The order for such a body at this relatively late date makes clear that there were advantages to such bodies beyond tax saving and an increased petrol ration! This unique vehicle has remained in the ownership of its original family until the present day. It also gained fame in the BBC TV drama series *Strathblair* in 1992-1993, when it featured regularly as the Laird's car.

the curvature of the wing pressings. There were 26 examples in all, plus one to design B10R (on B63BC) which was visually similar.

CT29 (S Type Continental, 1956-1958) and CT30 (1958-1959)

In the beginning, Bentley Motors insisted that only two-door coachwork was suitable for the S Type Continental, and so all the first James Young bodies for this chassis conformed to that type.

The James Young two-door body started out as design CT29 and evolved into a CT30 with different rear window pillars in 1958. These bodies were built on 16 six-cylinder S Type Continentals, of which just

JONES BROS

By the end of the 1940s, the coachbuilding firm of Jones Bros was based at Willesden in London, and was largely focussing on commercial bodywork. It had originally been founded in the Bayswater district of west London by 1928, and built a variety of car bodies, notably including those for Austin 12/4 taxis. In the post-war era, it continued to build car bodies alongside commercial types, but went bankrupt in the mid-1950s and closed down.

Jones Bros built just two bodies on post-war chassis from Crewe, both being on the early short-wheelbase Rolls-Royce Silver Wraith. The earlier of the two was delivered in November 1950 and was a Touring Limousine with division on chassis number WYA9. This body showed a marked Hooper influence, particularly of their "pre-Teviot" design number 8034, and even incorporated that coachbuilder's characteristic rear quarter-window shape.

The second Jones Bros body was an estate car for Silver Wraith chassis number WYA24 and was delivered in February 1951.

MULLINER, PARK WARD

As Nick Walker suggests in his classic *A-Z British Coachbuilders 1919-1960*, when Rolls-Royce bought the HJ Mulliner coachbuilding company in 1959 it was probably a way of ensuring that it would continue to have access to traditional coachbuilding skills. The market for coachbuilt bodywork was, after all, shrinking very rapidly, and trained craftsmen were gradually drifting away into other occupations.

In 1961, Rolls-Royce merged HJ Mulliner with its Park Ward coachbuilding subsidiary to create HJ Mulliner, Park Ward Ltd, and moved the entire operation into the Park Ward works at Willesden. Mulliner, Park Ward built coachwork exclusively for Rolls-Royce and Bentley chassis, initially using designs from the two formerly separate companies. Bodies built by the merged concern nevertheless continued to carry the builder's plate of their "design parent" until well into 1963.

There were no genuinely bespoke designs from Mulliner, Park Ward between its creation in 1961 and the end of coachbuilding on separate-chassis models

The Koren Drophead Coupé, which had originated with Park Ward, became Mulliner, Park Ward design number 2045 when applied to the Rolls-Royce Silver Cloud III chassis. This one is LCSC85B, delivered in 1965. All the Rolls-Royce versions of the Koren design had a side trim strip, as seen here. (Simon Clay)

The Koren Drophead Coupé lines still looked beautifully balanced when the soft top was erected. (Simon Clay)

On the Rolls-Royce chassis, standard instruments were used, even though the steering column was specially raked to suit these bodies, which had originally been designed for the Bentley Continental. (Simon Clay)

Variations: on this 1965 body, the coachbuilder's plate is attached by four screws. This was not always the case, as a later picture on page 124 reveals! (Simon Clay)

in 1965; all the body designs were built in quantity. They were nevertheless still hand-built by craftsmen to the very highest standards, just as they always had been. Although individual coachbuilder's plates were in use until 1963 (and HJ Mulliner plates until 1965 on one design), by the time of the Silver Cloud III and S3 the merger between the two former coachbuilders was effectively complete.

From the former HJ Mulliner came four designs. What Mulliner, Park Ward knew as design 2007 was

the "beheaded" Silver Cloud Drophead Coupé that had originated as HJ Mulliner's design 7504. The Flying Spur sports saloon became design 2042, and the Drophead Coupé for the long-wheelbase Silver Cloud chassis became design 2033, having started life as HJ Mulliner's design 7484. There were also a few bodies to design 2012, which had earlier been HJ Mulliner's design 7514 for the Continental chassis.

From the former Park Ward came three more designs. These were the Koren-designed Fixed-head Coupé and Drophead Coupé, and the Limousine for the Phantom V chassis. The Phantom Limousine body took the new number 2003. On the Bentley Continental chassis, the fixed-head Koren body became design 2035, but for the Silver Cloud (from 1963) it became design 2041. The Drophead Coupé then became design 2006 for the Bentley S3 Continental and (again from 1963) 2045 for the Silver Cloud chassis. Both bodies were modified from their original configuration to take on the paired headlamps of the Silver Cloud III and Bentley S3, resulting in a very distinctive front-end style that earned these designs the nickname of "Chinese eye" types.

By the time of the Mulliner, Park Ward division's creation, the only other British coachbuilder still active was James Young, and it should therefore be no surprise that the majority of coachbuilt bodies on Rolls-Royce and Bentley chassis after 1961 were created by Mulliner, Park Ward.

HOW MANY BODIES?

The figures below have been calculated by chassis type.

Rolls-Royce		Bentley	
Silver Cloud III	302	S3 Continental	291
S Cloud III LWB	5		
Phantom V	112		
Phantom VI	366		
Total	**785**	**Total**	**291**

Drophead Coupés

The two-door Drophead Coupé conversion of the standard saloon body introduced in 1959 on the six-cylinder Silver Cloud became the Mulliner, Park Ward division's design number 2007 for the Silver Cloud III chassis. There were no major changes, although the front end sheet metal and the tail lights were those associated with the parent chassis. Electrically operated door windows and power operation of the convertible top both remained optional extras in this period.

There were 38 Drophead Coupé bodies to design 2007 on the Silver Cloud III, plus one on the Bentley S3. They were built as a batch in 1962-1963, the first one being delivered in July 1962 and the last at the end of 1963.

The Koren-designed Drophead Coupés were much more numerous. Initially available only for the Bentley Continental chassis as design 2006, they were then

With the addition of the paired headlamps associated with the third generation of the S Type chassis, the Flying Spur became part of the Mulliner, Park Ward repertoire. Two-tone paint finishes such as this one, on BC172XA, made for some pleasant variation. This car was new in 1963. (Simon Clay)

made available for the adapted Silver Cloud III (with the Continental's more raked steering column) from the 1963 Earls Court show as design 2045. The two designs were identical externally, with the exception of the grilles, bonnets and badges, but design 2006 on the Continental had plain body sides and design 2045 on the Silver Cloud had a bright trim strip above the wheelarches. The Silver Cloud bodies also had standard saloon instrumentation rather than the more comprehensive array associated with the Continentals.

There were 86 of these "Chinese eye" bodies to design 2006 on the Bentley Continental S3 chassis (28 of them with left-hand drive), and a further quantity on the Silver Cloud III.

Between 1962 and 1965, there were also five four-door Drophead Coupé bodies on the long-wheelbase Silver Cloud III chassis, all to Mulliner, Park Ward

design number 2033. However, this design had originated with HJ Mulliner as that company's design number 7484, and all five cars carried HJ Mulliner builder's plates.

The first two of these cars were ordered by the Australian Government for use on Her Majesty the Queen's tour of Australia. Delivered in December 1962, these did not have the latest Silver Cloud III front end but had the taller radiator grille associated with the earlier Clouds, together with their single headlamps and sidelights on the wing tops. They also had the earlier "cathedral" style of rear lamp units. Both had separate rear seats, which could be raised so that the occupants could be more easily seen during parades and processions.

The three later cars all had standard Silver Cloud III front ends and standard rear light units. The first was delivered in 1964 and the other two in 1965, the last one in May that year.

The Flying Spur

The Flying Spur sports saloon, now design 2042, took on the four-headlamp front end of the Silver Cloud III and Bentley S3 but was otherwise very much as it had been built by HJ Mulliner. There were 51 examples on Rolls-Royce chassis (with the more raked Continental-type steering column) and a further 82 on the Bentley S3 Continental. The four-light version of the Flying Spur became design 2011/E, and there were 11 examples on the Continental chassis, of which just three had left-hand drive. A small number of these bodies were made with quarter-lights of reduced size.

There is a modern ICE head unit in this dashboard, but it cannot detract from the appeal of the figured woodwork. As this body is on a Continental chassis, a rev counter is fitted outboard of the steering wheel. (Simon Clay)

The rear seat on the Flying Spur bodies was quite different in design from the one on the Koren-designed coachwork. (Simon Clay)

More conventionally finished in a dark single colour, this Flying Spur is on S3 Continental BC134XC and was new in 1965. Simon Clay)

This type of rear number-plate box was characteristic of former Mulliner designs, and is here complemented by the S3 badge on the right. (Simon Clay)

Compare and contrast: the coachbuilder's plate on this Flying Spur is attached by only two screws, not the four seen on the 1965 Koren drophead pictured earlier on page 120. (Simon Clay)

There was also a very rare variant of the Flying Spur with small rear quarter-lights, for those who wanted a little more privacy in the back seat. This was considerably rarer than either the standard six-light design or the less common four-light type, and is seen here on a late 1962 S3 Continental chassis.

The Koren Fixed-head Coupé is seen here on a Bentley Continental chassis, BC12LXC from 1964. The absence of a trim strip was not noticeable with dark colours like this, but on light-coloured cars tended to give a slab-sided appearance. (Simon Clay)

Today, using the term "Chinese eye" to describe one of these bodies on the S3 Continental chassis is likely to be met with accusations of racial stereotyping – but it is not hard to see how the description arose. (Simon Clay)

Fixed-head coupés

There is a question of nomenclature here. Rolls-Royce tended to prefer the description "two-door saloon", even though the Koren-designed cars at least were perhaps more accurately described as Fixed-head Coupés because they did have a closely related Drophead Coupé variant.

The majority of the closed two-door bodies from the Mulliner, Park Ward division had the Koren design, but for customers who wanted a two-door Bentley Continental S3 and were not impressed

Detail: the Bentley versions of the Koren bodies had a winged B between each pair of headlamps, matched by an RR badge for the Rolls-Royce versions. (Simon Clay)

The straight-through wing lines gave a hint of a tail fin, adding a contemporary air to these bodies without looking too extreme. (Simon Clay)

An enviable place to be… behind the wheel of a "Chinese-eye" Continental. This is BC46XA. (Simon Clay)

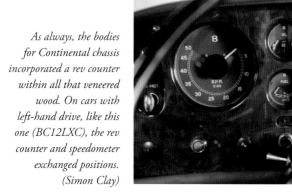

As always, the bodies for Continental chassis incorporated a rev counter within all that veneered wood. On cars with left-hand drive, like this one (BC12LXC), the rev counter and speedometer exchanged positions. (Simon Clay)

by the Koren design, the division kept the older HJ Mulliner design (number 7514) in production for a time. Closely related visually to the four-door Flying Spur, this now became design 2012. However, only 11 examples were built before it became clear that the Koren design could continue to attract the required volume of sales on its own.

The Koren "saloon" was initially built as design 2035 and only for the Bentley S3 Continental chassis, but it became available for the adapted Silver Cloud III chassis at the same time as the drophead version did in 1963. For the Silver Cloud, it became design

This is the Rolls-Royce equivalent, built on a standard Silver Cloud III chassis but with more steeply raked steering column. The car is CSC65B, which was new in 1965. (Simon Clay)

This view of the dashboard in the Rolls-Royce bears comparison with that of the dashboard in the Bentley S3 Fixed-head Coupé pictured earlier. (Simon Clay)

The hooded tail lamp arrangement remained unchanged from Park Ward days, although there were no Park Ward versions of the body on Rolls-Royce chassis. (Simon Clay)

In this case, the backplates for the headlamps have been painted to match the coachwork – and of course they feature small "RR" badges. (Simon Clay)

The tail treatment is of course subtly different from that of the Continental versions, with a "Silver Cloud III" badge on the boot lid and an "RR" in the centre of the bumper. (Simon Clay)

2041, and the Bentley and Rolls-Royce versions had the same differences as on the drophead bodies: the Rolls-Royce had a bodyside trim strip but did not have the Bentley's more comprehensive instrumentation.

Mulliner, Park Ward built 104 Koren "saloons" on the S3 Continental chassis (including 27 with left-hand drive), and a further quantity on the Silver Cloud III chassis. There was also a single body to design 2035/F, essentially a Koren "saloon" shortened to suit long-term customer RG McLeod's preferences. This was built on chassis number BC38XC.

The Phantom V limousines

From the start of the VA-series chassis in 1963, the Mulliner, Park Ward division began to deliver a new design of seven-seater limousine on the Phantom V chassis, numbered 2003. This was essentially an update of Park Ward's earlier design 980, most readily recognisable by the paired headlamps which were introduced at the same time on the standard Silver Cloud III saloons. The new sidelamps mounted in the front wings, and the larger rear tail-light units, were also borrowings from the latest Silver Cloud and

One of the most famous Phantom V models was the one owned by John Lennon of the Beatles, who bought a 1964 car in unremarkable Valentines Black and then had it customised in the psychedelic style of the mid-1960s. (Rolls-Royce Motor Cars)

The Mulliner, Park Ward body for the Rolls-Royce Phantom V was an amalgamation of elements from Park Ward and HJ Mulliner designs. This is a late example, with the twin-headlamp design used from 1963.

Two special variants of the Mulliner, Park Ward Limousine on Phantom V chassis were built for HM the Queen, with the codename of Canberra. This is one of them. The roof was raised and there is a Perspex rear section, as well as a Perspex section in the roof above the rear doors.

This is the spacious rear compartment of a Phantom V seven-passenger Limousine. The electric door windows shown here were an optional extra.

helped to reinforce the family resemblance.

Nevertheless, there were important changes elsewhere in the design, which was the work of Martin Bourne on John Blatchley's styling team at Crewe. There was a new shape for the windscreen, and slim chrome frames for the door windows replaced the painted type on the Park Ward bodies. The rear of the body was also restyled, with rounded rear quarters and a razor edge for the boot. Design 2003 remained readily recognisable as the original Park Ward design, and the resulting cars were familiarly known at Crewe as "Phantom V½" models!

A total of 112 examples were built between 1963 and 1968, and the body design was then carried over to the new Rolls-Royce Phantom VI chassis. Every Phantom V in the chassis series from VA to VF had one of these bodies, except for 125 built by James Young (see under that coachbuilder) and one that was built as a hearse by Woodall Nicholson.

The Phantom V Landaulettes

The Mulliner, Park Ward division inherited Park Ward's Landaulette design number 1104 and renumbered it as 2047, but it appears that only two were built, on 5LVD33 (January 1965) and 5VD83 (August 1966) for the Ruler of Bahrain.

Meanwhile, Mulliner, Park Ward had drawn up their own design, numbered 2052 and described as a State Landaulette. Although the lower body closely resembled that of the standard 2003 Limousine design of the time, the boot reverted to the more rounded design that Park Ward had used on their original limousine design 980. Another key feature was that the folding head was not just over the rear seat but began at the central door pillars, leaving a fixed roof section only over the driving compartment. An option was an electrically operated rear seat that raised the occupants by 3½in so that they could be seen better during parades and ceremonies. Four examples of this design were built, beginning with 5VD99 in September 1965 for the President of Tanganyika.

There were Landaulette
derivatives of the Limousine
body for the Phantom
chassis, too. This one
was built in 1974 on a
Phantom VI chassis.

The rear compartment of the Phantom VI Landaulette makes clear that the Mulliner, Park Ward coachbuilding skills were still very much intact in 1990. (Simon Clay)

This rare view shows the rear seat in the Phantom VI Landaulette, with the top down. (Simon Clay)

Just in case.... the Phantom VI Landaulette carries umbrellas clipped under the boot lid. (Simon Clay)

Special features in PMX10422 were these inlaid images of Rolls and Royce. (Simon Clay)

The Phantom VI limousines and saloons

Only eight Rolls-Royce Phantom VI chassis were not bodied by Mulliner, Park Ward, and of the 366 that were, 347 were built as standard limousines. A further two bodies were built to the same outward design but as saloons (with no division), and five more were built as armoured limousines. One special high-roof "Canberra" Limousine was built for Her Majesty the Queen.

The first Phantom VI bodies all had design 2003, which was carried over from the Phantom V chassis but with the addition of air conditioning for both front and rear compartments. However, a suite of changes was introduced in 1972 to comply with new European safety regulations, and the most obvious recognition feature of one of these later bodies (design 2003/1) is that the rear doors were hinged at their leading edges rather than at the rear as on earlier bodies. The first chassis with this revised body design was PRH4701. All early bodies had the Silver Cloud III style of rear light units, but later ones used the light units associated with the Rolls-Royce Corniche. Most bodies had leather upholstery for the front compartment but a variety of different materials were specified for the rear compartment seating. There were also some individual variations in the interior features.

The five armoured limousines were sold as "special limousines", and were developed as design 2053 under the code name of Alpha. Details of the changes to these bodies were understandably not released to the public, but they were not difficult to distinguish from the standard design 2003 Limousine of the

time. Although the armoured Phantoms shared most of their exterior lines with the contemporary 2003 and 2003/1 bodies, they had heavy chromed window frames to support two-inch-thick armoured glass, and a noticeably recessed rear window.

The single special state limousine for Her Majesty the Queen had coachwork along the lines of the two earlier "Canberra" limousines on the Phantom V chassis. This one was intended as a present to Her Majesty from the Society of Motor Manufacturers and Traders during the Silver Jubilee year of 1977, but was not in fact delivered until March 1978. Like the earlier cars built by Park Ward, it had a raised roof that gave four inches of extra headroom, with a Perspex rear roof. This time, the metal roof cover was a removable metal panel rather than the folding type used on the two earlier cars. This body was mounted on chassis PGH101, the first "production" Phantom VI to have the 6.75-litre engine and GM400 gearbox.

The Phantom VI Landaulettes

The Mulliner, Park Ward division also built 12 State Landaulette bodies on the Phantom VI chassis, all of them based on design 2052 which was carried over from the Phantom V chassis.

MULLINERS (BIRMINGHAM)

Mulliners Ltd of Bordesley Green in Birmingham is perhaps the least well known of the three Mulliner companies. In the late 18th century, the Birmingham company was founded by members of the same family as the others, but after 1924 it was reconstituted under Louis Antweiler. The company specialised in Weymann fabric bodywork, always preferring to build in volume rather than to bespoke commission, and during the 1930s was closely associated with Daimler and Lanchester, for whom it built most of the bodies on the less expensive chassis. Nevertheless, Mulliners did undertake the occasional special commission, and built a number of bodies on Rolls-Royce chassis plus a handful on Derby Bentleys.

After the 1939-1945 war, Mulliners' business was very largely for the Standard-Triumph group, which took the company over formally in 1957. In the meantime, however, the Bordesley Green works had built one body on a Bentley MkVI chassis. This was on chassis number B342NZ and was delivered in July 1952 to Standard-Triumph's Managing Director, Sir John Black. The Drophead Coupé body had a unique and contemporary design by Stuart Peck at Mulliners, supposedly inspired by French examples, and the door interiors had an Art Deco-style "sunburst" stitch pattern.

It is possible to tell a large part of the post-war Park Ward story through pictures of the company's Drophead Coupés. This is a 1949 body on the MkVI Bentley chassis, and shows the early style with separate front and rear wing volumes. (Rex Gray/WikiMedia Commons)

PARK WARD

Park Ward was one of the five major players in post-war coachbuilding on Rolls-Royce and Bentley chassis. Founded at Willesden in north London in 1919, the company rapidly began to stand out in its chosen field. In the first half of the 1920s, an approach from Rolls-Royce in connection with an abortive scheme to build standardised coachwork for the new Twenty chassis was a clear indication of the esteem in which the company was held.

From the mid-1920s, Park Ward began to focus on designs for Rolls-Royce and Bentley chassis, and 90% of the bodies it made by 1930 were for Rolls-Royce chassis. Nevertheless, within a few years the company was in difficulties, and an approach to Rolls-Royce led to that company buying a major stake in Park Ward. With support from the chassis maker, Park Ward developed all-steel saloon coachwork after 1933, making it available from 1936 on the Bentley 4¼-litre chassis. In 1939, Rolls-Royce bought the remaining shares in Park Ward.

After the war, the technology that Park Ward had developed for all-steel coachwork went into the Bentley MkVI with its standardised Pressed Steel body. The company continued to operate under its own name as a bespoke in-house coachbuilding division but its scope was limited as the Silver Cloud and S Type cars came on-stream, and it built no bodies for either type except on the six-cylinder Bentley Continental chassis, although the famous HJ Mulliner "beheaded" Drophead Coupés in fact came from a design exercise carried out by Park Ward, who built the first example of each.

There were no Park Ward bodies on the standard-wheelbase Silver Cloud II or S2 chassis, either,

HOW MANY BODIES?			
The figures below have been calculated by chassis type. Note that some of these bodies are sometimes attributed to the merged Mulliner, Park Ward division and that totals may therefore vary from those given elsewhere.			
Rolls-Royce		**Bentley**	
Silver Wraith	312	MkVI	172
S Wraith LWB	168	R Type	51
Silver Dawn	28	Continental	6
Silver Cloud	89	S Type	31
S Cloud LWB	87	S Continental	186
S Cloud II LWB	1	S Type LWB	23
Phantom V	132	S2 Continental	125
Total	**817**	**Total**	**594**

although there was one on a long-wheelbase Silver Cloud II. However, Park Ward did build 125 bodies on the Continental S2 chassis (some of which were strictly Mulliner, Park Ward products). In 1961, Park Ward was merged with Rolls-Royce's latest acquisition, HJ Mulliner, to form the Mulliner, Park Ward coachbuilding division.

Park Ward was responsible for some most elegant and satisfying designs in the 20 years after the war. Many of these were quite long-lived, being modified only slightly over the years but going through several different design numbers that are difficult to tell apart.

Drophead Coupés

Park Ward built Drophead Coupés to seven different designs on the Bentley MkVI chassis, although there were just three major styles, which had design numbers 65, 99 and 100. The position was much the same for the Rolls-Royce Silver Wraith, and there were three designs on the short-wheelbase chassis (numbers 201, 225 and 291) that were very similar to one another. There were then three more designs (numbers 547, 571 and 705) on the long-wheelbase Silver Wraith, spread over eight bodies.

Experimental (MkVI, 1947)

The earliest Park Ward Drophead Coupé for the MkVI chassis was built on experimental chassis 5-B-VI in mid-1947 and was very much a compromise, using as many parts from the standard steel body as possible in order to keep costs down. No design number for this body is known, although it certainly did anticipate the later design number 65, which was produced in quantity. However, this prototype body was considered unsatisfactory and was removed during 1948, being replaced by a standard Pressed Steel Saloon body that remained on the chassis for the rest of its life on test.

It seems probable that the body was subsequently fitted to chassis B132EY, and the completed car was then delivered to a new owner in October 1949. Presumably any remaining unsatisfactory elements of the body had been dealt with beforehand!

Design 16 (MkVI, 1947)

A second design of Drophead Coupé for the Bentley MkVI chassis was drawn up as Park Ward's number 16, and the surviving specification reveals that its framework was intended to be made of steel, while the body panels were to be of alloy. The design differed from the earlier experimental Drophead Coupé, with a more marked outsweep to the lower body and more rounded wings, while the folded convertible top sat lower down to give a smoother profile at the rear. All

this rather suggests that Park Ward were treating it as a way of exploring new ideas – but in practice the steel framework was not made and the car was built with alloy panels on a traditional ash wood frame. The sole example of design number 16 was mounted on a very early production MkVI, B10AK, and was delivered in August 1947. With further development, the design entered "production" as number 100.

Design 65 (MkVI, 1947-1949) and Design 66 (1948)

When the definitive Park Ward Drophead Coupé design was ready, it gained number 65 in the Park Ward canon. Clearly a further development of the ideas explored on the first Experimental body and then with design number 16, it had been most obviously redesigned at the rear, where there was a larger boot. The chrome waist moulding now terminated earlier, and many cars were fitted with spats. A side-mounted spare wheel was standard, and some cars had one on each side.

Park Ward built 23 of these bodies for the MkVI, the first being delivered in October 1947 and taking part in a Showing the Flag tour of the USA along with other British products. The last few were delivered in April 1949. Design number 65 never did appear on a show stand at Earls Court, an example of design number 100 being preferred at the only show where this would have been possible, in 1948.

Just one body was built to design 66 for the Bentley MkVI, and this was on chassis number B432CF. It was delivered to an owner in France in August 1948, but nothing else is known about the body design and no pictures of the car are known.

Design 99 (MkVI & R Type, 1949-1955)

Park Ward's next major Drophead Coupé design for the Bentley MkVI was number 99, of which the first example was delivered in June 1949. This became a demonstrator for Rolls-Royce, but it would be March 1950 before any "production" examples were delivered.

Design 99 was a major step forward, with a much more modern approach than number 65, which it replaced in the Park Ward catalogue. The front wing line swept back across the door to meet the spatted rear wing, and a chromed fillet decorated the bottom edge of the body on each side. There were 57 examples of this classic, elegant design on the Bentley MkVI chassis, and it was carried over to the later R Type as well. It appeared twice on the Park Ward stand at Earls Court, B4HR being the Show car in 1950 and B18MD having that honour in 1951. The last example numerically on the MkVI chassis was B501LNY,

This more flowing style became the norm around 1950. The 1951 car pictured has chassis B128LJ, but the body (to design number 99) is a few months newer and was originally mounted on chassis B186LJ. (Charles 01/WikiMedia Commons)

The classic Park Ward
Drophead Coupé design
number 100 is seen here
on a pair of Bentley MkVI
chassis. On the left is
B417FU, new in June
1950, and on the right is
B401DZ, delivered exactly
a year earlier.
(Klaus-Josef Rossfeldt)

which was delivered in June 1952, although both B499LNY and B467NY were delivered later that year.

Unsurprisingly, the Design 99 Drophead Coupé was made available for the Bentley R Type as that replaced the MkVI, and a further 25 examples of this body were built up to November 1953. Eighteen were on RHD chassis, and seven on LHD chassis. A number of these later examples of the body had no rear wheel spats, which gave them a quite different appearance, and some had hydraulic power assistance for the folding roof.

Design 100 (MkVI, 1948-1950)

Design 100 was a further development of the ideas pioneered by design number 16 in 1947, one obvious difference being the addition of rear-wing spats. It was introduced at the 1948 Earls Court Show, where Bentley MkVI chassis B140DA displayed it on the Rolls-Royce stand and B144DA did likewise on the Park Ward stand. Delivery of customer cars began in March 1949 and a total of 45 examples were built, the last one (on chassis B154LHR) reaching its owner in November 1950. The two 1948 Show cars had the

The flowing wing lines are seen here on Rolls-Royce Silver Dawn LSLE43, which was new in 1953. (Simon Clay)

The upholstery has the typical early 1950s combination of pleated seat backs with plain panels for the cushions. (Simon Clay)

In this case, bright metal trim along the bottom edges of the body and on the rear wheel spat adds welcome highlights to the design. (Simon Clay)

new feature of a power-operated hood, but it is not clear whether all the customer cars also had this.

Design 116 (MkVI, 1949) and Design 177 (1950)

There were two Drophead Coupé bodies with individual design numbers in 1949-1950, although the minor details that distinguished them from the volume-built designs of the time are not obvious. Design 116 was a slightly modified variant of design number 100, and the sole example was built on chassis number B375DZ to special order for the Prince

Regent of Belgium. It was delivered in August 1949. Design 177 was visually indistinguishable from design number 99. It was built on chassis number B498LFV and was exhibited at the Geneva Show in March 1950.

Designs 201, 225 (Silver Wraith, 1950) and 291 (1951-1953)

Park Ward's Drophead Coupé design for the short-wheelbase Rolls-Royce Silver Wraith chassis went through three design numbers, although the basic lines remained unchanged. It appeared first of all as

This Drophead Coupé was a 1954 confection for JD Rockefeller, and is unique in combining left-hand drive with a two-light configuration. It is on Bentley R Type chassis number B132LTN. (sicnag/WikiMedia Commons)

number 201, of which just one example was built, on chassis LWHD39 which was delivered in May 1950. A second body was delivered in August 1950, this time described as design number 225 and on chassis LWHD78.

There were then three more bodies to design 291, which was again hard to tell apart from the two earlier designs. The first of these was on chassis WME27, which was delivered in May 1951. WVH61 followed in April 1953, and the last example was delivered in May 1953 on WVH46.

Design 488 (R Type, 1953) and Design 511 (1953)

There were two one-off Drophead Coupé bodies on Bentley R Type chassis. These were design 488 (on B133LSP), which was broadly similar to Fixed-head Coupé design 466 but incorporated rear wheel spats; and design 511 (on B9TO) without spats.

Design 547 (Silver Wraith, 1954) and Design 571 (1954-1955)

There was just one Drophead Coupé body to design 547 on the long-wheelbase Silver Wraith chassis. This was delivered in April 1954 on chassis number BLW77, and was a masterful lesson in how to create an elegant Drophead Coupé on such a large chassis. The overall lines were typical of the Park Ward style at the time, and the folding roof sat flush with the top of the body to create a very pleasing look when the car was open to the elements.

Park Ward then built three examples of Design 571, with wing lines that echoed those of their contemporary closed bodies. The first one was delivered on chassis CLW40 in July 1954, and the last on DLW149 in May 1955.

Design 552 (R Type, 1953-1955)

Park Ward's design number 552 had a new wing line, where the line of the front wing met that of the rear in a gentler curve than before. These Drophead Coupés also differed from most earlier such Park Ward designs in featuring open rear wheel arches without spats. There were nine of these bodies, of which just one was on a left-hand-drive chassis (B202LWH).

Design 553 (R Type, 1953-1954) and Design 554 (1953-1955)

As always, Park Ward produced variations on their main designs, and there were two design 553 Drophead Coupés and four to design 554. All were elegant bodies on the Bentley R Type chassis, and were closely related to the mainstream design 552 of the time.

Design 647 (R Type Continental, 1954-1955)

For the R Type Continental chassis, Park Ward based its Drophead Coupés and Two-door Saloons on a common design. There were four Drophead Coupés

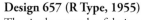

Design 657 (R Type, 1955)

The single example of design 657 on the R Type chassis was a throwback to earlier days, being essentially a design 100 Drophead Coupé adapted to suit the later chassis. It was built on chassis B310YD.

Design 700 (S Type Continental, 1955-1957) and design 889 (1957-1959)

For the S Type Continentals, the Park Ward designs were developed from John Blatchley's design for the late R Type Continentals, with just a few changes to suit the longer (123in) wheelbase of the new chassis. As for the earlier Continentals, the company used essentially the same styling for the Drophead Coupés as it did for the Two-door Saloons.

Park Ward's first Drophead Coupé body for the S Type Continental was for one of the two prototypes, 26-B. The body was completed in March 1955 but was removed after the car was severely damaged in a crash during endurance testing on the European continent in April 1956. The chassis was then rebuilt with an HJ Mulliner two-door Saloon body and the car was used for further testing. It was eventually sold

The sleek lines of Park Ward's Drophead Coupé on this 1954 Bentley Continental chassis make a marked contrast with those for the standard R Type chassis of the same period. (Anton van Luijk/ WikiMedia Commons)

in late 1954 and early 1955. Just one was built on the C-series chassis, and the other three were on D-series chassis. BC8D was nevertheless the first one delivered, in September 1954. The last one was BC25D, which did duty at the Brussels and Turin Shows. BC73C had special seating, and BC28D was at the 1954 Earls Court Show.

Very similar lines were carried over for the S Type Continental chassis. This one is on chassis BC7AF, and was first registered in October 1955. It was retained as the "trials car" (demonstrator) at the Rolls-Royce showroom in London's Conduit Street. Here pictured with its top up, it looks somewhat travel-stained.

This rear view of BC7AF shows the fins that were integral to the early body design but were not to every customer's taste.

The boot was large enough to suit a long-distance touring car, with the spare wheel located flat on the right under its own cover.

on in August 1962, becoming BC102AF.

"Production" Drophead Coupé bodies to design 700 were first delivered in September 1955, and a power-operated hood was fitted to some examples. Like their fixed-head equivalents to design 701, these bodies were built with discreet fins on the rear wings. On the earliest bodies, three separate tail lamps on each side were used, but later bodies (to design 889) blended the fins in more effectively by using standard saloon rear light units whose pointed tops fitted into the rear face of each fin. Nevertheless, the fins remained controversial and in some cases they were removed during later restoration.

The last of 89 Drophead Coupés on the S Type Continental chassis were delivered in July 1959; the total is 90 if the prototype is counted as well. Of those, 31 were built with left-hand drive.

Design 705 (Silver Wraith, 1956-1958)

Drophead Coupé design number 571 was updated with the latest Silver Cloud type of bumpers to become design 705 in 1956. There were no other significant differences, and four examples of this body for the long-wheelbase Silver Wraith were built in just over two years. The first was on chassis number ELW43 and was delivered in July 1956; the last was on LHLW26 and was delivered in October 1958.

Design number not known (Silver Cloud & S Type, 1959)

Park Ward investigated the possibility of converting the standard steel Saloon body of the Silver Cloud and S Type Bentley into a two-door Drophead Coupé, and built one example of each. The Bentley was the first, on chassis B568FA, and the Silver Cloud was

There were heavy-looking seats in these bodies to design number 700, as seen on the demonstration car BC7AF.

Park Ward were always good at creating a flush-fitting for the convertible top, and the effect contributed very much to the sleek lines of the open S Type Continental body.

Something completely new was needed for the V8-engined S2 Continental, and this was it – design 991 that originated with Vilhelm Koren. It was radically different from earlier Park Ward designs, and top management at Rolls-Royce had their doubts about it, but it turned out to be very successful indeed. This is a 1962 example, on BC119LCZ. (Simon Clay)

The curved sides of the Koren design prevented the straight-through wing lines from looking bland, and the peak over the tail lights reflected contemporary design themes elsewhere. (Simon Clay)

on LSJF60. Park Ward's conclusion was that the conversion was too time-consuming and expensive – although that did not stop HJ Mulliner from taking the design over (after they had been absorbed by Rolls-Royce) and putting it into production as the much-admired "beheaded" model.

Design 991 (S2 Continental, 1959-1962)

Park Ward's design for the S2 Continental chassis broke new ground in many areas. It was done within John Blatchley's styling department at Crewe, by a young Norwegian industrial designer called Vilhelm Koren. He had been recruited to Rolls-Royce in 1957

A snug-fitting soft top ensured that this very modern design always looked smart and sophisticated. (Simon Clay)

The driving appeal of the drophead coachwork to design 991 is immediately obvious from this picture… (Simon Clay)

The Park Ward coachbuilder's plate was simple but stylish. (Simon Clay)

after Blatchley and "Doc" Llewellyn Smith had been impressed with his coupé body for an Alfa Romeo chassis at the Turin Show.

Koren drew up both Drophead Coupé and closed versions of a body for the Continental chassis, but only the open car went into production for the S2 Continental. Somewhat inevitably, the design was known at Crewe and by the coachbuilder's staff as a Korenental.

The Koren design was characterised by a great simplicity, with straight-through wing lines leading from cowled headlamps on the wing fronts to fin-like cowls over stacked tail lamps. The body construction

The seat back could be folded down to create a platform for luggage when required. (Simon Clay)

The Koren design mixed simple lines with more ornate elements – such as these headlamp and auxiliary lamp recesses. (Simon Clay)

also marked a first for British coachbuilders, incorporating aircraft construction methods with extensive use of welded steel for the frame and fixed panels – and presaged the use of similar construction for the two-door Mulliner, Park Ward bodies on the later Silver Shadow and T Series family.

The neat convertible top had a Perspex rear window that could be unzipped, and was raised and lowered by an electro-hydraulic system, with a safety link to the gearbox to ensure that it could only be operated when the transmission was in Neutral. The interior also broke with Crewe traditions, featuring anatomically designed front seats, an instrument nacelle located directly ahead of the driver, and a vinyl-covered padded dashboard top.

125 examples of this design were built between 1959 and 1962, 65 with LHD and 60 with RHD. Park Ward's design number 991 was then transferred to the Mulliner, Park Ward division where it was built with paired headlamps as their design number 2006 for the Silver Cloud III and Bentley S3 chassis. In practice, bodies carried Park Ward identification until well into 1963.

Fixed-head Coupés

The Fixed-head Coupé was a rarity from Park Ward on the post-war chassis. There were just two (closely related) designs on the smaller chassis, and a third on the Silver Wraith.

Design 147 (MkVI, 1949-1952) and Design 149 (1950)

The Park Ward Fixed-head Coupé for the Bentley MkVI had design number 147, and was very much a closed version of the contemporary Drophead Coupé with design 99. Design 147 was introduced on the Park Ward stand at Earls Court in 1949, where the Show car was probably the first one built, on chassis B97EW. A total of 34 examples were made, the last ones being delivered in April 1952. In the intervening period, Design 147 figured twice more on the Park Ward stand at Earls Court: B6HLR was the 1950 exhibit, and B16MD was shown in 1951.

Like its Drophead Coupé equivalent, design 147 remained available for the Bentley R Type chassis, on which a further six examples were built between October 1952 and May 1954.

Park Ward's Fixed-head Coupé coachwork shared its lines with the Drophead Coupés in the late 1940s and early 1950s, and design number 147 looked supremely attractive from all angles. This example is on Bentley MkVI chassis B279FU, and was delivered in August 1950. (Klaus-Josef Rossfeldt)

Two-colour paint schemes lent a different look to design number 147. This example is probably on Bentley MkVI chassis B97EW.

Design 147 was also slightly modified to become design 149, of which a single example was built. This was on Bentley MkVI chassis B410LFV and was delivered to its owner in Switzerland in February 1950.

Design 173 (Silver Wraith, 1950)

Park Ward's only Fixed-head Coupé body on the Rolls-Royce Silver Wraith chassis was delivered in May 1950 on chassis number WGC94. This was a very neat-looking design which embodied all the Park Ward characteristics of the time, with full front wings, spatted rear wheels, and a most attractive two-tone colour scheme. It was essentially a closed version of the design 201 Drophead Coupé (see above).

Design 466 (R Type, 1952)

Alongside the 34 examples of design 147 on the R Type chassis, Park Ward built a single example of a Fixed-head Coupé to design number 466. This was on early chassis B14RT and was a most elegant design without the rear-wheel spats of other Fixed-head Coupés from Park Ward at the time. B14RT was one of the first few chassis that were described as "Bentley 7" types on the chassis record cards before the R Type name was adopted.

Landaulettes

Park Ward built only a small number of Landaulette bodies, all of them on the long-wheelbase Rolls-Royce Silver Wraith or Phantom V chassis.

Design 558 (Silver Wraith, 1954-1955)

The first design of Park Ward Landaulette was built on the long-wheelbase Silver Wraith chassis and appeared in September 1954. Just two examples of design 558 were built, each with free-standing headlamps. These were on chassis CLW36 (for the Emperor of Ethiopia) and DLW126, which was delivered in July 1955 for the Governor of the Gold Coast.

Design 727 (Silver Wraith, 1957-1958)

The second Park Ward Landaulette design was very much like the first, but had built-in headlamps and different rear lights. The top of the boot was also lower down and the boot itself was deeper. All six examples were delivered for ceremonial use, the first (on FLW61) in January 1957 and the last (on LGLW24) going to Queen Juliana of the Netherlands in March 1958.

Design 1000 (Phantom V, 1961-1962)

Two State Landaulettes were constructed on the Rolls-Royce Phantom V chassis, to design number 1000. The first one was on chassis 5BV7, and was delivered in 1961 to the Governor of Hong Kong. The second was on 5LCG51 and went to the President of Tunisia in 1962. Design 1000 remained available after the merger of HJ Mulliner and Park Ward, and later examples were attributed to the merged concern.

Design 1104 (Phantom V, 1962)

The special State Landaulette built on Phantom V chassis 5CG37 for the Queen Mother had Park Ward design number 1104. Delivered in February 1962, it was perhaps strictly a Mulliner, Park Ward body, and its design was taken over by that concern and was renumbered as 2047.

The first post-war Limousine design was not an aesthetic success, but Park Ward redesigned it with flowing wing lines and in this guise it carried on until 1950. This is one of the later examples, delivered in June 1950 on Silver Wraith chassis WHD11. (Klaus-Josef Rossfeldt)

Limousines
Design 17 (Silver Wraith, 1947-1948)

Park Ward's first post-war Limousine design was for the Rolls-Royce Silver Wraith chassis and had design number 17. It turned out to be a disappointingly dumpy-looking shape despite an appropriate degree of haughtiness and reserve. Nine examples were built, the first one being on chassis WTA33 in March 1947 and the last on WYA60 in March 1948. One example, on chassis WVA20 that was built for the High Commissioner of India in November 1947, was described as a Touring Limousine.

Design 51 (Silver Wraith, 1948-1950)

That first Limousine design was redrawn early in 1948, retaining the original body shape but greatly enhanced by more sweeping wing lines with running-boards and cutaway rear spats. The front doors were still hinged on the centre pillar, and the rear doors still opened in the same direction, giving maximum access to the rear compartment. This one lasted in production for two years, and earned 36 orders; at least ten cars went to the funeral service of the Scottish CWS as mourners' cars, where they worked alongside other Silver Wraiths with that company's own hearse coachwork.

The first body with design 51 to be delivered was on Silver Wraith chassis WYA54 in April 1948, although there were two chassis that were earlier numerically, and the last one was on WHD11, delivered in June 1950. This design was then modified yet again to become number 146.

Design 146 (Silver Wraith, 1949-1952)

Design 146 took the basic elements of that original 1947 design for the Silver Wraith right through to 1952, now with softer lines around the boot and the rearmost side windows. The first one was delivered on chassis WGC20 in December 1949, and the last of

The extra length of the long-wheelbase Silver Wraith gave Park Ward's Limousine designs room to breathe, and this is a later seven-passenger model to design 551. It was photographed outside the coachbuilder's premises.

11 bodies to this design was delivered on WOF46 in January 1952. Like its two predecessors, this design had free-standing R100 headlamps.

Design 213 (Silver Wraith, 1950)

As always, Park Ward responded to requests for individual coachwork, and produced a single Limousine body to design 213 for an Egyptian customer. This was delivered in September 1950 on Silver Wraith chassis LWHD30.

Design 408 (Silver Wraith, 1952-1953)

The arrival of the long-wheelbase Silver Wraith gave Park Ward greater scope, and the company's first Limousine design for it took number 408. The tail followed the lines developed for design 146 on the short-wheelbase chassis, but the rest was mostly new. The front doors were now hinged at their leading edges and the extra length was accommodated in the rear doors, while a full wing line swept across both and a bright lower body trim added an extra touch. The headlamps were also built into the front end.

The first of these bodies was on chassis ALW5 in May 1952, and the last on BLW18 in September 1953. There were nine examples in all, the design being replaced during 1953 by the very similar number 551.

Design 551 (Silver Wraith, 1953-1955)

Design 551 was the replacement Limousine for design 408 on the long-wheelbase Silver Wraith chassis, and in all important respects it looked exactly the same as its predecessor. The key difference was that the radiator grille was set further forward on design 551, so creating a longer bonnet and a rather grander appearance. Spat design varied from car to car, and one example (on chassis CLW42 in June 1954) had a modified design recorded as 551/593. Design 551 was

further developed into design 704, and in this guise the original Limousine shape for the long-wheelbase Silver Wraith chassis continued until the end of 1958.

There were 35 of these bodies, the earliest delivered in October 1953 and the last in April 1955. Several late examples were delivered for the use of HM Ambassadors overseas.

Design 594 (Silver Wraith, 1954)

Just one Limousine body was built to design 594, and was delivered to Liverpool Corporation in March 1954 on Silver Wraith chassis BLW82.

Design 704 Silver Wraith, 1955-1958)

Design 704 was the third and last iteration of Park Ward's "standard" Limousine for the long-wheelbase Silver Wraith chassis. It was very much in the mould of design 551, which it replaced in the autumn of 1955, although the boot was larger and more rounded, and the rear wings were altered to suit that additional length.

Thirty-six examples of this body were built, the first one being delivered on chassis ELW4 in October 1955. The last one was on LHLW42, which was delivered in December 1958 to HM Ambassador in Rio de Janeiro and was one of several delivered for the use of British Ambassadors.

Design 980 (Phantom V, 1959-1961)

Park Ward was given the task of building coachwork for one of the two Rolls-Royce Phantom V prototypes that were built in 1958, and the body it built went initially onto chassis 45EX, later being swapped with the Hooper body on 44EX.

This body was the prototype of design 980, which went on to become the "standard" Phantom V Limousine design from the merged Mulliner, Park Ward division and later became the basis of

Park Ward's design 980 for the Rolls-Royce Phantom V was a classic piece of work, and its lines were preferred over those of the contemporary HJ Mulliner Limousine when the Mulliner, Park Ward division had to focus on a single design. This one is on chassis 5AS7, which was delivered in July 1961 and was the second example of this coachwork type.

the "standard" design for the Phantom VI as well. Remarkably well balanced, and sharing much of its overall approach with the contemporary standard Silver Cloud design, design 980 was used on 126 Phantom V chassis before becoming the "property" of Mulliner, Park Ward in late 1961. There were some variations among these bodies, and at least two examples were built with rear quarter-lights of reduced size which gave the rear-seat occupants greater privacy.

The first production example was on chassis 5AS5 and was displayed on the Rolls-Royce stand at Earls Court in 1959. The last one (numerically) attributed to Park Ward alone was on 5LBX100 and was delivered in October 1961, although the last one actually delivered was on 5LBX96 in Feb 62. Design 980 was also the basis of two "Canberra" Limousines for HM The Queen.

Canberra (Phantom V, 1960-1961)

Design 980 was developed further to create two special State Limousines for HM The Queen with the code name of Canberra. These two bodies were similar to the standard 980 type below the waist, but they had a raised roof line and a Perspex rear section. This section could be covered by a folding metal roof panel which was stowed in the boot when not in use. The two cars were deliberately identical, "Canberra II" actually being delivered first in May 1960 on chassis 5AS33, and "Canberra I" on 5AT34 following in February 1961.

Saloons

Saloons were prominent among Park Ward's early post-war bodies. The company also built one experimental Sports Saloon for the second experimental Rolls-Royce Silver Wraith, 2-SW-1, and delivered it in September 1947. This Sports Saloon had some similarities to the coachbuilder's contemporary "production" bodies for the Silver Wraith, but had larger blind rear quarters, a deeper boot, and side-mounted spare wheels.

However, Park Ward generally kept clear of building Saloon bodies for the Bentley MkVI chassis, concentrating instead on Drophead and Fixed-head Coupé types. There was nevertheless some involvement with the MkVI prototypes: Park Ward completed the Pressed Steel body on 3-B-VI in 1947, adding twin spare wheels and removing the chrome waist moulding. The company also built a pair of one-off Saloon designs.

They also built seven prototype Saloon bodies for the Rolls-Royce Silver Cloud (two) and Bentley S Type (five), although there were no substantive differences from the standard type that went into volume production at Pressed Steel. A few examples of the Park Ward body for the long-wheelbase versions of the Rolls-Royce Silver Cloud and Bentley S Type were built as Saloons, but the majority were Touring Limousines and the design (number 858) is discussed in the section on those types.

Design 13 (Silver Wraith, 1947-1949)

Park Ward's first post-war Saloon design was number

13, for the Rolls-Royce Silver Wraith chassis. This was a plain but elegant Sports Saloon, with separate front and rear wings, and rear-hung doors that swept outwards to cover the running-boards and flanked a central pillar with a distinctive triangular base. The first example was delivered in April 1947 on chassis WTA15, and had the side-mounted spare wheels also seen on the body for the second Silver Wraith prototype; the others, however, did not. The last of 26 bodies to design 13 was on WDC38 in April 1949, by which time the basic design had already been modified to become design number 45 in 1948.

Design 20 (Silver Wraith, 1947-1948)

Saloons to design 20 were more or less contemporary with the Sports Saloon design number 13, and the first example was delivered in August 1947 on Silver Wraith chassis WTA4. This was essentially the same as design 13 but was distinguished by a division. The last of seven examples was delivered in February 1948 on chassis WVA47.

Design 45 (Silver Wraith, 1948-1949)
and Design 46 (1948)

Design 45 for the Silver Wraith chassis was really an evolution of the original post-war Saloon design 13, and was available alongside it for about a year. While the main body remained more or less unchanged, the front wings now blended gracefully into running-boards that met the rear wings, and cutaway rear-wheel spats added a stylish element. The boot was larger and squarer, and several examples were delivered with two-tone colour schemes.

The first of these bodies was delivered in February 1948 on chassis WYA15, and the last of 61 examples in October 1949 was on WFC71. The design was further modified, with a division, as number 46. There were just four of these bodies built over the middle of 1948, the first on chassis WYA72 delivered in April. WZB18 was delivered in August but the earlier chassis WYA78 was not delivered until September, so becoming the last example.

Design 101 (Silver Wraith, 1948)

Like every other coachbuilder, Park Ward wanted to make an impression at the 1948 Earls Court show, and the design it developed for the purpose was a full-width Saloon body to which it gave the name of Wentworth. The upholstery had a very American look to it, with two different colours of leather.

Design number 101 was mounted on an unidentified chassis with left-hand drive for the purposes of the motor show, but it was too extreme for the tastes of the

time and no orders ensued. A customer was found for the sole example of the body, which was re-mounted on right-hand-drive Silver Wraith chassis number WGC47. At the same time, the original slab sides were re-worked and a swage line was added.

Estoril (Experimental, 1949)

By 1949, Rolls-Royce were becoming increasingly aware that coachwork design was moving on and that the style then in production for the Bentley MkVI would soon look outdated. Among the experiments they conducted was to have Park Ward design a new four-light saloon in a more modern idiom for an experimental chassis numbered 7-B-VII. The "VII" in this number indicates that it was considered to be a next step on from the MkVI, which at that stage was envisaged as a six-cylinder car on a 121-inch wheelbase and had the code name of Estoril. (It was not strictly a predecessor of the R Type, which the factory knew as the Bentley VII.)

Park Ward's four-light saloon body was completed by about April 1949 and reflected the company's latest style with front wings that swept back across the doors to meet the rear wing pressings low down. There were full spats over the rear wheels and the traditional radiator shell gave way to a cowled front with vertical grille bars that were recognisably Bentley. Overall, though, the lines were more rounded than those of contemporary Park Ward Saloon bodies. The car apparently did little real testing and was probably scrapped in 1951 when the Estoril disappeared from Crewe's forward products plan; there was no direct follow-up of its body style.

Design 113 (Silver Wraith, 1949-1950)

The Saloon design for the Silver Wraith continued with design 113, which was an evolution of design 45 with a more rounded rear to the body and an equally rounded boot. Chassis WFC72 was the first to have it, in August 1949, and WGC66 was the last of 20 examples, in April 1950.

Design 114 (Silver Wraith, 1949)

Although design 101 for the 1948 Earls Court Show was not a success, some of its features were retained for a second prototype body on the Silver Wraith chassis< which was shown at Earls Court the following year. The window lines, the shape of the boot, and the combination of front-hinged front door and rear-hinged rear door were all the same. However, instead of the slab sides came separate front and wing volumes, linked by a graceful downsweep that ran across the doors. A more conventional front end helped, and

Design 144 was one of Park Ward's most successful and most satisfying, and was introduced in 1950. This example dates from December 1951 and is on Silver Wraith chassis WOF36. (Charles01/WikiMedia Commons)

although design 114 was not repeated, it did lead on to the later Park Ward design 144. As Lawrie Dalton suggested in *Rolls-Royce, the Classic Elegance*, it may well have influenced James Young's WR25 design, and there is no doubt that it was the inspiration behind Freestone & Webb's design 3070 as well. The single example was built on chassis number WGC28.

Design 144 (Silver Wraith, 1950-1953) and Design 314 (1951)

The main impact of design 114 was on Park Ward's own design 144, a hugely successful evolution of the earlier style that saw out the production life of the short-wheelbase Silver Wraith. Its combination of six large windows, a high wing line, and wheel spats of varying designs was extremely elegant and distinctive, and elements of it filtered across to other Park Ward body styles of the early 1950s. It offered plenty of interior space, too. Deliveries of Saloons to design

144 began in early 1950, the first being on chassis WGC56 in January that year. Park Ward built 117 examples of this body, delivering the last one in December 1953 on WVH112 (although WVH113 was the last chassis numerically).

Inevitably, there were variations on the 144 theme. Two early bodies were built as 144s with a four-light version of the design, which later became design 262 and also spawned design 259. Late examples of the six-light 144 had a larger back window. When design 144 was built with a division, it became design 314, which was numerically the last Saloon design for the short-wheelbase Silver Wraith chassis. This was built only once, for chassis WME41, which was delivered in July 1951.

Design 230 (MkVI, 1950) and Design 238 (1951)

Park Ward seems to have been too busy providing coachwork for the Rolls-Royce Silver Wraith to

Also dating from December 1951 is this example of design 144, on Silver Wraith chassis WOF19. These two views of the car show the superb balance that Park Ward achieved with the lines of this six-light Saloon. (Greg Gjerdingen/ WikiMedia Commons)

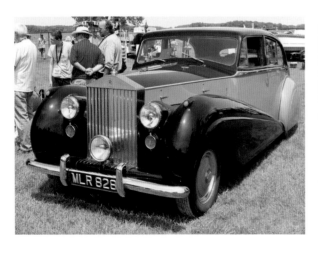

Unmistakably Park Ward, this four-door Saloon was built to design 230 and was delivered in November 1950 on Bentley MkVI chassis B93GT. (Anton van Luijk/ WikiMedia Commons)

spend much time on its smaller Bentley MkVI sibling. As a result, the company only ever built two Saloon bodies for this chassis, both of them six-light types and both of them with clear similarities even though they were actually to two different designs. Both were typical early-1950s shapes with the front wings sweeping back across both doors to join the rear wing pressings low down; they were clearly related to the Drophead Coupé design 100 and to the Fixed-head Coupé design 147.

The earlier car was on chassis B93GT and its body had design number 230. This body had both rear spats and a chrome moulding along the bottom edge of each side, and was in many ways a Saloon version of the Drophead Coupé design number 99. It was delivered in November 1950.

Park Ward's second six-light Saloon body for the Bentley MkVI was built to design number 238, which had the same bright lower moulding but did not have the rear-wheel spats. This one was on chassis number B235HP and was delivered in July 1951.

Design 259 (Silver Wraith, 1951) and Design 262 (1952-1953)

The four-light version of design 144 had a further life in the Park Ward repertoire as designs 259 and 262. There was just one body to design 259, on chassis WME56 delivered in July 1951, and it seems to have been a prototype for the later two bodies to design 262. The first of these was on WVH2, delivered in December 1952, and the second was on WVH 115, which was delivered in August 1953.

Design 295 (R Type, 1953)

There was a single example of six-light Saloon design number 295 on a Bentley R Type chassis, B61SP. This had instantly recognisable Park Ward lines echoing those of the contemporary Drophead Coupé and Fixed-head Coupé bodies.

Design 483 (Silver Wraith, 1953)

Park Ward built only three examples of its first Saloon design for the long-wheelbase Rolls-Royce Silver Wraith, and all of them were on B-series chassis that were delivered in autumn 1953. This was design number 483, which was really a long-wheelbase derivative of the popular design 144 on the earlier Silver Wraith with the shorter wheelbase.

Design 550 (Silver Wraith, 1953-1955) and Design 598 (1954-1955)

Strictly speaking, design 550 was a Touring Saloon, incorporating a half-height division without a glass section. The first example was built on a prototype long-wheelbase Silver Wraith, 41EX, and the design was then introduced to the public at Earls Court in 1953. Recognisably from the same school of thought as design 483 and design 144 which had preceded it on the shorter chassis, design 550 had different wing lines, with the downsweep from the front meeting the rear wing higher up, and fully exposed rear wheels instead of the spatted type.

This was another successful design, and there were 27 examples in addition to the experimental prototype for Rolls-Royce. The first example was on chassis BLW49 and the last was delivered on LDLW163 in June 1955. But Park Ward could never be accused of

This is a Touring Saloon to design 550, with an attractive two-colour finish to set off its lines. Changing its half-division (not visible here) for a full-height division allowed Park Ward to turn it into a Touring Limousine. This example is probably Silver Wraith DLW52, the 1954 Scottish Show exhibit.

not making the most of a good design, and design 550 was adapted to make a Saloon with Division, number 598. There were 17 of these bodies, the earliest on chassis BLW76 in April 1954. The last examples were delivered in summer 1955, DLW168 in June 1955 being the last in date order, although the last in chassis number terms was on DLW170, which went to the entertainer George Formby in May that year.

Further evolutions of design 550 then produced the design 702 Touring Saloon and the design 703 Touring Limousine.

Design 702 (Silver Wraith, 1955-1958)
Touring Saloon 550 evolved into Touring Saloon 702 in 1955, and Silver Wraith ELW15 introduced it at that year's Earls Court show. The two bodies were very similar indeed to look at, although the later variant had the latest style of bumpers, as designed for the Silver Cloud. Less visibly, design 702 also had different spare wheel stowage arrangements, with the wheel concealed below the boot floor instead of on display inside the boot. There were just seven examples of this body, and the last one was delivered in March 1958 on chassis LGLW2.

Touring Limousines
Design 703 (Silver Wraith, 1955-1958)
Park Ward adapted its design 702 Touring Saloon to make a Touring Limousine, leaving the outside unchanged but extending the division from half-height to full height. There were 14 of these bodies, the first on chassis ELW9 in October 1955 and the last in July 1958 on LHLW9.

Design 858 (Silver Cloud LWB and S Type LWB, 1957-1959)
When Rolls-Royce decided to create a Touring Limousine by extending the Silver Cloud and Bentley S Type chassis, Park Ward was given the job of modifying the standard saloon body to suit. This was known as design 858, although at the Park Ward works it was also called the 4SSC, which apparently stood for "4-inch stretched Silver Cloud". The work involved fitting a longer roof, floorpan and rear doors, while retaining the lines of the original body, and the transformation was so successful that it was not always easy to distinguish the long-wheelbase model from the standard type at a glance.

There were 87 of these bodies on the long-wheelbase Silver Cloud and a further 23 on its Bentley equivalent. The design was carried over to the Silver Cloud II but the only example, on LLCA12 in January 1960, was built as a Saloon with Division. There were no examples on the Bentley S2. The design remained in production for the Silver Cloud III (and Bentley S3), although it was by then a product of the merged Mulliner, Park Ward division. Most of the bodies to design 858 were built as Touring Limousines, but there were also some built as Saloons without a division.

Two-door Saloons
As far as Park Ward were concerned, two-door Saloon bodies were for the Bentley Continental chassis only. The company built examples on both the R and S Type Continental chassis, but there were none on the S2 Continental, even though design 991 (the Koren Drophead Coupé) did appear on that chassis. The closed version of this design would not appear on S2 Continentals until after the Mulliner, Park Ward merger.

Design 648 (R Type Continental, 1954-1955)
Park Ward two-door Saloon coachwork for the R Type Continental chassis shared a common design with the company's Drophead Coupés. This commonality ensured that the closed models had a three-box shape rather than the fastback style that distinguished the Mulliner-bodied Continentals.

There were just two two-door Saloon bodies, both

The close relationship between the closed body (design 701) for the S Type Continental and its drophead equivalent (design 700) is immediately obvious by comparing this example with the earlier pictures. This was a highly successful design, even if the tail fins were somewhat controversial.

on D-series chassis. BC24D was delivered first, in September 1954, and the second car was BC29D, which is thought to have been on the Park Ward stand at the 1954 Earls Court Show.

Design 701 (S Type Continental, 1955-1957) and Design 872 (1957-1959)

Park Ward's all-aluminium bodies for the Bentley S Type Continental were developed from John Blatchley's design for the late R Type Continentals, with just a few changes to suit the longer (123in) wheelbase of the new chassis. Among those changes was that the door handle on the S Type bodies was above the swage line rather than below it. These bodies had discreet tail fins above separate circular stop/tail lamp, reflector, and turn indicator lamps. Many cars were delivered with two-tone paintwork, with the two colours divided by the swage line that ran along the body sides.

Two-toning of the coachwork on the S Type Continental made for a most attractive appearance. (Luc106/WikiMedia Commons)

There were 69 examples of the Park Ward two-door Saloon body to design 701, beginning with one on chassis BC10AF in October 1955. Of these, 24 had left-hand drive. There were two variants (known to Park Ward as Issue 1 and Issue 2). The earlier bodies had three individual tail lamps on each side, but the later ones used the tail light units from the standard saloons, which blended into the small fins on the rear wings and provided a neater appearance.

Design 701 was then modified in 1957 for the 1958 season, becoming design 872. The alterations were famously carried out using an airbrush on a photograph of the earlier design. The changes were at the rear of the passenger cabin, where the quarter-lights were enlarged and a wraparound rear window was added, leaving much slimmer rear pillars than on the original design. There were 27 examples of this body, of which 11 were on left-hand drive chassis. The final examples reached their owners in July 1959, the last one numerically being BC24GN.

Another two-colour body to design 701 is seen on an S Type Continental chassis in Australia. (Jeremy/WikiMedia Commons)

Bearing Harold Radford's personal registration plate HAR 1, this is probably the very first of the Mk I Countryman bodies, on a 1948 Bentley MkVI chassis.

RADFORD

Harold Radford had been a Rolls-Royce and Bentley dealer in London's West End during the 1930s, and during the 1939-1945 war he supplied estate car-type conversions to the armed forces. He had the bodies for these built under contract by small coachbuilders and, after the war, he started out by modifying war surplus vehicles

Perhaps inspired by the vogue for wooden-bodied "utility" estate cars, which were exempt from Purchase Tax in the late 1940s, he drew up a body design along these lines for the Bentley Mk VI. He had the first one constructed for him in 1948 by a small Southgate coachbuilding company called Seary & McReady (see below). An enthusiastic Radford took it to that year's Cannes concours d'élégance, where it won first prize. Two years later Radford acquired Seary & McReady to form Harold Radford (Coachbuilders) Ltd, and in 1951 exhibited a new version of his coachwork at the Earls Court Motor Show.

Rolls-Royce designated Radford as an official coachbuilder, and during the 1950s and early 1960s the company focussed on versatile conversions of standard Rolls-Royce and Bentley coachwork, which bore the name of Countryman. In 1954, Radford sold a controlling interest in his company to the Provincial Traction Co, and finally sold out to the Swain Group in 1957. Sales were then handled by the HR Owen dealer chain, itself owned by the Swain Group.

Radford also became involved with the estate cars built on six-cylinder Silver Cloud chassis in 1959 by HJ Mulliner. The Countryman conversions remained available until 1965, but from 1963 Radford entered a new era of popularity with his customised Mini Coopers, which created a new and popular vogue for such cars among wealthy celebrities.

The MkI Countryman, 1948-1949

The first Countryman bodies were produced for Bentley MkVI chassis between mid-1948 and mid-1949. There were nine of them, all fully coachbuilt, with alloy panels clad with oak or beech trim and a choice of mahogany or walnut veneer at the rear so that they looked like wooden-bodied estate cars. They also had a two-piece tailgate and a folding rear seat, which allowed maximum use of the rear load area. Electric windows were among the options.

The MkII Countryman, 1951-1953

Once again built on the Bentley MkVI chassis, the Mk II Countryman was introduced to the public at the 1951 Earls Court show by B40MD. This time, the design was metal-panelled, and was a four-door saloon rather than a utility estate like the Mk I. The design incorporated picnic and other items carefully stowed in compartments within the body. A total of nine examples were built, the last one being on B495NY, which was delivered in February 1953.

The coachbuilt MkII Countryman was a stylish machine. This one is on Bentley MkVI B207LH and was delivered in March 1952. It was the only MkII to be delivered with a conventional boot. (©Jack Snell/Flickr)

All closed up, only the opening lines around the rear window for the "hatchback" seemed a little unusual.

The Countryman MkII was a very different style of body from the MkI, and was essentially a modern-looking four-door Saloon. This one was photographed in 1951 and may well be the first of its kind.

Picnic tables could be fitted to the backs of the front seats, and the rear armrests doubled as storage compartments.

The boot lid on the MkII was arranged to open right up and give access to a load floor that could be extended by folding the rear seats down.

The rear load area of the MkII Countryman was remarkably capacious, and made the Radford body much more versatile than any other Saloon on offer at the time.

The later Countryman Saloon was based on a standard Bentley R Type (or Rolls-Royce Silver Dawn) saloon, and there is nothing immediately visible here to suggest that this 1954 car has been modified…

… but in this rear view of the same car (with a standard R Type in the background), the changes are more obvious.

Picnic sets were high on the Radford agenda, as on this MkIII model.

The MkIII Countryman, 1952-1953

When the R Type (and "big-boot" Silver Dawn) were introduced in 1952, Radford continued to plough the same furrow. The Countryman was redesignated a MkIII type, and Radford offered a menu of options, with the result that no two cars had to be exactly the same. Among these options were picnic tables, drinks cabinets, an electric kettle, and a razor. Ten of the MkIII Countryman bodies were built on the Bentley chassis, and three more on the Silver Dawn.

The Countryman Saloons

The MkI, MkII and MkIII Countryman models delivered by Radford had fully coachbuilt bodies, but during the currency of the Bentley R Type chassis, Radford developed a way of offering most of their benefits at a more attractive price.

He started with a standard steel saloon, converting it by enlarging the boot upwards and dividing its lid into two sections, the lower hinging downwards. The upper section was combined with the rear window, and this assembly hinged upwards like a hatchback. The rear seat backrest was typically split into two and could be folded down electrically, while the front seats backs could be folded down to form a bed. There were 11 of these conversions, all on the R Type chassis.

Silver Cloud and S Type conversions

Radford retained the principle established by his earlier R Type conversions for his work on the Silver Cloud and Bentley S Type. This meant that standard bodies were modified to suit the customer's wishes, using an extensive range of options. In the later 1950s, it appears that many of these alterations were carried out for Radford by HJ Mulliner at Chiswick. However, by the early 1960s there is evidence that some work was being done at the former Freestone & Webb works in Willesden. (By this stage, Freestone & Webb had ceased coachbuilding but the company had joined Radford in the Swain Group.)

Each car was specified from a list of 38 options designed to make the car more useful for a country lifestyle. These included a boot lid that was three inches deeper than standard, front seats that reclined fully to make a bed, split-folding rear seat backs, a Tudor Webasto folding fabric sunroof, fine lines painted along the wings, and a fishing rod container carried below the doors. Inside the car, the options included an expanding sunglasses pouch for either sun visor, a folding wire mesh dog's cage, an extending picnic table (that slid out from the boot floor), a picnic kit of kettle and washbasin in the boot, and removable "toadstool" cushions that fitted onto the rear over-riders. Customers could also order magazine pockets behind the front seats, a cubby box within the centre rear armrest, and compartments let into the front doors that were typically used to carry glasses, decanters and flasks.

Most conversions were carried out on nearly-new cars already registered in their owner's name in order to avoid the Purchase Tax that would otherwise have been levied in Britain. However, the exact number of cars that had this type of Radford conversion remains in dispute, not least because no detailed records survive. Bernard King quotes totals of 35 Silver Clouds (including two long-wheelbase cars) and 37 S Types (including one long-wheelbase car).

The Safari estate cars, 1959

Radford also put his name to a total of four estate bodies on the six-cylinder Silver Cloud chassis, two of them on the long-wheelbase variant. These were

known as Safari Town & Country types, and in this case it was HJ Mulliner who did the metalwork of the conversion, while Radford did the interior trimming and added the special equipment. All four bodies had a split-folding rear seat.

On the standard wheelbase, HJ Mulliner knew the design as number 7506, and the two estates were delivered in April and May 1959, on chassis LSLG112 and LSMH65 respectively. The first car was displayed at the 1959 New York Auto Show, and in fact all four Safari estates were built on left-hand-drive chassis. The bodies for the two long-wheelbase estates had design number 7503, and both LCLC38 and LCLC42 were delivered in August 1959.

The folding seat back allowed additional luggage to be stowed in the rear of the MkIII conversion.

There were four estates on the Silver Cloud chassis, built with the assistance of HJ Mulliner. This is one of the two standard-wheelbase examples.

REALL

Reall had started out building bus bodies in West London in the 1920s, when it was known as R.E.A.L. – a name derived from its founder, RE Allman. In the first half of the 1930s, the company broke into the car market but went into voluntary liquidation in 1936. It emerged from this as Reall, with new premises in Cippenham (Buckinghamshire), and focussed its activities on hearses, school buses and commercial bodies. The company eventually closed in 1966.

Reall built just one hearse body on a Rolls-Royce Silver Wraith chassis, which was ELW42 of January 1957. It was delivered to a customer in Ireland.

RIPPON

Rippon Bros of Huddersfield in Yorkshire was Britain's oldest coachbuilding company, with a history that could be traced back to 1555. The company became a royal carriage supplier, and built its first motor car body on a Rolls-Royce chassis in 1905.

Rippon worked on most of the grand chassis of the 1930s, becoming known for robustly made, slightly heavy bodies which focussed on luxury and comfort rather than style. These included several hundred bodies for Rolls-Royce and Bentley chassis. Customers were largely drawn from the wealthy mill owners of Yorkshire and Lancashire, and Rippon coachwork was acknowledged as in the very top class.

After the war, the company resumed coachbuilding but quantities were very much more limited. Between 1948 and 1951, Rippon regularly showed both a Silver Wraith and a MkVI Bentley on its stand at the Earls Court Show, but in 1952 there was only a Silver Wraith, which was the last body this coachbuilder

This fascinating picture gives an insight into coachbuilding at Rippon in the late 1940s. The four-light Saloon body is being completed on Bentley MkVI B372EY, which would represent the company at Earls Court in 1949. (Huddersfield Examiner)

constructed for either of the two marques.

Rippon Bros withdrew from coachbuilding in 1958, but continued to function as a dealership. They then became part of the Appleyard Group and were the main supplier of spares for pre-1965 Bentley and Rolls-Royce cars until that business was transferred to Jack Barclay Ltd in the mid-1990s.

Four-light Saloons

There were two four-light Saloon bodies on Bentley MkVI chassis in 1948-1949, the earlier one on B22BH being the first design that Ronnie Matthews did after his appointment as Rippon's chief designer. This car was displayed on the Rippon stand at Earls Court in 1948, with Silver Wraith Touring Limousine WYA86 (see below). It was delivered to its first owner in December 1948.

The second and very similar body was built on B372EY during 1949, differing from the earlier one mainly in the addition of rectangular vents below the horn grilles at the front. This one was shown on the Rippon stand at Earls Court in 1949 (with Silver Wraith WFC29, see below), and was delivered to its new owner in January 1950.

More insight into the Rippon workshops comes from this picture, showing the Touring Limousine body on Silver Wraith WYA86 in preparation for display at the 1948 Earls Court show.

HOW MANY BODIES?
The figures below have been calculated by chassis type.

Rolls-Royce		Bentley	
Silver Wraith	5	MkVI	5
Total	**5**	**Total**	**5**

Rippon's last coachwork for the Bentley MkVI was this Saloon on Bentley MkVI B2MD, a design derived from a Park Ward original.

One of the two Rippon exhibits at Earls Court in 1951 was this most elegant Saloon on Silver Wraith chassis WOF4.

Six-light Saloons

Rippon built three six-light Saloon bodies, of which one was for a Bentley MkVI and the other two for Rolls-Royce Silver Wraith chassis.

Both Saloon bodies on Silver Wraith chassis had the curved sloping boot characteristic of this coachbuilder. Their upper bodies had close similarities, and both bodies had cutaway rear spats. However, the 1951 body (on WOF4, delivered in May 1952) had a higher wing-line than the 1952 body (on WVH4, delivered in November 1952), which in consequence actually looked older.

WOF4 was on Rippon's stand at the 1951 Earls Court Show, together with Bentley MkVI B2MD (see below). WVH4 was alone on the 1952 Earls Court Show stand, and was the last Rolls-Royce chassis to be bodied by this coachbuilder. According to a report in the Huddersfield Daily Examiner, it took nearly 12 months for this body to be built by Ronnie Matthews, who was the foreman of the Body Shop and the company's chief designer, with two apprentices, twin brothers Trevor and Malcolm Gibson.

While these two bodies were quite distinctive, the sole six-light saloon body on the Bentley MkVI chassis appears to have been a copy of a 1950 Park Ward design (number 230, on MkVI chassis B93GT). The Rippon body was built on chassis B2MD in 1951 and was displayed at that year's Earls Court Show along with Silver Wraith WOF4 (see above). It was delivered in December 1951 and was the last Rippon body on a post-war Bentley chassis.

Wood and metal panels combine here to make the attractive "Touring Saloon" body on Bentley MkVI B91FU, built in 1950. (copyright unknown)

Touring Limousine

Rippon's single Touring Limousine was a somewhat upright and formal body on a Rolls-Royce Silver Wraith, not dissimilar to those that the company had built in the later 1930s. It was on chassis number WYA86 and was displayed on the company's stand at Earls Court in 1948 together with Bentley MkVI four-light Saloon B22BH (see above).

Touring Saloon

Rippon built three "Touring Saloons" in 1950-1951, but in reality these bodies were estate cars of the type then popular because they allowed owners to avoid Purchase Tax (for further details, see the entry for David Joel). They incorporated metal panels but were made to look as if they were built of wood. The first

The third and last of Rippon's "Touring Saloons" was on Silver Wraith chassis WHD87, and was different from both the coachbuilder's other bodies of this type.

one was on a Bentley MkVI chassis and was delivered in May 1950. There was one other on a MkVI and a single example on a Rolls-Royce Silver Wraith, and both of these dated from later in 1950.

The first of the Bentley Touring Saloons was built on MkVI chassis B91FU, and had the dubious distinction of being the only post-war Rippon body on either of the two marques that was not displayed at the Earls Court Motor Show. The second Bentley was on chassis B349GT, and it was shown on the coachbuilder's stand at Earls Court in 1950 together with the similarly-bodied Silver Wraith before being delivered in December 1950. Both these bodies on MkVI chassis seem to have used the wings of the Standard Steel cars, but there were some differences between them, notably around the rear end.

The Touring Saloon for the Silver Wraith was on chassis number WHD87, and was the last of the three bodies of this type to be delivered, going to its new owner in March 1951. This body differed from the one for the Bentley with which it shared the 1950

Earls Court stand in having a more sweeping design, and was, unusually for an estate, built with spatted rear wheels.

Two-door Saloon
Familiar descriptive problems come into play for this single body on the Rolls-Royce Silver Wraith chassis. Sometimes described as a Fixed-head Coupé, it is probably more accurately described as a two-door Saloon. Built on chassis number WFC29 in 1949, it was delivered to its first owner in March 1950. The sloping boot was typical of Rippon designs but separate front wings were distinctly conservative by this time and made the body look rather old-fashioned. The car was displayed at Earls Court on the Rippon stand in 1949, together with Bentley MkVI four-light Saloon B372EY (see above).

RONALD KENT
There is no hard evidence at all about this coachbuilder, who built a single body on a Bentley MkVI chassis. It might be reasonable to suppose that the company was based in Northamptonshire, as was the customer, but that is no more than speculation. The Bentley Motors records show the body as a Saloon, but no photographs have ever been found to confirm this, and (as Bernard King suggests), the body might well have been a shooting brake of the type popular at the time to avoid taxation. The chassis number was B290BH, and the completed car was delivered in September 1950.

SCOTTISH CWS
Commercial body building was a sideline of the Scottish Co-Operative Wholesale Society, and was carried out at workshops in Broughton. Between 1949 and 1951, these workshops constructed the hearse bodies on a fleet of Rolls-Royce Silver Wraith hearses that was used by the funeral business of the Scottish CWS.

There were 27 of these remarkably square-rigged hearse bodies, which were clearly designed to be functional rather than elegant. The earliest was completed in April 1949 on chassis WYA3, and the last in October 1951 on WHD70, although the last chassis numerically was WHD74.

SEARY & MCREADY
Seary & McReady was a small coachbuilding company with premises at Chase Road, Southgate, in north-west London. Its main claim to fame was that it was sub-contracted by Harold Radford (qv) in 1948 to build the bodies for his Town & Country estate cars on Bentley MkVI chassis. In 1950, Radford bought

a controlling interest in the company, renamed it Harold Radford (Coachbuilders) Ltd, and moved its workshops to Ealing.

However, Seary & McReady also built a pair of estate car bodies under their own name in 1950 and 1951, on Bentley MkVI chassis, probably during a lull between the MkI and MkII Radford Countryman models. No pictures of these have come to light, and so it is impossible to say whether they differed significantly from the estate cars built on behalf of Radford. They were on chassis numbered B75FU and B95JN.

SIMPSON & SLATER

Simpson & Slater was a Nottingham coachbuilder that had been active since at least 1925, and is best known today as a prominent builder of hearses. The company was responsible for rebodying a number of Rolls-Royce chassis as hearses in the 1950s and 1960s

This coachbuilder built just one body on a new Silver Wraith chassis, which was a six-light saloon for WDC69. The completed car was delivered in June 1950. The body design was fairly conservative for the period and incorporated a rear side window shape that may well have been inspired by Hooper and has sometimes caused this body to be attributed to that company.

VANDEN PLAS

A tortuous series of business manoeuvres led to the establishment of Vanden Plas (England) 1923 Ltd, ultimately descended from the Belgian Vanden Plas coachwork company but after 1923 independent of it. The British company enjoyed a fruitful relationship with the original Bentley company, and during the 1930s also built 200 bodies for Derby Bentley chassis. Their bodies for Rolls-Royce chassis in this period were far less numerous, however.

After the Second World War, Vanden Plas put in an unsuccessful bid to build the standard bodies for the Bentley MkVI before becoming part of the

Austin Motor Company in 1946 and subsequently the builder of its limousine bodies. Its only post-war bodies for either of the marques based at Crewe were 21 on the Bentley MkVI chassis in 1946-1948. These shared common design features that, unsurprisingly, had marked similarities to some of the designs that the company also produced on Austin chassis. They consisted of 14 Saloons, six Drophead Coupés, and a single Fixed-head Coupé.

Drophead Coupés

The six Drophead Coupé bodies were built to Vanden Plas design number 1727. The earliest chassis, B12AK, was actually the last example delivered and was later fitted with a removable hardtop, but it is not clear whether this was actually made by Vanden Plas. Deliveries began in August 1947 and all were completed by the end of the year except for one, which took place in March 1948.

Fixed-head coupé

Bentley MkVI B269BG was delivered in March 1948 with a Vanden Plas body that has always been described as a Fixed-head Coupé. However, there are some reasons for thinking that this was actually another Drophead Coupé with a removable hardtop, exactly like B12AK described above (which was delivered in the same month).

Saloons

The saloon body by Vanden Plas for the Bentley MkVI was a four-light type with design number 1732, and there were 14 examples of it. These bodies seem not to have proved very durable, and a former owner has suggested that their frames, made of Canadian pine, rotted very quickly.

The very first (on B8AK) was delivered in October 1946 and was also the very first post-war body that Vanden Plas built; it had originally been intended for the new owner-driver Rolls-Royce model that was not put into production (and later appeared as the

The number-plate reads "BM 1946" (Bentley Motors, 1946), so this Vanden Plas Saloon body can only be on Bentley MkVI B8AK.

The sole Simpson & Slater body on a new post-war Rolls-Royce chassis was this one on Silver Wraith chassis WDC69. (Klaus-Josef Rossfeldt)

Silver Dawn). With a single exception, the remainder were delivered between August and December 1947, and the last example (on B285BG) was delivered in June 1948. It was also the last Vanden Plas body on a Bentley chassis

VINCENTS

William Vincent Ltd was established as a coachbuilding company in Reading in 1806 and built its first motor car body in 1899. Its first body on a Rolls-Royce chassis followed just seven years later. During the 1920s, Vincents became one of Britain's largest coachbuilders for both luxury cars and commercial vehicles, but from the middle of the 1930s its focus was increasingly on the commercial side and it was particularly well known for its horse boxes.

After the 1939-1945 war, the company returned to its core business and continued to build on Rolls-Royce chassis. There were no bodies on new Bentley chassis, although Vincents did build some shooting brake types on older examples. There was a Vincents stand with a Silver Wraith at every Earls Court Show from 1948 to 1952, but the company bodied only two other Silver Wraith chassis, one a hearse and one for a member of the Vincent family. As demand for coachwork slowed, so Vincents withdrew from the business in the mid-1950s and the business developed into a chain of car dealerships.

Although Vincents were listed as approved coachbuilders in the first sales catalogue for the Bentley R Type, no bodies are known to have been built for that chassis. All seven Vincents bodies on post-war Rolls-Royce chassis were for the Silver Wraith. Their designs were rather upright and formal, and sometimes reminiscent of HJ Mulliner, although

This was the first post-war Vincents body on a Rolls-Royce chassis. This six-light Saloon on Silver Wraith WTA40 looks heavy and old-fashioned by the standards of 1948, when it was built.

some had a certain awkwardness about them. There were Saloons with both six- and four-light designs, and a single Hearse.

Four-light Saloons

Five of the Vincents bodies on the Silver Wraith chassis were four-light Saloons, although they were not all to the same design. WZB30 was at Earls Court in 1948, WOF1 in 1951, and WVH3 – the last Rolls-Royce chassis that the company bodied – in 1952. The other two were on chassis WFC63 and WGC64, and both were delivered in June 1950. WGC64 had been Vincents' 1949 Earls Court show exhibit.

Hearse

The single Hearse body was delivered in February 1949 and was on chassis number WZB20. It was later shipped to the USA, where it was converted into a station wagon for further use.

Six-light Saloon

Vincents' single six-light Saloon body on chassis WTA40 was delivered in January 1948 and was the company's first body on a post-war Rolls-Royce chassis.

WESTMINSTER

The name of Westminster Motor Supplies is attached to a single Bentley MkVI chassis, and very little is known about either the coachbuilder or the car itself. We do know that Westminster Motor Supplies were at 29 Battersea Bridge Road in south-west London, but that is all.

MkVI chassis B372BH was delivered in January 1948 and the Bentley Motors records list it as a Saloon.

Vincents built just one hearse body, on Silver Wraith WZB20. It was pictured in the USA after its new life as a station wagon had begun.

However (as Bernard King notes) there is a good possibility that this was actually a utility estate body of the type that avoided Purchase Tax and attracted a greater ration of petrol than ordinary private cars. There are no known pictures of the Westminster body, although the chassis survives as the basis of a "special".

WINDOVER

Windover had been founded in 1796, and had been a carriage builder in Huntingdon throughout the 19th century. Recognising the desirability of having representation in the capital city, it opened new workshops in Colindale, north-west London, in 1924. During the 1930s, Windover worked on many quality chassis, and built several hundred bodies on Rolls-Royce chassis, plus a smaller number on Bentleys.

Best known for its formal limousines, and always ready to add an air of formality to its body designs of all kinds, the company had close links with Vanden Plas, a near neighbour in Cricklewood, and used that company's designs on occasion. Some bodies were built for stock and some to individual order, but standardised bodies were never a Windover speciality.

After the war, Windover never recovered to its pre-war levels of car body production. There were just four bodies for the Silver Wraith chassis and four more for the Bentley MkVI, and the last of these eight was for a Silver Wraith in 1950. Meanwhile, Windover had diversified into passenger coach bodywork after 1947, quickly earning a reputation for distinctive designs and a high standard of finish. There were bodies for Beardmore taxis and hearses, and in the early 1950s for some of the Green Goddess fire appliances built for Civil Defence. However, Windover sold out to the London car dealer Henly's in 1956, and coachbuilding work ceased that year.

(Note: This coachbuilder is often referred to as "Windovers", and this name appeared on at least some of the maker's plates for its post-war bodies on Rolls-Royce and Bentley chassis. The company seems to have been rather inconsistent with its own name in this period. One late advertisement refers to a "Windover enclosed limousine" on a Silver Wraith chassis, and yet the company name is shown as "Windovers Ltd".)

Drophead Coupé

Windover built just one Drophead Coupé body in this period, to its design number 101 for the Bentley MkVI chassis. This was delivered in August 1947 on chassis B108AK. Recognisably from the same stable as the 1947 two-door Saloon body on B74AK, this body nevertheless had a longer tail that balanced the lines very well.

Limousines

Three of the four Windover bodies on the Silver Wraith chassis were six-light Limousines. Two had design number 135 in 1947-1948, but the design number of the third body is not known. These Windover bodies were distinctly conservative, perhaps even rather old-fashioned, in their design.

Design 135

Design number 135 featured outswept lower door panels with lines that were otherwise razor-edged and formal. All four doors were rear-hinged. The two bodies to this design were on chassis numbered WTA 80 (delivered in November 1947) and WVA 69 (March 1948).

Design (number not known)

The third Limousine body was built on chassis number WCB9 and delivered in August 1950. It is very similar indeed to the two early bodies built to design number 135 and may well be yet another to that design, modified with cutaway rear wheel spats. It became the last Windover body on a Rolls-Royce chassis.

Saloon

There was just one Saloon body, which was a six-light razor-edge type for Bentley MkVI chassis number B313CD. The design number is unknown. Although its overall shape brought no surprises, it had an unusual vee-windscreen that was matched by a split rear window. Windovers thought highly enough of it to have it represent them at the 1948 Earls Court Show. B313CD was delivered to its first owner in February 1949. It became the last Windover body on a Bentley chassis.

Two-door Saloons

There were two Windovers two-door Saloons on the Bentley MkVI chassis, and one on the Silver Wraith. All three were built to different designs.

The lines of Windover's sole Drophead Coupé on a Bentley MkVI are very pleasing, and also very much of their time. (Klaus-Josef Rossfeldt)

Design 35

The earlier body was built on chassis B95AJ and was delivered in April 1947. It was built to design number 35, which was not a very happy one, featuring lockers in the tops of the front wings and some strange sculpted lines that were somewhat self-consciously modernistic.

Design 110

The second two-door Saloon body had Windover's design number 110 and was built on chassis number B74AK. The completed car was delivered in June 1947, and the coachwork design was altogether more conventional than the earlier design number 35. It had rounded lines and separate wings typical of the time, plus dummy landau irons. Some commentators have described it as a pillarless coupé.

Design (number unknown)

The third and last of the Windover two-door Saloon bodies was on Rolls-Royce Silver Wraith chassis WYA17 and was delivered in July 1948. It featured a reverse-rake trailing edge for the rear quarter-windows, and cutaway rear wheel spats in the fashion of the time.

WOODALL NICHOLSON

Woodall Nicholson was established in Halifax in 1873, absorbing an earlier coachbuilding business. After a financial crisis in 1933, the company began to specialise in building hearse bodies on second-hand Rolls-Royce chassis, and after the Second World War became one of Britain's major hearse builders. The company was bought out in 1982 by its major competitor, Coleman Milne, and was closed down in 1987.

The company built just three hearses on post-war Rolls-Royce chassis. The first two were on Silver Wraith chassis WYA38 in 1948 and WGC78 in 1950. The third was on Phantom V 5VC29 in 1964, and was the only hearse known to have been built on a new post-war Phantom chassis.

Woodall Nicholson also converted a number of Rolls-Royce Silver Cloud models from standard Saloons into hearses in the 1960s and 1970s.

Woodall Nicholson is the only coachbuilder known to have built a hearse body on a brand-new Rolls-Royce Phantom V chassis. This is it, pictured appropriately on duty at the funeral of a Rolls-Royce enthusiast.
(Klaus-Josef Rossfeldt)

Chapter Four

Coachwork by Overseas Coachbuilders A-Z

Many overseas buyers of a Rolls-Royce or Bentley chassis were content to take it with British-built coachwork as well, perhaps because it added to the "Britishness" of the whole vehicle. Nevertheless, a number of buyers – particularly in continental Europe – decided to have coachwork built in their own countries.

There must have been several reasons for this. At this level of the market, lower costs can probably be discounted as a motive. Patriotism or the wish to support local trade must have been among the main reasons. Another might have been habit; and yet another would have been the wish simply to have something different or unusual. A few American buyers patronised continental European coachbuilders – particularly when Italian coachwork was fashionable in the 1950s – and a small number had coachwork built in the USA.

The largest number of bodies (51) came from France, which was justifiably proud of its coachbuilding tradition. Second in terms of overall number was Switzerland, with 36 bodies; coachbuilders here had specialised in Cabriolet bodies for many years and produced a number on the post-war Rolls-Royce and

---

WHO AND HOW MANY? OVERSEAS COACHWORK ON ROLLS-ROYCE AND BENTLEY CHASSIS FROM 1945

The totals here reflect the number of bodies actually built and not the number of chassis involved.

Some of the bodies were new ones on older chassis, or, in one case, an older body transferred to a new chassis.

Country	Coachbuilder	Bentley	Rolls-Royce	Total	Country	Coachbuilder	Bentley	Rolls-Royce	Total
Belgium	Van den Plas	0	1	1		Pinin Farina	6	1	7
France	Chapron	0	4	4		Vignale	0	1	1
	Facel Metallon	10	0	10	**Netherlands**	Roos	1	0	1
	Figoni & Falaschi	1	0	1	**Sweden**	Gustaf Nordberg	0	1	1
	Franay	17	13	30	**Switzerland**	Beutler	2	0	2
	Poberejsky	1	1	2		Graber	30	1	32
	Saoutchik	1	1	2		Köng	4	0	4
	Vanvooren	2	0	2		Worblaufen	4	0	4
Germany	Wendler	1	0	1	**USA**	Brewster	0	1	1
Italy	Bertone	1	0	1		Inskip	0	3	3
	Ghia	1	2	3	**Totals**		**83**	**30**	**113**

The Arnolt Bentley was certainly individual in its appearance. The rear-hinged rear doors were very much of their time, but the inset auxiliary driving lamps were unusual for the period. Michelotti's lines look best in a dead side view, where the shape of the rear wing pressing makes best sense. (Simon Clay)

The Bertone badge was fitted to each front wing. (Simon Clay)

Bentley chassis. There were 12 bodies from Italian coachbuilders, 3 from American companies, and just one each from Belgium, Germany, the Netherlands and Sweden. These are the confirmed totals, but there were probably at least two more: the names of the coachbuilders are not known for one Bentley MkVI chassis delivered to Belgium (B374DA, in 1948), and one delivered to France (B64CF, also in 1948).

The availability of left-hand-drive chassis from 1949 may have improved export sales of the two marques but seems not to have made any appreciable difference to the number of customers who ordered coachwork from companies outside Britain.

BERTONE

Although Bertone had been a major player among Italian coachbuilders in the 1930s, the company struggled to re-establish itself in the difficult climate after 1945. Nuccio Bertone took over as head of the company from his father Giovanni in 1950, and as a last ditch attempt to keep the business alive, father and son bought a pair of MG TDs and clothed them with new bodywork in time for the 1952 Turin motor show. The gamble paid off: US importer SH "Wacky" Arnolt placed an order for around 100 bodies on the later MG TF chassis, and followed this a year later with orders for a design on the Bristol 404 chassis. In

The three-piece rear window was needed because glass making technology could not cope with a curved one-piece screen of such a size at the time. Arnolt was familiarly known as "Wacky" Arnolt, as the rear number-plate shows. That number-plate also suggests, incorrectly, that the chassis was a Bentley MkVI. (Simon Clay)

The bench front seat was perhaps inspired by the common American practice of the time. (Simon Clay)

Arnolt was not averse to advertising his company discreetly on the Bentley…

… and was similarly keen to claim ownership of it. (Simon Clay)

The metal dashboard painted to match the exterior panels was characteristic of Italian coachbuilding at the time, although the wooden centre panel was not. (Simon Clay)

Arnolt stamped his identity all over the car. Each of the three hip flasks is engraved with his initials…

… and of course there was a corresponding stowage box for Madame's essentials. (Simon Clay)

due course, there would be a Bertone-bodied Aston Martin for Arnolt as well.

At the time, Giovanni Michelotti was working freelance for Bertone, and he was responsible for the MG design. Arnolt liked it enough to have Bertone and Michelotti design a scaled-up version of the body with four doors as his personal car. He had this constructed on a 1953 Bentley R Type chassis. The high waistline and shallow windows did not adapt well to the proportions of the Bentley and, as Rob de la Rive Box and Richard Crump put it in The Automotive Art of Bertone, "one gets the impression that Bertone lacked courage with the product."

The Arnolt Bentley has variously been described as being on a Bentley MkVII and even a Bentley R Continental chassis. It is in fact on a standard left-hand-drive R Type, number B43LSP. It was also the only Bertone-bodied Bentley or Rolls-Royce built in this period.

BEUTLER

Brothers Fritz and Ernst Beutler both spent time learning their craft with a variety of Swiss coachbuilders, most notably when they were employed by the Worblaufen coachworks between 1937 and 1942. As the end of the war in Europe brought the prospect of new opportunities, the two brothers set up their own business at Thun, in the canton of Berne.

Like so many other Swiss coachbuilders of the period, the Gebrüder Beutler (Beutler Brothers) coachworks was always best known for Coupé and Cabriolet bodies. Most were one-off designs, and that was the case with their two bodies for the Bentley MkVI – which were both mounted on the same chassis.

The 1960s were hard times for coachbuilders in Switzerland, and Beutler changed the focus of its business to bodywork repairs. Fritz Beutler died in 1986, and his brother closed the business for good in 1987.

The first Beutler Cabriolet body on MkVI chassis B139BG was constructed in 1947 for a leading Swiss enthusiast. It was a typically neat Swiss design, with a well-fitting convertible top and flowing front wings that were perhaps a little avant-garde when the car was new. However, the owner was clearly keen to have a car that reflected the latest styling trends, and in 1949 or 1951 (experts differ on the date) he took the car back to Beutler to have a new body constructed. This second body was again a Cabriolet and again very much in the latest idiom, an all-enveloping style that would not have looked out of place on a 1950s chassis.

BREWSTER

The Brewster coachbuilding firm was long extinct by the end of the Second World War, having closed in 1937. Founded as a carriage maker in 1810, the company became a Rolls-Royce sales agent in 1914 and subsequently became the main body suppliers for US-built Rolls-Royce chassis. The company also built its own complete luxury cars, although sales were limited and in 1925 Brewster sold out to Rolls-Royce of America. After that company closed, Phantom II chassis were shipped direct from Britain to the Brewster workshops in Long Island City.

In the early 1930s, a Brewster-bodied Rolls-Royce became a symbol of wealth in the USA, and the market for them slumped in the early 1930s as the Great Depression brought a marked reaction against the wealthy and their possessions. Sales collapsed, and in 1934 Brewster's sales director, JS Inskip, took charge of the company in an attempt to save it.

Inskip bought 135 Ford V8 chassis and designed a special Town Car body for them, with stylish front wings and a heart-shaped grille. This was a hit at the 1934 New York Auto Show; sold through the Rolls-Royce showrooms, it became a success with New York celebrities. However, the Ford-based Brewster came too late to save the company, and Brewster folded in 1937. JS Inskip, meanwhile, was able to retain the Rolls-Royce dealership, which now took his name and remained at the old Brewster premises in Long Island City.

One wealthy New York lady liked her Brewster-Ford Town Car so much that she had its visible elements transferred to a brand-new Silver Wraith chassis in 1948. The chassis was shipped out to the Inskip dealership, who did the work, doubtless using former Brewster craftsmen to ensure a top-quality job. Wheel trims apart, Silver Wraith WYA19 looked exactly like a Ford-based Brewster of the mid-1930s, and presumably gave its owner a great deal of satisfaction. It was, at least, the only one of its kind.

The original 1947 Beutler body on B139BG had a tight-fitting cabriolet top typical of Swiss coachbuilders, plus sweeping wing lines that would not reach British coachbuilders until later.
(via Klaus-Josef Rossfeldt

Elegant lady, elegant car: this picture could only have been taken in France in the early 1950s, and shows the Chapron Drophead Coupé on Silver Dawn LSTH79. (Copyright unknown)

CHAPRON

If France had had a royal coachbuilder, it would have been Chapron. Noted for the restrained good taste and supreme elegance of his designs, Henri Chapron was selected to produce most of the special presidential limos and parade cars in his workshops at Levallois in the 1950s and 1960s.

In the 1930s, his primary focus had been on Delahaye chassis, although he had also done some coachwork for Rolls-Royce (but not Bentley) to individual order. His close association with the Delahaye marque continued after World War II, when he did not rush to embrace new design trends, but preferred to assimilate elements of them gradually, blending modernity and conservatism in some exceptionally pleasing designs.

He built a Drophead Coupé on the Silver Dawn chassis in the early 1950s, a Touring Limousine on the long-wheelbase Silver Cloud in 1958, and then did two different Limousines on the Phantom V. All of these bodies were very respectful of British designs, and there were few features that were characteristic of Chapron. There were no Chapron bodies on the separate-chassis Bentleys in this period. Interestingly, however, it appears that Harold Radford (see Chapter 3) approached Chapron to make the estate bodies for his Safari conversions on Silver Cloud chassis before concluding an arrangement with HJ Mulliner.

Also of note is that Chapron rebuilt the HJ Mulliner fastback body on a Bentley R Type Continental after it had been involved in an accident. The car (BC63LC) was turned into a cabriolet in 1956, and was given a squared-up rear wing treatment that did not sit well with the curves of the original body. (The fins incorporated in the rear wings, fashionable at the time, have since been removed.) This car, as originally modified by Chapron, is thought to have inspired author Ian Fleming to give his creation, secret agent James Bond 007, just such a model in his 1961 novel, *Thunderball*. It had Chapron design number 5296.

The Silver Dawn Drophead Coupé

The single Chapron body on the Silver Dawn chassis was an attractive Drophead Coupé that may well have been inspired by HJ Mulliner's design number 7296. Its restraint perhaps counted against making it particularly distinctive, but it was undoubtedly well-proportioned and elegant. The body was built in 1954 on chassis number LSTH79.

Chapron's remodelling of the damaged rear end on Bentley R-type Continental BC63LC has always been controversial. (Bentley Motors)

The long-wheelbase Silver Cloud

Chapron's only body for the Silver Cloud was a Touring Limousine on the long-wheelbase chassis built in 1958. It was, as usual, a very restrained design which did not deviate too much from the norms established by Britiish coachbuilders, although notable features were the rakish rear roofline and the way the rear door windows blended into the rear quarter-lights. The front doors were also longer than those on the standard long-wheelbase body of the time.

This single body was built on chassis number LBLC22.

Recognisably a long-wheelbase Silver Cloud, even if built by Chapron, this is the Touring Limousine body on LBLC22. (Copyright unknown)

The Phantom V Limousines

Both Chapron bodies on the Phantom V chassis were Limousines, although they could hardly have been more different. The earlier one was actually ordered from Hooper, who stopped coachbuilding before they had built it. So the design, essentially the work of Hooper's designer Osmond Rivers, was handed over to Chapron to build. Chapron added their own touches, most notably the distinctive stacked headlamps and auxiliary lamps with a slatted plate between them. Overall, though, this was unmistakably a Hooper design, similar in many respects to their number 8570 that had been displayed on a Silver Cloud II chassis at Earls Court in 1959. It was built on chassis number 5LAT4.

Chapron's second Phantom V was built in 1961 and was based on the Hooper design of the earlier car, although its wing lines were higher and the rear wings more bulbous. A distinguishing feature was the same

stacked lighting with decorative backing plate that the French coachbuilder had used on his earlier Phantom. This second car was on chassis number 5LAT50.

Chapron made an excellent job of the Limousine coachwork on Phantom V 5LAT50, which was completed in 1961. (sicnag/WikiMedia Commons)

The rear view of Chapron's Limousine coachwork on 5LAT50 shows that the French coachbuilder was completely at ease with the design for a chassis much larger than any created in France. (dave_7/WikiMedia Commons)

Based on a MkVI chassis, the Bentley Cresta had its own sales brochure. The cover car was one of the Facel Metallon examples, with a Bentley grille.

The double F logo on B447CD represents Facel and Farina. (Klaus-Josef Rossfeldt)

FACEL METALLON

The name of Facel comes from the initials of the Forges et Ateliers de Construction d'Eure et Loir (Forges and assembly workshops of the Eure and Loir region) which was set up by Jean Daninos in 1939. Daninos joined forces with Metallon in 1945 with the intention of building car bodies, and over the next decade Facel Metallon built many thousands of bodies under contract to French manufacturers who did not have the capacity to meet post-war demand.

From 1948, the company established a luxury coachwork department where many later designs were created by Daninos in collaboration with the chief engineer of Facel Metallon, Jacques Brasseur. Cars were built at Dreux and Colombe, with pressings

from Amboise. It was in this period that the company became involved with the Bentley Cresta project (see Chapter 1), building 11 bodies in all on the Bentley MkVI chassis.

After a major contract with Panhard came to an end in 1953, Daninos established his own car marque, and from 1954 manufactured the Facel Vega luxury sports models. However, the business eventually ran into financial trouble and closed down in 1964.

Bentley Cresta Coupés

For the Bentley Cresta project, Facel Metallon built a total of 11 Coupé bodies on Bentley MkVI

The fastback shape of the Coupé body is clear here. This is one of the five examples with left-hand drive.

The fastback rear of the Cresta bodies was clearly an influence on HJ Mulliner's fastback for the Bentley Continental. It is interesting to compare this picture with HJ Mulliner's design 7210, also claimed to have influenced the Continental shape. This is B447CD, delivered in June 1948 and the first of the Cresta cars built by Facel – although its construction may have been started in the Farina workshops. (Klaus-Josef Rossfeldt)

chassis between 1948 and early 1951. The French coachbuilder took over the two-door Coupé design from Pinin Farina during 1948, and displayed the first one from its own workshops at the 1949 Geneva show.

All these bodies had aluminium panels on steel framework. They had the upright grille associated with Bentley instead of the wide style on the Pinin Farina-built cars, and they also carried special double-F coachbuilders' badges, the letters standing for Farina and Facel. The first of the French bodies, on B447CD, is thought to have been a genuine joint effort, started by Pinin Farina but finished by Facel.

Five of the eleven bodies were on left-hand-drive chassis, and one (B441LEW) went to Prince Rainier of Monaco. One of the later examples (on chassis B98KM in 1950) was a special two-seater, with a notchback rather than fastback style; it was constructed for the wife of Jean Daninos, owner of Facel Metallon. The last of the Facel Metallon bodies was delivered on chassis B167JN in February 1952.

FIGONI & FALASCHI

The Parisian coachbuilder Figoni & Falaschi was established in 1935, when Ovidio Falaschi joined forces with Joseph Figoni, who had already developed a well-respected business on his own. The company quickly acquired a reputation for building stylish coupés and cabriolets with flowing and voluptuous lines. They experimented with colour and employed the latest metallic paints to add drama to the looks of their cars. From the mid-1930s, Figoni & Falaschi built several show-stopping bodies on the latest Delahaye 135 chassis, with all-enveloping teardrop-shaped wings that were augmented by strips of chrome.

After the war, the company continued to build the dramatic designs for which they had become famous, notably on Delahaye and Talbot Lago chassis. Their sole body for a Bentley chassis was built in this period. However, the market for such extravagances had

shrunk drastically, and in 1950 Falaschi decided to retire. Figoni continued in business with his son for a while, but closed the coachbuilding business after a low-volume contract with Simca came to an end. He subsequently took on the Lancia franchsie for France.

The single body on a Bentley MkVI chassis by Figoni

FRANAY

Carrosserie Franay was a leading French coachbuilder in the first half of the 20th century. Based in the Paris suburb of Levallois-Perret, the company bodied a few Rolls-Royce chassis in the 1930s and became known after the Second World War for some sensuously flamboyant coachwork on French chassis such as Delahaye and Talbot-Lago. However, Marius Franay died in February 1954, and the company's stand at the 1955 Paris Salon was its last; Franay closed down in 1956.

Franay built 25 bodies on post-war Rolls-Royce and Bentley chassis, and it is notable that in many cases he was clearly unwilling to venture far beyond the norms established by British coachbuilders. For three of his Bentley R Type Continentals, he actually used panels shipped out from Britain by HJ Mulliner.

Particular mention must be made here of the fine analysis of the Franay-bodied Bentleys by André Blaize in *Flying Lady* magazine for September-October 2011.

HOW MANY BODIES?			
The figures below have been calculated by chassis type.			
Rolls-Royce		**Bentley**	
Silver Wraith	8	MkVI	8
Phantom IV	1	R Type	2
		R Continental	5
		S Continental	1
Total	**9**	**Total**	**16**

This Figoni & Falaschi Coupé was built on Bentley MkVI B9AJ. The bright metal lower body mouldings are fairly typical of the way that Figoni & Falaschi adorned their coachwork. (Bonhams Auctioneers)

& Falaschi was delivered to a French customer in July 1948 on chassis number B9AJ. It was a two-seater coupé with dummy landau irons, sweeping wings tipped with chrome flashes, double-bladed bumpers and a long sloping tail. Although much of the design was similar to the coachbuilder's contemporary work on French chassis, the overall result was much more restrained; the design was dramatic without being spectacular.

The Franay All-weather body on the Rolls-Royce Phantom IV chassis was really more of a parade cabriolet. The right-hand rear seat could be moved forwards hydraulically and swivel to make it easier for the occupant to get out of the car.

The lines of the Franay Cabriolet coachwork on Bentley MkVI B136LEY are just visible behind the lady adding to the glamour of this French concours event.

All-weather (1952)

It seems almost disrespectful to describe the distinctly grand Franay coachwork for Rolls-Royce Phantom IV 4AF22 as an All-weather type, although that is the description traditionally given to what some have called a four-door cabriolet. The front windows at least wind down into the doors, and there is a division between front and rear compartments. The rear compartment has a hydraulically-operated swivelling seat which enables easier access and exit, and it also incorporates a pair of occasional seats. This car was delivered to the Saudi royal family in 1952 or 1953 and remained unique.

Cabriolets (1947-1952)

Of the five Cabriolet bodies on Bentley MkVI chassis, the first was the most spectacular. This was on chassis number B20BH and was displayed at the 1947 Paris Salon. It featured a vee screen and enveloping pontoon wings with chrome accents for all four wheels, like those used by Figoni & Falsachi on pre-war Delahaye chassis. (The chrome accents have since been enhanced in a later restoration.) B26BH followed later the same year, with essentially the same body shape but overall it was a less flamboyant creation with exposed front wheels and different chrome accents on the wings. Both these cars were two-seaters with a sideways-facing occasional rear seat.

There is controversy about the next one, which was a slab-sided Cabriolet which Franay displayed at the 1948 Paris Salon. It was probably on chassis B64CF, the body for which otherwise remains unidentified.

One of Franay's less successful efforts was this slab-sided Cabriolet on a 1948 Bentley MkVI, B341GT.

One way or the other, Franay made a much better job of adapting the American fashion for slab sides than some British coachbuilders did at the time.

For B136LEY, displayed at the 1949 Geneva Show, Franay reverted to a more traditional style, with clearly defined front and rear wings. For this car, he added a painted radiator shell that helped to give a slightly more streamlined look. However, there were slab sides again for B341GT, this time with the lines of sweeping wings pressed into them. The coachbuilder was proud enough of this car to display it at the Paris Salon twice, in 1950 and 1951, but it is hard to understand why. It was controversial at the time, not least because of its protruding front bumper, and more recent modifications to the

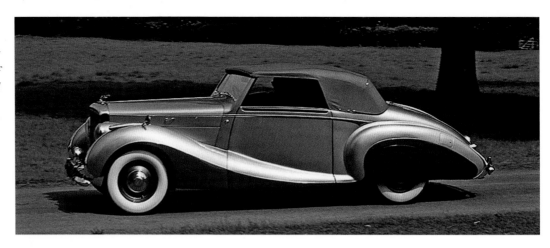

Franay described the body on B26BH as a Cabriolet, and the lines of this 1947 body were fully worthy of both the coachbuilder and the Bentley chassis. (Klaus-Josef Rossfeldt)

coachwork have again been controversial.

The last of the Franay Cabriolets on the MKVI was B324LMD, which was different yet again. This 1952 car was bodied as a four-door Cabriolet (Britons might be tempted to call it an Allweather) in a rather upright style that suggested a British coachbuilder rather than a French one.

Drophead Coupés (1947-1949)

Franay built just two Drophead Coupés or cabriolets on the Rolls-Royce Silver Wraith chassis, each different from the other. The earlier one was on chassis WVA63 in 1947, and it featured sweeping wings, rear wheel spats, and chrome accents on all four wings. This car was displayed at the Paris Salon in 1947.

The later body was much more restrained and upright, and was built in 1949 to replace the Poberejsky sedanca de ville body that had been mounted earlier. The chassis had been built with right-hand-drive for display purposes (and appeared at the 1948 Earls Court Show); it retained its right-hand drive with the Poberejsky body but was converted to left-hand drive

before delivery to Franay, becoming LWAB63.

For many years, the Drophead Coupé body on WYA69 was thought to be by Franay, but it has now been conclusively proved to be the work of Epps Bros.

Limousines (1949-1959)

All four Franay Limousines on the Silver Wraith chassis were built to different designs, which span the development of styling on Rolls-Royce chassis during the first decade after the war.

The earliest example was built on chassis WZB26 in 1949, and is a Touring Limousine that has more than a passing resemblance to contemporary British designs, especially HJ Mulliner's Touring Saloon of the period. The second car was built on WHD53 in 1950 for a customer in Monaco, and was a six-light Limousine with a rather unhappily proportioned rear end.

The two later cars were built on long-wheelbase Silver Wraith chassis. The earlier one was delivered in 1953 or 1954 on chassis LBLW70 and was a Limousine for Middle Eastern royalty. Its general lines were very similar to those of the 1952 Sedanca de Ville on LALW31 and it may have been deliberately intended as the second of a pair.

The last Franay Limousine on Silver Wraith chassis was a Touring Limousine for an American customer. Although built on a 1955 chassis, LELW2 was not delivered until 1959 – three years after Franay had closed for business. The reason is said to be that the customer had several changes of mind about what she wanted. This body looks at first glance more like one that might have been built for a Silver Cloud chassis, its general shape and proportions echoing the work of British coachbuilders on those models.

Saloons (1950-1954)

The sole Franay Saloon body for a Bentley MkVI was not a great success. For B43LFU in 1950, the

Very Franay, perhaps, but not very Bentley… this is the Saloon body on MkVI chassis B43LFU.

coachbuilder created a somewhat graceless, rotund design. There were no repeat orders.

There were also two four-light Saloon bodies for the Bentley R Type, the only bodies that Franay built on this chassis. Both were on 1954 chassis, and both were delivered to French customers. They were on chassis numbered B73YA and B321LYA.

Saloon Coupé (1949)

No pictures of Bentley MkVI B138BH with its original Franay Saloon Coupé coachwork have been found. Delivered in May 1949, it was rebodied a couple of years later by Graber as a Cabriolet.

Sedanca Coupé (1951)

Franay's sole Sedanca Coupé for the Bentley MkVI chassis was a discreetly elegant design, with dummy landau irons and old-fashioned carriage lamps on the scuttle sides. B182LLJ was built for the wife of Greek shipowner Aristotle Onassis, and was on the coachbuilder's stand at the 1951 Paris Salon. It was a fine demonstration of what Franay could do when given the chance.

Sedancas de Ville (1952-1954)

There were two formal Sedanca de Ville bodies on the Silver Wraith chassis. They shared the same overall design, which owed something to British razor-edge designs and featured cutaway rear wheel spats.

The first one, built in 1952, was destined for Middle Eastern royalty and was the most expensive car displayed at the 1952 Paris Salon. This body was on Silver Wraith LALW31. The second body was built in 1954 on chassis number LBLW12.

Two-door Saloons (1954-1955)

Franay built five two-door Saloon bodies on the Bentley R Type Continental chassis, which made this coachbuilder the most prolific outside Britain on that chassis. He followed these up with a single body for an S Type Continental.

The three bodies assembled from panels supplied by HJ Mulliner were mounted on chassis BC51LC, BC20D and BC66LD. The first two were completed in 1954 and the third car in 1955. It is not clear why this arrangement was made with Franay, although the French coachbuilder did not leave the British design entirely alone. Even though the body on these three cars closely follows the lines of the HJ Mulliner design, Franay incorporated a "rib" along the lower edge between the wheels, and abandoned the fastback shape in favour of a more conventional boot and a wraparound rear window incorporating two vertical

dividing bars. These cars seem strangely more upright and less sporting than the HJ Mulliner originals.

Franay also developed a unique design for the R Type Continental, which had a conventional boot and was characterised by a three-piece semi wrap-around rear window. Both BC21D and BC9LE were completed in 1955, but there is a story that BC9LE (which was the very last R Type Continental) was actually completed by Chapron. Certainly, it had some differences from BC21D, the most obvious being small fins on the rear wings.

The sole Franay body for an S Type Continental chassis was a fairly conventional booted two-door coupé with a distinctly stern appearance. The car was built in 1955 on chassis number BC17LAF, and at one stage belonged to the artist Salvador Dali. It was the second to last car from the Franay workshops, the very last being a special French Presidential limousine on a Citroen 15/6 chassis, to a design by Philippe Charbonneaux.

The rear of the body on B43LFU seems too heavy, but no doubt met the customer's wishes in 1950.

B20CD was one of the R Type Continental chassis that Franay bodied with the aid of panels supplied by HJ Mulliner.

The Ghia Limousine on Silver Wraith chassis had an imposing appearance, although the rear wing lines jarred rather on British sensibilities.

GHIA

Carrozzeria Ghia SpA was one of the most famous Italian design and coachbuilding companies for a period of around half a century. Established in Turin in 1916, it gradually built up a reputation and by the 1930s was creating some extravagant special coachwork for Italian chassis.

In 1943, its Turin factory was destroyed by Allied bombing, and Giacinto Ghia died of a heart attack in February 1944 while supervising rebuilding work. However, his widow was determined that the family business should carry on, and passed what remained of it to Felice Mario Boano, whom Ghia had chosen as his eventual successor, and to Giorgio Alberti, another of his close associates.

With Boano in charge of styling, these two now began to look beyond the Italian borders for new customers. Among other ventures, they established a subsidiary (Ghia-Aigle) in Switzerland to meet demand there, and in the early 1950s built concept designs for several American manufacturers.

Ghia's two bodies on Rolls-Royce and one on Bentley chassis were all built in this period, specifically between 1950 and 1952. All appear to have been individual commissions, although at least one of the bodies on a Rolls-Royce was also used to advertise the company's wares at a motor show.

The single Ghia body on a Rolls-Royce Silver Wraith chassis was a Limousine that was built for film director Roberto Rossellini. It was a most elegant six-light design and featured pre-war-style P100 headlamps, rear-hinged rear doors, and a stylised rear wing design that was quite unlike anything British coachbuilders were doing at the time. The car was on chassis number LWOF48 and was delivered in June 1952, after being displayed on the Ghia stand at that year's Turin show.

The six-light Ghia Limousine on Silver Dawn chassis LSHD22 was clearly related to the one built for Roberto Rossellini on a Silver Wraith chassis. It nevertheless had standard-sized headlamps and a simpler rear wing design. It was made to look larger and grander than it really was by the use of a longer bonnet and by mounting the radiator shell 6in forward of its normal position. The radiator shell was also reduced in height by 3¼in. These non-standard arrangements seem to have led to cooling problems, and as a result some rather ugly cooling vents were let into the front wings behind the wheelarches. The car nevertheless won the Grand Prix d'Honneur at the Villa Borghese in Rome in 1952.

Unfortunately, very little is known about the body that Ghia built on Bentley MkVI chassis B299FU for an Italian customer; not even the body type is known. The car was delivered in February 1950. Although the chassis survives, it now carries a Park Ward Drophead Coupé body.

GRABER

Carrosserie Hermann Graber is probably the best-known of the great Swiss coachbuilders. Graber took over his father's coachbuilding business at Wichtrach, near Berne, in 1925, and soon began to specialise in cabriolet bodies. There were a small number on Rolls-Royce and Bentley chassis in the 1930s.

After the Second World War, Graber focussed his attention largely on British-built chassis, becoming best known for his Alvis designs. He became the most prolific of the overseas coachbuilders on Bentley chassis, but bodied only one Rolls-Royce, perhaps because the upright Rolls-Royce grille blended less harmoniously than the Bentley type with the curved lines that he favoured. Most of the Graber bodies for the two marques were Cabriolets, but there were some highly attractive Coupés as well. The Bentley chassis were normally sourced through Garage Bellevue AG in Berne.

HOW MANY BODIES?
The figures below have been calculated by chassis type.

Rolls-Royce		Bentley	
Silver Cloud	1	MkVI	17
		R Type	7
		R Continental	3
		S Type	2
		S Continental	1
		S3 Continental	1
Total	**1**	**Total**	**31**

Some body swaps, probably by Graber himself, and some rebuilds in later years have caused a certain amount of confusion about how many of these cars were built.

Cabriolets

Graber's earliest post-war design for the two marques was a Cabriolet for the Bentley MkVI that made its appearance in 1946. This was distinguished by separate "pontoon" wings, and was replaced (probably from 1948) by a Cabriolet design with the more integrated lines that would become common in the 1950s. This second Cabriolet design was carried over for the R Type chassis, and a very similar design also appeared on the R Type Continental. There were then two later designs for S Type chassis, another for the Rolls-Royce Silver Cloud, and a final one some years later for the Bentley S3 Continental.

The first of five Cabriolets with the pontoon-wing design was on MkVI chassis B86AK and was delivered in November 1946, and the last was delivered in January 1948 on B190CF. There were then eight with "straight-through" wings, beginning with B82FV in late 1949. A ninth MkVI (B138BH from 1947) was rebodied to this style, probably also in 1949. Two more on the R Type chassis from 1953 (B89RS and B42RT) brought the total of these bodies to 11. There were variations from one body to another in details such as the position of the headlights and the shape and style of the horn grilles. Three more on the R Type chassis from 1953 (B89RS, B42RT and B342SR) brought the total of these bodies to 12. Graber converted the body on B342SR to a Coupé in 1954.

Using very much the same lines that he was using

on the standard R Type chassis at the time, Graber also built three Cabriolet bodies on the R Type Continental chassis. The first was on BC55C and was displayed at the Geneva Show in 1954. The second, BC77C was built as a two-seater. BC68D, new in 1955, was turned into a Coupé in 1957 by the coachbuilder Köng in Basle. The Graber lines then remained readily recognisable on the two Cabriolets that he built for standard S Type chassis in 1956. The first of these, on chassis B478AN, was displayed at that year's Geneva show. The second car, B462LAN, had left-hand drive.

Also built in 1956 was Graber's sole body on the six-cylinder S Type Continental chassis. It was a Cabriolet, perhaps somewhat more grand than earlier designs for Bentley, but again instantly recognisable as a Graber creation. The single car was on chassis number BC25BG and was the only S1 Continental not bodied

The later design of Cabriolet with straight-through wing lines was extremely sleek and graceful. This is on Bentley MkVI B138BH and was built in 1949 as a rebody on an earlier chassis. (Thesupermat/WikiMedia Commons)

For the R Type chassis, the Cabriolet body evolved further, with repositioned headlamps – but the Graber style remained unmistakeable. (John Lloyd/WikiMedia Commons

by a British coachbuilder. The only Graber-bodied post-war Rolls-Royce was also completed in 1956, and was a Cabriolet on an early left-hand-drive Silver Cloud chassis, numbered LSWA30. It was very much in the Graber style of the time but with its own distinctive features. The chassis was obtained through Franco-Britannic in Paris rather than from his usual supplier.

There was then a gap of 11 years before the last Graber Cabriolet for a Bentley chassis was built on a late S3 Continental. This was an unusual confection, more recognisable than ever as a Graber creation because it was really an enlarged version of his Alvis designs, complete with vertically stacked Alvis headlamps, wire wheels and an electrically lowered reverse-rake rear window. The car was on chassis number BC202LXC and was ordered by one Baptista Fritze, who had the winged B on the radiator surround modified into a winged F. It was delivered in 1967.

Coupés

Graber created a Coupé for the Bentley MkVI chassis which shared the basic shape he had created for the Cabriolets with "straight-through" wing lines. There were four of these bodies on the MkVI chassis from 1951 (one a two-seater) and two more on the R Type three: B82SR, B340SR, B197LSP. A seventh coupé body was built in 1951 on the chassis of a 1947 MkVI (B190BH) which had originally been delivered as a standard saloon in France. This was the only Graber-bodied Bentley MkVI to have left-hand drive. B184MD, the two-seater, was at the 1952 Geneva Show and B82SR was at the 1953 Geneva Show.

GUSTAF NORDBERG

Gustaf Nordbergs Vagnfabrik was founded in Stockholm, in 1901, and soon progressed from wagon building to car bodywork. Gustaf was joined in the business by his sons Nils and Carl, and during the 1920s they built the coachwork for a small number of Rolls-Royce chassis. There were bodies on imported American chassis during the 1930s, too, and although Gustaf himself died in 1935, his sons carried the business on.

Little known outside Sweden, the Nordberg business bodied around 1000 cars in all, its very last body being on a long-wheelbase Rolls-Royce Silver Wraith in 1953. This was a six-light Limousine, which had imposing if somewhat upright lines, with spatted rear wheels. As Sweden was a right-hand-drive country until 1967, it is interesting that the chassis was ordered with left-hand drive. It was delivered in May 1953 on chassis number LALW14.

INSKIP

JS Inskip was actually the New York distributor for Rolls-Royce, but had built a handful of bodies to order on Rolls-Royce chassis during the 1930s. When pressed once more to produce special coachwork in the post-war period, the company assembled a team of former Brewster craftsmen and obliged three customers, delivering three bodies with Inskip badges in 1948-1951.

All three Inskip bodies were on Silver Wraith chassis and shared the same design of coachwork. This was a two-door, four-seater, that has often been described as a Drophead Coupé or Convertible because of its winding door windows. However, the lines of the body, and in particular the cut-down windscreen, convertible top, and waistline dip suggesting a doortop cutaway, are all more reminiscent of a Tourer. The flowing wings, accompanied by spats at the rear, were decorated with chromed swoops that were clearly inspired by French coachbuilders such as Figoni &

Still recognisably Graber, this is the 1956 Cabriolet body on a Bentley S Type. (Luc106/WikiMedia Commons)

Unquestionably flamboyant, with strong echoes of French coachbuiding practice, this is the Inskip body built in 1951 on Silver Wraith WZB36. (Rex Gray/WikiMedia Commons)

This most unusual Limousine coachwork was built in Sweden in 1953. (Klauss-Josef Rossfeldt)

The cutaway door tops suggest a roadster or Tourer body, although the Inskip Silver Wraith is more generally described as a Convertible.
(Rex Gray/WikiMedia Commons)

Falaschi or Saoutchik.

The first car was on chassis WYA20, and the second, on chassis WYA26, was completed in 1948 for the eccentric millionaire Tommy Manville, Jr and later became part of the Blackhawk Collection. This car was displayed at the 1949 New York Show. The third car was delivered in January 1951 on chassis number WZB36 and became the last separate-chassis Rolls-Royce to carry a coachbuilt American body.

KÖNG

Walter Köng took over his father's coachbuilding business at Basle in Switzerland in 1935, having learned his craft with French, Italian and American companies. Like many other Swiss coachbuilders in the 1930s, the company became known mainly for its cabriolet bodies on a variety of upmarket British and French chassis.

Köng returned to coachbuilding after the war, and among his earliest work was on Bentley chassis. His most famous body, a daring "transformable coupé" with Plexiglass roof and other highly individual features, was supposedly originally intended for a Bentley but was actually built on a Riley 2½-litre chassis. The company built two bodies on new Bentley chassis, plus at least two more as re-bodies.

However, the traditional coachbuilding business was slow, and Köng re-focussed his activities to become a restorer of classic cars. After his death in 1989, the business survived for a further ten years in the hands of shareholders before being sold to another Basle coachbuilding company, Rudi Wenger.

Cabriolets

Köng's first known body on Bentley chassis after the war was a Cabriolet built for a Swiss customer on chassis B237AJ and delivered in March 1947. The body was

not particularly adventurous and had some quite old-fashioned characteristics, including a vee windscreen and a spare wheel mounted alongside the bonnet.

There appears to have been a second Köng Cabriolet on an unidentified Bentley chassis, in this case a re-body.

Sedanca Coupé

Sedanca bodies were not a particular Köng speciality, but the coachbuilder's second body on a new post-war Bentley chassis showed that he could be adaptable. For chassis B284CF in early 1948, he came up with a semi- razor-edge design of very formal appearance. The original buyer was Swiss, but the car later found its way into the Schlumpf Collection at Mulhouse in France.

Estate

Estate bodies were not a Köng speciality, either, but at a time when business was hard to come by, the coachbuilder agreed to re-body a MkVI Bentley as an estate car. B56BH had started life with a Saloon Coupé body by James Young, and was supposedly rebodied to suit the wishes of its French-domiciled owner. The date of the rebody is not known, but the car later became an exhibit in the Verkehrshaus Museum at Lucerne.

PININ FARINA

This Italian coachbuilder was correctly known as Pinin Farina until 1960, Pinin being the nickname of owner Battista Farina: it is Piedmontese slang for the youngest son of the family. After 1960, the company became Pininfarina, and Signor Farina legally changed his own surname to Pininfarina as well.

Pinin Farina the company was founded in Turin in 1930, and in the ensuing decade gained a reputation for aerodynamic designs. In the late 1940s and early 1950s, it produced a number of one-off designs for

Pinin Farina certainly captured the essence of the Continental chassis with this close-coupled Coupé body for chassis BC49C in 1954.

Even though it dates from 1949, and therefore was later than the Cresta designs, this Drophead Coupé on Bentley MkVI B435CD has more conservative lines, with similarities to those on the fastback coupé for Silver Dawn chassis on the next page. The lines are typical of the coachbuilder's creations in this period, and suit the MkVI chassis very well. (André Blaize via Klaus-Josef Rossfeldt) (Author)

companies ranging from Alfa Romeo through Rover to Cadillac, in the hope of securing a volume contract. But no such contract was forthcoming, and Farina's attempt to persuade Rolls-Royce to grant him such a contract led to nothing. Meanwhile, the Torinese firm built a handful of bodies to individual commission on both Rolls-Royce and Bentley chassis.

However, the first Pinin Farina-bodied Ferrari was built in 1952, and in 1954 a gentlemen's agreement between Ferrari and Farina – no contract was ever signed – saw Pinin Farina becoming the Ferrari house stylist. This arrangement provided the coachbuilder with all the work he could handle, as well as an ideal showcase for his talents. From that point Pinin Farina no longer bothered to pursue Rolls-Royce and Bentley work, and there were no more bodies on the separate-chassis models after 1954.

Pinin Farina built a total of seven bodies on the two marques in the period between 1945 and 1965. These were on the Bentley MkVI (5), Bentley R Type

Continental (1), and Rolls-Royce Silver Dawn (1). The MkVI bodies included some that were built for the Bentley Cresta project (see Chapter 1).

Close-coupled Coupé

Pinin Farina built just one body on the R Type Continental chassis. This was a close-coupled Coupé which had some similarities to the coachbuilder's 1952 Fixed-head Coupé on MkVI chassis – notably the wrapover rear window. The Continental's body nevertheless looked sleeker and longer. It was built on chassis BC49C in 1954 and had design number 1136.

Drophead Coupé

The single Drophead Coupé body on Bentley MkVI chassis was fairly typical of Pinin Farina's designs at the time, with a divided windscreen and clearly defined wing pressings in the side panels. It was on chassis number B435CD and was displayed at the Geneva Show in 1949.

This picture of BC49C shows the wrapover rear window. The picture was taken outside the premises of HJ Mulliner in Chiswick.

Pinin Farina's only body for a Rolls-Royce chassis in this period was this 1951 Coupé on Silver Dawn SCA43. The proportions worked very well.

This rear view of the Coupé on the Silver Dawn chassis emphasises its interesting mix of sleek lines with wing shapes that hark back to late 1940s practice. The body was built in 1951. (Tentenths/WikiMedia Commons)

This most attractive body on Bentley MkVI B323CD was Pinin Farina's first contribution to the Bentley Cresta project. The wide grille undoubtedly would have offended purists, but worked very well with the lines of the body.

Fastback Coupé

There was only ever one Pinin Farina body on a separate-chassis Rolls-Royce, and that was a two-door fastback design on Silver Dawn SCA43. The buyer asked Pinin Farina to base the design on a short-wheelbase Rolls-Royce Phantom II.

The car was very pretty but also hugely expensive – supposedly costing about three times as much as a standard Silver Dawn. It was displayed at Pinin Farina's home show in Turin in April 1951, but discussions about building more came to nothing. A key reason is said to have been the unpredictable fluctuations in the exchange rate between Pounds Sterling and the Italian Lire.

Fixed-head Coupé

Pinin Farina built just one Fixed-head Coupé on the Bentley MkVI chassis. This was a special commission for a Swiss customer and was a three-box design with a wrapover rear window. It was on chassis number B332MD and was delivered in 1952.

Saloon Coupés

There were three two-door fastback Saloon Coupés on the special Cresta version of the Bentley MkVI chassis, built in 1948 and 1949. The Cresta had been drawn up at the request of Walter Sleator of Franco-

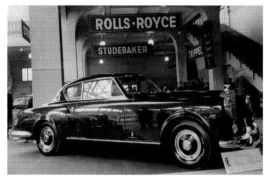

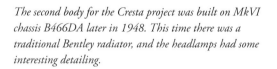

The second body for the Cresta project was built on MkVI chassis B466DA later in 1948. This time there was a traditional Bentley radiator, and the headlamps had some interesting detailing.

Britannic Autos in Paris, and featured left-hand drive, a lowered bonnet line and a steeply raked steering column.

The first body, on B323CD, had the wide radiator grille that was a Pinin Farina characteristic of the time but the later two did not. The last car, B476DA, featured rear wheel spats and its chassis was converted to left-hand drive specially by Rolls-Royce. The fastback design was later licensed to Facel Metallon in France (see above).

POBEREJSKY

Jacques Poberejsky made his name and a sizeable fortune through his Société Superflexit, which made specialised aircraft components such as high-pressure hoses and self-sealing fuel tanks. Although domiciled in Paris, Poberejsky was of Russian descent, having been born in Odessa in 1885.

In 1936, he had the coachbuilder Henri Binder create a special body for him on a Rolls-Royce Phantom II chassis, with a removable front end that hinted at the American Cord 810, and this is recognisably the origin of some of the ideas that he carried over for a pair of highly controversial bodies that bore his name. One was on a Rolls-Royce Silver Wraith chassis, and the other on a Bentley MkVI. They were displayed together at the Geneva Show in March 1949 – right next to another controversial car, the Riley bodied by Swiss coachbuilder Walter Köng.

The Bentley was the earlier of the two. Poberejsky had taken delivery of a standard-steel MkVI saloon (B124BH) in July 1947, removed its body, and arranged for a two-door Saloon of his own design to be constructed on it. This incorporated several unusual styling features, together with a front end that again harked back to the "coffin-nose" design of the Cord

This is the Poberejsky Silver Wraith, a Sedanca de Ville design.

810. It also suppressed the Bentley grille altogether, and the overall effect was of a black beetle, as American Motor Industry magazine rather brutally put it.

The Silver Wraith had a Sedanca de Ville body along generally similar lines. This was on chassis number WAB63, which had started life as a specially prepared display chassis for the 1948 Earls Court Show. After that show was over, Rolls-Royce decided to have it given a special body so that it could be used as a show car again the following year. For reasons that are no longer clear, the chassis found its way to Jacques Poberejsky. Like the Saloon on the Bentley chassis, this Sedanca de Ville was almost universally condemned as ugly.

It is unlikely that Poberejsky constructed these two bodies himself, and Klaus-Josef Rossfeldt (in *The Flying Lady* for January-February 2016) has suggested that both may have been constructed by the Parisan coachbuilder Letourneur. As for Jacques Poberejsky, he died soon after the Geneva Show in 1949. His son arranged for the Bentley Saloon to be displayed at the Paris Salon later that year, but the Silver Wraith went back to Rolls-Royce, who removed the body and converted the chassis to left-hand drive as LWAB63. It was then sent to Franay, who rebodied it in a more conventional style (see above). That car survives, but the Bentley has been lost since 1954.

The sleek lines of the Roos Cabriolet body for Prince Bernhard of the Netherlands were penned by the Prince himself. (copyright unknown)

ROOS

Chris Roos had been active as a builder of van and trailer bodies in the Hague, Holland, since 1927. After the Second World War, he turned his hand to building car bodywork, and got off to what looked like a flying start by earning a commission to body a Bentley for HRH Prince Bernhard of the Netherlands.

Roos also converted one of the royal Daimlers into a landaulette and rebodied a pre-war Alfa Romeo chassis, but decided against continuing in the coachbuilding business. He returned to his earlier occupation and eventually closed his company in 1958.

The single Bentley bodied by the Roos coachworks was a Cabriolet, built to a design by HRH Prince Bernhard himself, who had a taste for fast cars. The Bentley chassis was number B311CD, and the car was completed in late 1948. It had commendably sleek lines, and featured a faired-in sloping radiator grille that was reminiscent of Lagonda practice. The car was displayed at the Brussels Show in 1949.

This is the Saoutchik Bentley MkVI Tourer. The swoops and sweeps are ditinctive, but the car is still recognisable as MkVI.

SAOUTCHIK

The Parisian coachbuilder Saoutchik was among France's most important and best known by the time he came to body a Rolls-Royce Silver Wraith and a Bentley MkVI in 1948. These were by no means his only bodies for the British marques: he had bodied his first Rolls-Royce chassis in 1913 and his first Bentley in 1935.

Saoutchik deliberately confined his attentions to high-quality chassis, and in the 1920s and 1930s developed a reputation for flamboyant designs which made extensive but tasteful use of ornamentation. He did his best to continue in the same vein after 1945, but the market had changed and the coachbuilder was unable to survive on his traditional business. Despite some small series work for Pegaso, by which time founder Jacques had handed over control of the company to his son Pierre Saoutchik, the company closed down in 1955.

Saoutchik was not surprisingly patronised by the flamboyant John Gaul, a Briton with a taste for the high life who lived in the south of France. Gaul requested a Sedanca Coupé on Silver Wraith chassis WTA45, and Saoutchik did not disappoint. The body was notable for the extraordinarily curvaceous shapes of its rear side windows, and for the fake cane panelling on the doors and the body sides behind them. It was the essence of elegance and flamboyance – just as its buyer had intended – and was delivered in March 1948.

However, sedanca styles were gong out of fashion in the late 1940s and WTA45 was later returned to Saoutchik to be turned into a Fixed-head Coupé with sliding sunroof. Fortunately, the original lines of the body were retained.

The only Saoutchik body on a post-war Bentley chassis was not actually designed by the coachbuilder but by the client, with the assistance of his son. It was

Saoutchik's only body for a post-war Rolls-Royce was this Sedanca de Ville, pictured when relatively new. It was subsequently converted to a Fixed-head Coupé, losing the faux cane panelling and gaining rear wheel spats at the same time.

a two-door Tourer, featuring cutaway door tops in the tourer idiom. Chrome sweeps on the wings and a bold two-tone paint scheme may have been Saoutchik's idea, but the result was an unusual and most attractive car. Built on chassis number B440CF, it was delivered in the same month as the Saoutchik Silver Wraith – March 1948.

VAN DEN PLAS (BRUSSELS)

Van den Plas was one of the great Belgian coachbuilders of the early 20th century, established out of a successful carriage making company as Carrosserie Van den Plas in 1898. Quality of construction was an early hallmark, and after 1924 there were some superbly proportioned bodies for quality chassis that included Rolls-Royce. Meanwhile, a British branch was set up in 1913, and ten years later was re-established under British owners as Vanden Plas (England) 1923 Ltd.

The Belgian branch continued its existence quite independently of the British branch, forging a close relationship in the 1930s with Belgian chassis maker Minerva, which invested in the coachbuilder. Van den Plas returned to coachbuilding after the 1939-1945 war, and produced a number of individual bodies in the late 1940s. Many of these are said to have been designed by the Brussels coachbuilder d'Ieteren. The last Van den Plas bodies were built in 1949, and the coachbuilder then closed down.

Among those individual bodies was a Cabriolet on a Rolls-Royce Silver Wraith chassis, number WYA5. The car was ordered by Charles, the Prince Regent of Belgium, and was a neat but unremarkable design with all-steel construction. It was delivered in 1948.

VANVOOREN

In the 1930s, Vanvooren had been one of France's great coachbuilders, and its ability to build structurally solid bodies that were also light in weight had attracted the

The only body for a post-war Rolls-Royce built by Van den Plas in Brussels was this Cabriolet for the Prince Regent of Belgium.

attention of Rolls-Royce. From about the middle of the decade, the company bodied a large proportion of the Rolls-Royce and Bentley chassis sold in France, and forged a close relationship with the parent company in England through its French importers, Franco-Britannic in Paris. As war broke out in 1939, Vanvooren was poised to build the lightweight bodies for the streamlined Corniche model, and a co-operative arrangement with Park Ward, Rolls-Royce's favoured British coachbuilder, was on the cards.

Sadly, the war put paid to all of that. The Vanvooren workshops in the Parisian suburb of Courbevoie were badly damaged by bombing in 1943, and the company did not resume coachbuilding until 1947. Vanvooren's output never reached its pre-war levels again, and it survived by rebuilding pre-war cars and constructing a handful of bodies to special order. Finding that the market for coachbuilt bodies had shrunk to unviable levels, Vanvooren closed for good in 1950.

The mighty had certainly fallen in this case, although the two bodies that Vanvooren built on Bentley MkVI chassis were fully worthy of the great coachbuilder. Only one of them was on a brand-new chassis, and that was a typically discreet and elegant Saloon Coupé with sweeping front wings and spatted rear ones. It was built in 1950 on chassis number B332LEY, although it is hard to see the echoes of the Hooper Empress Line in its appearance that some commentators claim to have detected.

The second body replaced a standard steel body on chassis B53BG, which had been delivered in late 1947. It was built for a customer in France and its Cabriolet body appears to have retained at least the front wings of the original Saloon. The exact date of this body is not known.

VIGNALE

In the 1950s, Carrozzeria Alfredo Vignale was one of Italy's best-known coachbuilders. Alfredo Vignale had worked for Stabilimenti Farina before founding his coachworks in Turin in October 1946, and he established his reputation through some most attractive if somewhat flamboyant coachwork on Ferrai chassis in the early 1950s. His company built individual commissions, small-run batches and derivatives of mainstream models to which it applied its own name.

Most of Vignale's work in the 1950s was on Italian cars, and its reputation remained intact in the 1960s. However, the company ran into financial difficulties later in the decade, and in 1969 was sold to De Tomaso. Sadly, Alfredo Vignale himself was killed in a car accident just three days after the sale was concluded.

The design sketch for the car was signed by Giovanni Michelotti.

The deliberate resemblance to a Mercedes "Fintail" is immediately obvious in this view of the Wendler estate body on a Bentley S2 chassis. (Mr.choppers/WikiMedia Commons)

The sole Vignale body on a post-war Rolls-Royce chassis was built for an American customer in 1955 on long-wheelbase Silver Wraith chassis number LCLW14. The body was a six-light Limousine with division and was clearly intended to be an eye-catcher – although not necessarily to be attractive as well. The design sketch is signed by Giovanni Michelotti, who

was at the time a freelance designer and did some work for Vignale under contract. The car is said to have been displayed at the Turin Show in 1954.

The rear window and rearmost pillar of this body were raked rearwards and set well back to create a very long passenger cabin, and there was an excessively long rear overhang to accommodate a full-sized boot. These had the unfortunate effect of unbalancing the lines. The rear window was also retractable. Meanwhile, the front end featured a pair of huge P100 headlamps flanked by foglights in the wing fronts.

Bizarrely, the interior of this car featured a toilet with gold-painted toilet seat under the right-hand rear passenger seat. Allegedly, this was only ever used as a champagne cooler by the original owner.

WENDLER

During the 1950s, the German coachbuilder Wendler was best known for its work on racing Porsches, but it was also building a few bodies to individual order. Founded in Reutlingen as a carriage maker in 1840, Wendler had turned to car bodies in the 1920s and had built a number of special streamlined bodies in the 1930s. In the 1940s and 1950s, the company focussed on one-off bodies for individual customers and on prototype work for car manufacturers. It continued with similar work into the 1960s.

Wendler's only coachwork on a post-war Bentley chassis was a quite remarkable estate car for an American customer. This customer had already commissioned Wendler to build an estate body of different design on a Mercedes-Benz 300S chassis.

The brief was straightforward: the body had to incorporate elements of the then-new Mercedes-Benz 300SE "Fintail" saloon. (No estate version of the "Fintail" range was then available, although IMA in Brussels did produce one from 1965.) Wendler's interpretation was creative and surprisingly elegant, incorporating the stacked headlamp clusters of the Mercedes alongside a traditional Bentley grille. The car remained unique, and was constructed in 1960 on S2 chassis LLBA9.

WORBLAUFEN

The carriage works at Worblaufen near Berne in Switzerland was founded in 1900 by Fritz Ramseier. When his sons took over the business in 1929, they gradually transformed it into one of Switzerland's most respected coachbuilders. The plates they applied to their coachwork gave prominence to the Worblaufen name, but the company's full title was Fritz Ramseier & Cie, Carrosserie Worblaufen, and as a result the business has often been called by the Ramseier name.

Like so many other Swiss coachbuilders, Worblaufen specialised in elegant cabriolet bodies. In the 1930s their output was mainly on French, Italian and German chassis, but in the more difficult trading conditions after the war they also bodied a few British chassis, and among these were four MkVI Bentleys.

Demand for coachbuilt bodies gradually dried up in the 1950s, and Carrosserie Worblaufen constructed its last car body in 1958. The company remained in business, carrying out repairs and building commercial bodywork until it closed in 1983.

All the Worblaufen bodies on Bentley MkVI chassis were Cabriolets. Two were built in 1947, and two more in 1950 to a different design. All four were for Swiss customers.

The 1947 bodies were on chassis B181AJ and B401BG. There were minor differences between the two cars, but the most obvious was that B181AJ had cutaway rear spats while the later B401BG had open rear wheelarches. B181AJ was displayed at the 1948 Geneva Show. In later years, a US owner added cutaway spats and chrome mouldings to B401BG.

The two 1950 bodies were on B88LFV and B412FV. Both of these cars had a more slab-sided body that reflected the pontoon style of the times. B88LFV had fashionable squared-off tops to its wheelarches, and cutaway rear wing spats. B412FV differed by having round tops to the wheelarches and full rear spats.

The Cabriolet body on B88LFV is very different indeed, with a rather heavy look that was more typical of German coachbuilders than their Swiss counterparts. (Luc106/WikiMedia Commons)

CARROSSERIE WORBLAUFEN F. Ramseier & Cie. · Tel. (031) 7 04 14

This sales brochure for a Worblaufen-bodied Bentley almost certainly illustrates the Cabriolet on B401BG, with an early style of coachwork.

Related titles from Herridge & Sons

A-Z British Coachbuilders by Nick Walker

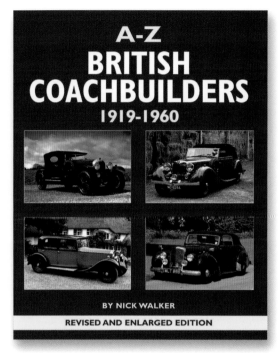

A comprehensive study of coachbuilding, and coachbuilders, in Britain. It gives a unique A-Z coverage of over 300 British coachbuilders. In addition, there is useful advice on assessing the condition of a coachbuilt body today. A glossary of coachbuilding terms completes the picture. This enlarged and revised edition contains new entries and photographs.

"Required reading for anyone interested in a fascinating subject."
The Automobile

- 224 pages, hardback
- 280 x 210mm
- 50 colour & 370 b/w illustrations
- ISBN 978-0-9549981-6-5
- £35

A-Z European Coachbuilders by James Taylor

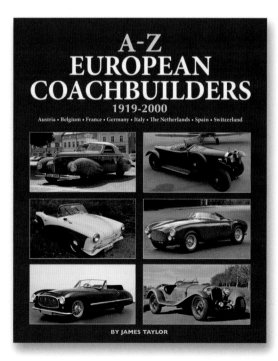

From ACB of Paris (1934-91) to Zschau of Leipzig (1878-1939), by way of great names like Ghia, Erdmann & Rossi, Kellner, Pininfarina, Saoutchik and Zagato, this is an alphabetical reference guide to the major coachbuilders of western continental Europe – Austria, Belgium, France, Germany, Italy, the Netherlands, Spain and Switzerland.

The A-Z entries provide details of the history, activities and specialities of each coachbuilder, with more than 450 illustrations.

"...a solid overview."
The Automobile

- 240 pages, hardback
- 280 x 210mm
- 450 illustrations
- ISBN 978-906133-78-8
- £40

Coachwork on Derby Bentleys by James Taylor

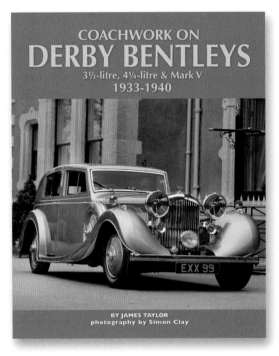

From Abbey of Acton, West London, to Worblaufen of Switzerland, by way of great names like Barker, Gurney Nutting, H J Mulliner and Saoutchik, this book covers all the British and overseas coachbuilders on the Bentley chassis, with chassis numbers, and reviews the bodies they built on the 3½-litre, 4¼-litre and the short-lived Mark V.

There are some 280 colour photographs, including in-detail shoots of selected outstanding cars, and 80 black-and-white illustrations from the archives.

"...easily accessible information in an attractive volume."
Bentley Drivers Club Review

• 200 pages, hardback
• 270 x 210mm
• 280 colour & 80 b/w illustrations
• ISBN 978-1-906133-75-7
• £40

Bentley 3¹/₂ & 4¹/₄ Litre In Detail by Nick Walker

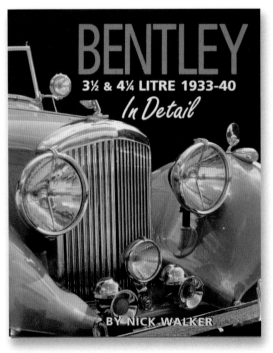

The Bentleys built by Rolls-Royce during the 1930s proved to be an extraordinary success for the company. This success was due to the performance and manners of the cars, to the excellence of their engineering and construction, and to the wonderful variety of body styles offered by a host of coachbuilders.

The book covers the 3½ Litre, 4¼ Litre and short-lived Mark V.

"No owner or admirer of these fine cars will wish to miss having a copy of this excellent book"
The Bulletin, VSCC magazine

• 160 pages, hardback
• 270 x 210mm
• 70 colour & 150 b/w illustrations
• ISBN 978-0-9541063-1-7
• £50

Bentley Four-Cylinder Models In Detail by James Taylor

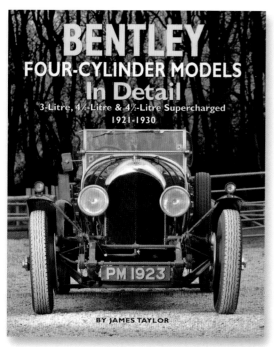

For nearly 100 years these legendary Bentleys, the creation of the celebrated W O Bentley, have remained the object of fascination and desire of all motoring enthusiasts.

This book covers the four-cylinder models – the 3 Litre of 1921, the 4½ Litre and the 4½ Litre "Blower" Bentley. The author studies the evolution of the models, their competition history and the wide range of coachwork fitted, with detailed colour photography of ten outstanding examples of the cars.

"Undeniably comprehensive."
Octane

- 176 pages, hardback
- 270 x 210mm
- 120 colour & 185 b/w illustrations
- ISBN 978-1-906133-30-6
- £40

Original Rolls-Royce & Bentley 1946-65 by James Tayor

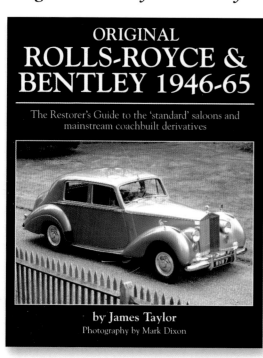

The essential companion to these supremely elegant cars, which survive in large numbers thanks to their mechanical longevity and peerless quality of construction. The aim of this book is to reveal how the various models altered through the course of production. Over 250 specially commissioned colour photographs show the detail changes to these cars to provide a valuable reference source for owners, buyers and restorers.

"...an amazing piece of research"
The Automobile

- 160 pages, hardback
- 295 x 225mm
- 250 colour illustrations
- ISBN 978-1-906133-06-1
- £35